Bey[ond]

Early Reading

You might also like the following books in our *Critical Teaching* series

Teaching Systematic Synthetic Phonics and Early English
Jonathan Glazzard and Jane Stokoe
978-1-909330-09-2 In print

Primary School Placements: A Critical Guide to Outstanding Teaching
Catriona Robinson, Branwen Bingle and Colin Howard
978-1-909330-45-0 In print

Teaching and Learning Early Years Mathematics: Subject and Pedagogic Knowledge
Mary Briggs
978-1-909330-37-5 In print

Most of our titles are also available in a range of electronic formats. To order please go to our website www.criticalpublishing.com or contact our distributor, NBN International, 10 Thornbury Road, Plymouth PL6 7PP, telephone 01752 202301 or email orders@nbninternational.com.

Beyond
Early Reading

David Waugh
Sally Neaum

CRITICAL
TEACHING

First published in 2013 by Critical Publishing Ltd

British Library Cataloguing in Publication Data
A CIP record for this book is available from the British Library

ISBN: 978-1-909330-41-2

This book is also available in the following e-book formats:

Kindle ISBN: 978-1-909330-42-9
EPUB ISBN: 978-1-909330-43-6
Adobe e-book ISBN: 978-1-909330-44-3

Cover and text design by Greensplash Limited
Project Management by Out of House Publishing
Printed and bound in Great Britain by T J International

Critical Publishing
152 Chester Road
Northwich
CW8 4AL
www.criticalpublishing.com

MIX
Paper from responsible sources
FSC® C013056

Contents

Meet the editors

David Waugh is a former deputy headteacher who worked in Initial Teacher Training (ITT) from 1990 at the University of Hull, where he led the PGCE course and became Head of Department. In 2008 he was appointed as a National Strategies Regional Adviser for ITT. He is currently Director of the Primary PGCE at Durham University, where he is also subject leader for English. He has published extensively in primary English, and has developed e-learning resources for National Strategies for English, mathematics and mentoring and coaching.

Sally Neaum is Senior Lecturer in Early Childhood Studies at the University of Teesside. She has worked as a nursery and primary school teacher, and as an adviser in early years, inclusion, and intial teacher training. Sally has published extensively in early years and primary education.

Meet the authors

John Bennett is a lecturer in education at the University of Hull. His main roles are in primary initial teacher training (ITT), particularly providing primary English teaching courses for post-graduate and undergraduate trainees. He previously spent 25 years working in schools, as a teacher, an advisory teacher and a primary headteacher.

David Boorman is a primary school teacher at Moss Hey Primary School, Bramhall. He also works as a marker for the Key Stage 2 English SATs and is currently undertaking a fractional secondment at Edge Hill University, working as a senior lecturer on their Maths Specialist Teacher programme.

Eve English a former head teacher, is a lecturer in English on the PGCE (Primary) and BA (QTS) courses at Durham University. She has published extensively on primary English.

Daniel Harrison has been Headteacher at Ox Close Primary School in Spennymoor, County Durham since June 2011; his first headship. He is also closely involved with ITT. He lectures part time on Durham University's Primary PGCE course and is a Professional Tutor on High Force Education's Primary SCITT programme.

Steven Higgins is Professor of Education at Durham University. He has undertaken a number of research projects in primary schools investigating the impact of digital technologies on children1s learning in literacy and mathematics. A former primary school teacher, he has a particular interest in the development of children's thinking and reasoning.

Jemma Rennocks is an Advanced Skills Teacher at Moss Hey Primary School in Bramhall. She has provided expertise on numerous outreach partnership projects with classroom teachers in the Stockport area and has taken a leading role in the successful *Everybody Writes* and *Every Child a Writer* projects.

Martin Richardson is the Director of Education Studies at the University of Durham. He teaches and writes on the history of education, citizenship, culture and identity. He is also the architect of Harry Potter and the Age of Illusion, the only university module of its kind in Europe.

Craig Small is a coaching and educational psychologist with a long running interesting in behaviour, literacy, social inclusion and the psychology of collaboration and change. He has experience of leading local authority psychology services and has been seconded to government projects focused on meeting the behaviour challenge in schools, and the integration of children's services to improve outcomes. His doctorate research looked at using a solution focused approach to support teacher development in schools. He currently works in a range of fields where psychology can add social value.

Jayne Stead is Director of Drama and Performing Arts at Arnold Hill Academy in Nottinghamshire. She has taught English and performing arts across Key Stages 3, 4 and 5 in a wide variety of schools. She has undertaken extensive outreach work in primary schools and has advised on creative arts programmes at both secondary and primary levels. In her present role she has initiated a full *Primary Liaison for the Arts* package between secondary and primary phases.

Seven Stories is the National Centre for Children's Books. Its mission is to champion children's books as an essential part of our childhood, our national heritage and our culture. Staff are custodians of the only collection in the world dedicated to telling the story of British children's literature from the 1930s to the present day. The collection includes the original manuscripts and illustrations of many writers and artists including Judith Kerr, Enid Blyton, Philip Pullman, Kaye Webb and David Almond. Situated in a converted Victorian warehouse in Newcastle-upon-Tyne, its seven floors have been carefully restored to house galleries for exhibitions, performances and creative space, and a specialist children's bookshop.

Claire Warner is an education consultant for primary English. Her recent roles include working as a senior adviser for literacy with the National Strategies, and as a senior lecturer and leader of undergraduate ITT programmes at Chester University.

Acknowledgements

The editors are very grateful to everyone who has contributed to this book as authors of chapters. In addition, we would like to thank teachers and trainee teachers who allowed us to use examples of their teaching as case studies. Particular thanks go to Laura Coote, who wrote case studies of her Harry Potter-themed lessons for Chapter 6, and to Lauren Sinden for her contributions on parental involvement to Chapter 9.

Introduction

A current key focus in primary education is the teaching of systematic synthetic phonics to early readers. For some children, this has been done within *a broad and rich language curriculum that takes full account of developing the four interdependent strands of language: speaking, listening, reading and writing and enlarging children's stock of words* (DfES, 2006, 70). However, others may have been less fortunate, enduring a literacy curriculum lacking engagement with texts beyond those which are easily decodable, and featuring limited opportunities to hear their teachers bring texts to life in reading sessions. This book is designed to offer both ideas and a rationale for developing children's reading once they have mastered the early stages, and to show how teachers can engage children with texts, perhaps when they have become disillusioned by an earlier 'thin' diet.

In Chapter 1, Prof Steve Higgins describes the role research can play in helping us to identify problems and issues. He cites a key piece of international research (the PIRLS survey), which shows that children in England perform well compared with their peers in other countries. However, the study also shows that while the highest attaining pupils in England do as well as the best countries in the world for reading, we are not as good as these countries in supporting the reading achievement of our lower attaining pupils. Children's attitudes to reading are also more negative in England than in many countries. There is clearly much that needs to be done both to address the needs of low achievers and to engage the interest of those who can read well, but often choose not to read at all.

In Chapter 2, David Waugh focuses on the development of vocabulary. English is a rich language with a large lexicon acquired from many other languages. Good readers draw upon wide vocabularies to enable them to read well, but what strategies can teachers use to develop children's understanding of words and their meanings? The chapter looks at how words are created and at ways of applying our lexical knowledge when we meet new words. A strong case is made for vocabulary development to take place in a language-rich environment, set within meaningful contexts

In Chapter 3, Eve English explores a range of meaningful activities to engage children's interest in reading and aid their understanding of texts. She also stresses the importance of teachers' knowledge and understanding of texts and the value of demonstrating that they are readers too. The chapter includes a discussion about parental involvement in reading, a theme developed in Daniel Harrison's later chapter.

Claire Warner's Chapter 4 explores reading comprehension and in particular the role of adults in making the reading process visible by explicitly modelling and teaching a range of strategies for comprehension. Claire looks at key aspects of comprehension and provides practical guidance on developing readers' abilities to use a range of strategies to help them understand texts.

In Chapter 5, John Bennett examines the nature of modern children's reading, looking at children's reading beyond books. John explores ways in which we can develop the skills needed to read digital texts as effectively as possible. He concludes that the reading curriculum must look towards future reading activities, not just those with which the majority of children currently engage.

Chapter 6 looks at the phenomenally successful Harry Potter series to explore how the themes children have become so familiar with, through both the books and films, might lead teachers to capitalise upon children's interest in Potter in order to engage them in a range of literary themes. Martin Richardson, together with teacher Laura Coote, looks at the potential for discussing character, relationships and social and moral issues, using J.K. Rowling's stories as a starting point.

We are fortunate, in north-east England, to have Seven Stories, the National Centre for Children's Books, nearby. This is a superb resource, not only for local children but also for children all over Britain, since much of the staff's work involves schools around the country. Having seen the Seven Stories staff captivating children with imaginative and inspirational activities, we asked them to contribute a chapter to this book. The result is a chapter that provides a rationale for using a range of stimulating activities designed to engage children as creative and cultural readers for pleasure.

In Chapter 8, David Boorman and Jemma Rennocks examine ways in which children can be successfully engaged in reading by exploring texts actively. They focus on a series of classroom projects that increase children's engagement with reading, and find that active reading and plenty of 'talk' about texts can be harnessed to improve writing skills at text, sentence and word level.

In Chapter 9, headteacher, Daniel Harrison, describes a school's project to engage its children and parents in reading and writing. The school identified a need to work innovatively to encourage enthusiasm and enjoyment of reading. To achieve this, teachers made use of local places of interest including Seven Stories, Antony Gormley's iconic and huge *Angel of the North*, and a local Premier League football club, its stadium and educational facilities. The chapter describes the challenges teachers faced and the successes they and their pupils achieved.

In Chapter 10, educational psychologist, Craig Small, describes a project to develop an authentic approach to reading for children in alternative educational provision. This approach echoes a lot of other work on starting from the child's interests in order to engage reluctant readers.

There are implications here for teachers in mainstream provision who seek approaches to engage disengaged readers.

Jayne Stead, a secondary English and drama teacher, shows in Chapter 11 ways in which teachers can tune into children's interest in narrative forms and use this to develop their engagement with texts. In particular, she describes how this can be achieved in the transition from primary to secondary school.

Each chapter provides critical questions, points and reflections to encourage you to consider your own practice in light of what you have read. There are also case studies to demonstrate how teachers and trainee teachers have used the ideas in the classroom. Many chapters include recommended further reading, to enable you to develop stronger insights into how teachers can help children move beyond early reading to become fully engaged with the pleasures of reading.

1 What can we learn from research?

STEVE HIGGINS

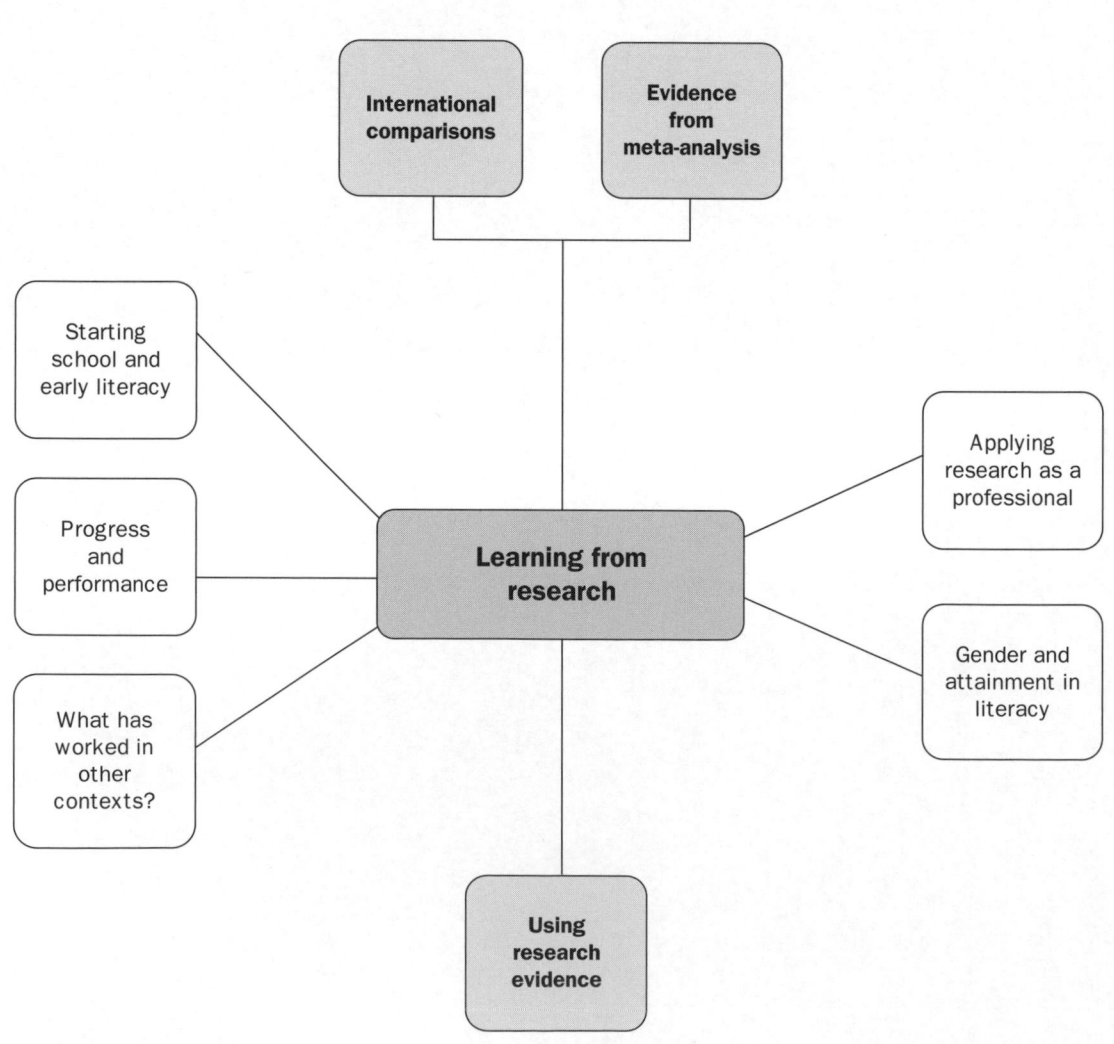

Teachers' standards

2 Promote good progress and outcomes by pupils

- demonstrate knowledge and understanding of how pupils learn and how this impacts on teaching

3 Demonstrate good subject and curriculum knowledge

- demonstrate a critical understanding of developments in the subject and curriculum areas, and promote the value of scholarship

4 Plan and teach well-structured lessons

- reflect systematically on the effectiveness of lessons and approaches to teaching

Critical questions

» *What can we learn from research into early literacy?*

» *What do international comparisons tell us?*

» *What can we learn about the teaching of early literacy?*

» *How can this information be used effectively?*

Why do we need research?

Imagine going to see your local doctor and hearing her (or him) say, *Oh I don't keep up to date with research. I just use the things that I know work for my patients. I learned what I know on the job, so I'm not really interested in how research can help me or my patients.* Would you be impressed? Of course, medical research and educational research are different, but we can still learn valuable lessons from what research tells us will help make us more effective teachers, which will keep us up to date with evidence as it develops, and which will help keep us effective and fresh as teachers through trying out and evaluating new ideas.

In this chapter, you will find evidence from research that will help you reflect critically on the teaching of literacy in schools, by comparing what we do with what happens in other countries and by looking at some examples of research evidence about what has helped in the teaching of literacy.

International comparisons

There are a number of large-scale international comparisons of educational performance. The oldest is the Trends in International Mathematics and Science Study (TIMSS), which was first administered in 1995 by the International Association for the Evaluation of Educational Achievement (IEA) to allow the countries involved to compare their pupils' educational attainment in mathematics and science. The IEA also manages the Progress in International Reading Literacy Study (PIRLS), which assesses 9- and 10-year-olds in reading and literacy (see below). The Programme for International Student Assessment (PISA) is another international study, undertaken by the Organisation for Economic Co-operation and Development (OECD), of 15-year-old school pupils' attainment in mathematics, science and reading. It was first administered in 2000 and then repeated every three years. These studies can help us to understand how our children are learning compared with progress in other countries. They also can shed light on other debates, such as the age that children start school, and on the teaching of the subjects that are assessed, including literacy. The tests and the design of the sampling of pupils aim to make the fairest comparisons possible, given differences in language and culture.

Progress in international reading literacy study (PIRLS) 2011

The Progress in International Reading Literacy Study (PIRLS) is an international study of reading. It is conducted by the International Association for the Evaluation of Educational Achievement (IEA). It has measured trends in the reading and literacy achievement of 9- and 10-year-olds every five years since 2001. It also collects information about reading and literacy policies, teaching practices in schools and home experiences. In 2006 PIRLS tested over 215,000 pupils from 45 countries.

In 2011, the results showed that only five out of the 45 countries involved performed significantly better than England. These countries were Finland, Hong Kong, Northern Ireland, the Russian Federation and Singapore.

England's performance improved between 2006 and 2011. Only the United States and Chinese Taipei showed greater improvement in this period.

Pupils in England had a wider spread of attainment than the top performing countries. The highest attaining pupils in England were similar to those in Singapore and higher than the best readers in the three top performing countries (Finland, Hong Kong and the Russian Federation). However, low attaining pupils in England scored less well than the low attaining pupils in other countries.

This indicates that overall progress in reading at primary school in England and Northern Ireland is good compared with other countries around the world (Scotland did not take part in PIRLS). It also suggests that although the highest attaining pupils in England do as well as the best countries in the world for reading, we are not as good as these countries in supporting the reading achievement of our lower attaining pupils. England had one of the largest proportions of pupils reaching the Advanced International Benchmark (18 per cent). However, the proportion of pupils in England who did not reach the Low International Benchmark (5 per cent) is similar to the proportion that do not achieve level 3 or above in National Curriculum tests of reading in England at the end of primary school. Overall this international evidence therefore suggests that this is an area where we could improve our overall performance, and at the same time provide a more equitable education system for our children. In other countries, the gap between the highest and lowest attaining pupils is not as wide as in England.

Activity 1: Why do you think we are not as good as other top performing countries at supporting the progress in reading of low attaining pupils?

» *As a pupil in school yourself, and most likely a successful reader, did you see or experience anything that you think might help you to understand this?*

» *In your more recent experience, have you seen anything in schools that might explain why low attaining pupils do not make such good progress with their reading and writing?*

Gender and attainment in literacy

International comparisons can provide information about more than overall national per-formance or the spread of scores however. We worry a lot in the UK about the underper-formance of boys and the difficulties that boys seem to have in literacy, in particular in early reading and writing, but what is the evidence for this from PIRLS? It is certainly true that in England girls performed significantly better than boys in PIRLS, but this is true for almost all other participating countries, with scores for girls on average about 3 per cent better than boys. So, girls all over the world, on average, do a little bit better on tests of literacy at age 10. It is also true that the difference between the attainment of boys and girls is a little bit bigger in England than in most other countries, and this has stayed about the same in all three PIRLS surveys. So the problem is an international one, and we do a little less well than other countries at solving it. The difference between the UK and the average of the other countries is just less than 1 per cent however. So, although there is a difference, and that difference hasn't really changed since 2001, it is a very small difference. It is also true to say that the difference between boys and girls is not as great as the 'gap' between low attaining and high attaining pupils' results in PIRLS. We have 5 per cent of our pupils who don't even reach the low benchmark, whereas 99 per cent of the pupils in Hong Kong and 98 per cent of the pupils in the Russian Federation, Sweden and the United States do.

Activity 2: Do you think people worry more about gender differences or about the attainment 'gap' between high and low attainers?

» *What issues have you picked up as important in schools in terms of differences in attainment?*

» *What about how this is represented in the media? What makes the news?*

» *What are your own views? Which difference do you think is more important?*

Other findings from PIRLS

* PIRLS assesses different kinds of reading: reading for literary purposes and reading to acquire and use information. In 2011, pupils in England performed equally well on both scales and this was better than they did in 2006. This was not true of all countries.

* In terms of reading comprehension, pupils in England were particularly good at the more challenging aspects of comprehension such as interpreting, integrating and evaluating information. Surprisingly, they were not quite as good at the more basic skills of retrieving information and inferencing.

* Pupils in higher performing countries spent less time on reading activities than the average, suggesting that these countries are both very efficient and very effective

at teaching reading. It may also be that reading skills are also developed through other activities in these countries. Alternatively some of the differences may be due to differences in the languages involved. Finnish, for example, has almost perfect phonemic orthography where a single letter represents each speech sound, so teaching phonics is relatively straightforward. Other languages, such as Chinese and Japanese, are logographic where each symbol or character represents a word or a morpheme. Both of these differences may make aspects of learning to read less complex than in English where the correspondence between sound and symbol is more variable.

•   Internationally, the average achievement scores were the same regardless of whether or not computers were available for use in reading lessons. Average achievement in England was similar for pupils who did and who did not have access to a computer for reading lessons.

•   PIRLS also asks questions about children's wider experience of schooling, including bullying. In England, reports of bullying from pupils were very similar to international averages and about 45 per cent of pupils reported that they were almost never bullied. However, 20 per cent reported that they experienced bullying behaviours about weekly. This suggests that, on average, one in five children in each class experience bullying each week in school.

Summer-born children

There are other issues that international studies can also shed light on that are not so well known or talked about. International studies indicate that it is a disadvantage to being the youngest in the class. School systems in different parts of the world start at different times of the year, but those who are youngest in the year tend to do less well. How much does this matter?

FOCUS ON RESEARCH

Does it matter in which month you are born?

A study of longitudinal data on 3,187 children in Flemish primary education in Belgium (Verachtert et al., 2010) found that there were season-of-birth effects on both grade retention and achievement during the first two years of primary school. (Grade retention is where pupils have to repeat a school year and do not progress with their peers.) Because the Flemish cut-off date is 31 December, children born in the last quarter (October to December) invariably are among the youngest in their grade age group. Almost 20 per cent of these children born towards the end of the school year were found to have been retained or referred to special education by the end of Grade 2, whereas for the oldest children in the school year who were born in the first quarter (January to March), this was only 6 per cent. The study also investigated whether this effect was the same for teachers who provided different work for the children and those who did not, but differentiated teaching was not found to be related to any decrease in the disadvantage associated with the month in which the children were born.

In England, there is evidence that children born in July and August make slower progress at school, particularly for reading and writing. They are also more likely to be put in lower attaining groups and are more likely to be diagnosed with special educational needs (Crawford *et al.*, 2007).

If we consider, on average, the differences in the proportions of August-born and September-born children who reach the expected level at Key Stage 1, August-born children are about 25 per cent less likely to reach the expected level than September-born children in the same year group. On average, at Key Stage 1, about three-quarters of September-born but only about half of the August-born children attain the expected level. These differences are fairly consistent across ethnic groupings, but children receiving free school meals (which is used as an approximation for economic disadvantage) are even less likely to succeed. Boys born in August who receive free school meals (FSM) are 58 per cent less likely to reach the expected level by the end of Key Stage 1 compared with FSM-eligible September-born boys. These differences also persist into Key Stage 2 where August-born children are about 13 per cent less likely to achieve the expected levels.

Overall, the analysis indicates that there is a significant disadvantage in being born in August across all outcomes and at every age for children in English state schools. In terms of average scores and the proportion of children achieving the expected level, this disadvantage is largest when a child first enters school (about 25 per cent less likely) and it declines over time, but is still significant at ages 16 (about 6 per cent) and 18 (about 2 per cent), when students are making decisions about career choices and/or future study. Slower development in literacy makes it difficult for children to participate in the wider curriculum when this involves reading and writing

Of course, we have to start the school year at some point. The research from Belgium indicates that we could not solve the problem by changing the starting month of the school year. If we started the school year in January, the 'August-born' problem would become a 'December-born' problem. Also the routine kind of differentiation that teachers used in Belgium (see above) did not solve the problem. Although this affects children's progress in school generally, the impact is especially detrimental in terms of the development of reading and writing skills as these are fundamental to young children's learning at school.

Activity 3: What do you think about this issue?

» *In which month were you born? Do you think this affected you either positively or negatively?*

» *Why does this issue not capture the headlines? Had you heard of it before? The impact is much greater than the effects of gender and makes the disadvantage linked with FSM-status much worse.*

» *What could be done about this? Would it help to have different test times for children born at different times of year? Should we interpret test scores differently for children born at different times? How might you plan your literacy activities to take this into account?*

At what age should children start learning literacy?

The question of at what age children should start learning to read and write is a complex one. Although there is extensive research and debate in this area, it is hard to draw firm conclusions. Since the late nineteenth century, the UK has expected children to start school at an earlier age than most other countries. In England, children are legally required to be in school in the term following their fifth birthday, though most start when they are 4 years old. In Northern Ireland, children start school when they are 4 years old. In most of Europe, children do not start school until they are older; in Finland and most other Scandinavian countries this is as old as 7. Of course, the age at which children start school does not necessarily reflect the kind of literacy teaching that they experience or the way that they learn about books and print. Young children may be in an Early Years setting, which is less formal or teacher-directed than a more formal and didactic playgroup. The type of Early Years experience, such as whether it is a school or a playgroup, may not make as much difference as what happens within each setting. It is important that young children receive developmentally appropriate support to develop their early literacy skills, knowledge and confidence.

It is certainly the case that early literacy experience, and in particular knowledge of letters and sounds, is associated with greater progress in reading and writing. However, the question of how we can best help those who do not start school with this knowledge and literacy experience is much more problematic. In Finland, although children start school relatively late, they make more rapid progress from 7 to 10 years old (but bear in mind the note above about the phonemic orthography of Finnish). It is also the case that many of them will have attended kindergarten or some form of preschool setting from the age of 6. For most children, a later start does not seem to make much difference in the long run. Overall, the message seems to be that it is the *quality* of these early literacy experiences that makes the difference. The challenge is to make sure that when children start school early this does not increase the time in which they have to experience failure.

Overall, the question should really be what kind of literacy learning is appropriate for young children? And how can we ensure that this increases their chances of becoming successful readers and writers in school and in later life?

Evidence from research about effective teaching

There is a vast amount of research on the teaching of literacy in schools. It spans the educational research journals, the psychology literature and research into speech and language development. There is research on phonics, on reading comprehension and on dyslexia. It is not possible to be familiar with all of it. A single study is never going to be conclusive in education. Even when you find evidence that something has been effective, you have to consider the differences in the contexts in which the research was conducted and the setting where you might want to make improvements based on research. Just because something worked in Belgium, with 10-year-olds, even if 50 schools and 100 classes improved their first language reading comprehension of French, it does not guarantee it will help you teach your class of Year 6 children to read better, but it might contain ideas or techniques that would get you off to a good start.

A good idea is to start with summaries and overviews of research for teachers. There are a number of trustworthy sites available on the internet (please see links below and the references).

The New Zealand government funds the 'Best Evidence Synthesis' which aims to provide *trustworthy evidence about what works and what makes a bigger difference in education*. One distinctive feature of the programme and the reviews it contains is a focus on explaining the evidence about the influences on valued outcomes for diverse learners. The range of Best Evidence Syntheses is designed to be a catalyst for systemic and ongoing improvement in education.

www.educationcounts.govt.nz/topics/bes

The US government funds the 'What Works Clearinghouse' (WWC). This focuses on identifying thematic areas that represent challenging areas of interest in US education, such as 'beginning reading' or 'character education'. Within each selected topic area, the WWC collects studies of interventions that have research evidence. These include *programs, products, practices, and policies* that are potentially relevant to the area, and they also undertake comprehensive and systematic literature searches. The studies collected are then subjected to a three-stage review process. Where there is insufficient evidence, some areas do not get past the first stage; others are reported as meeting evidence standards.

www.whatworks.ed.gov

In the UK, the Sutton Trust and the Education Endowment Foundation (EEF) have produced the 'Teaching and Learning Toolkit'. This has been endorsed by the Department for Education and the government as a 'What Works' centre for education evidence in the UK. It aims to provide an accessible summary of educational research as guidance for teachers and schools on how to use their resources, in particular to improve the attainment of disadvantaged pupils. It is different from other summaries of research, in that it includes an estimate of the potential benefit in terms of months of progress, an estimate of costs, as well as an indication of the strength of the evidence. It is also unusual in that it reviews areas that the evidence indicates have *not* been effective, as well as those that show more promise.

http://educationendowmentfoundation.org.uk/toolkit

Activity 4: Review two of these sources for research evidence

» *What did you think? How easy were the sites to use to find evidence that interested you?*

» *Were there any surprises? Did the evidence match what you expected?*

» *How could you use these to inform your teaching?*

The Sutton Trust and EEF's 'Teaching and Learning Toolkit'

In this section we will look at one of these resources in more detail. The 'Teaching and Learning Toolkit' sets out a range of different approaches to improving learning in schools. It assesses the quality of the evidence, and identifies how well each approach has worked from over 60 detailed summaries of the impact of education research (these are 'meta-analyses' that pull together the quantitative findings from a large number of research studies).

The potential gain in attainment is presented in terms of the additional months' progress you might expect pupils to make as a result of a successful approach. For example, if an effective feedback intervention has an impact of nine months' progress, it means that, for two classes of pupils that were the same before the intervention, the class that adopted the effective feedback intervention would be better than the control class by a large margin after the intervention. The average pupil in a class of 25 pupils in the feedback class would now be equivalent to the 6th best pupil in the control class, having made 21 months' progress over the year, compared with an average of 12 months' normal progress in the other class. The Toolkit uses systematic reviews of research and detailed quantitative summaries ('meta-analyses').

Cost estimates are based on how much an approach for a class of 25 pupils would be estimated to cost. Where an approach does not require any additional resources, estimates are based on the cost of the training or professional development that may be required.

An estimate of the quality of the evidence is also made based on the methodological quality of the primary evidence and the reliability or consistency of this impact.

The findings

There are some surprises in the findings. For example, the deployment of teaching assistants (TAs) makes less of an impact than many schools expect, especially considering that this has been one of the most popular ways to spend additional funding from the *pupil premium* (additional funding given to schools for each pupil in receipt of FSM). On average, classes with TAs assigned to them make only the same progress as classes without TAs. This does not mean that teaching assistants do not have any effect on learning. It suggests about half are deployed in a way that has a positive effect, and about half in ways that are ineffective or detrimental to learning. A recent UK study revealed that the more support pupils with special educational needs (SEN) received from TAs the *less* well they did in terms of attainment, when compared with similar SEN pupils in classes without a TA. This means that it is vitally important to work out how support staff can best support pupils' learning as, on average, this does not happen just by them being present in the classroom or in the typical ways that schools choose to use them.

APPROACH	COST ESTIMATE	EVIDENCE ESTIMATE	AVERAGE IMPACT
Ability grouping	£	★ ★ ★	– 1 months
After school programmes	£ £ £ £	★ ★	+ 2 months
Arts participation	£ £	★ ★ ★	+ 2 months
Aspiration interventions	£ £ £	★	0 months
Behaviour interventions	£ £ £	★ ★ ★ ★	+ 4 months
Collaborative learning	£	★ ★ ★ ★	+ 5 months
Digital technology	£ £ £ £	★ ★ ★ ★	+ 4 months
Early Years intervention	£ £ £ £ £	★ ★ ★ ★	+ 6 months

APPROACH	COST ESTIMATE	EVIDENCE ESTIMATE	AVERAGE IMPACT
Extended school time	£ £ £	★ ★	+ 2 months
Feedback	£ £	★ ★ ★	+ 8 months
Homework (primary)	£	★ ★ ★	+ 1 months
Homework (secondary)	£	★ ★ ★	+ 5 months
Individualised instruction	£	★ ★ ★	+ 2 months
Learning styles	£	★ ★ ★	+ 2 months
Mentoring	£ £ £	★ ★ ★	+ 1 month
Meta-cognition and self-regulation	£ £	★ ★ ★ ★	+ 8 months
One-to-one tuition	£ £ £ £	★ ★ ★ ★	+ 5 months
Parental involvement	£ £ £	★ ★ ★	+ 3 months
Peer tutoring	£ £	★ ★ ★ ★	+ 6 months
Performance pay	£ £ £	★	0 months
Phonics	£	★ ★ ★ ★	+ 4 months
Physical environment	£ £	★	0 months
Reducing class size	£ £ £ £ £	★ ★ ★	+ 3 months
School uniform	£	★	0 months
Small group tuition	£ £ £	★ ★	+ 4 months
Social and emotional aspects of learning	£	★ ★ ★ ★	+ 4 months
Sports participation	£ £ £	★ ★ ★	+ 2 months
Summer schools	£ £ £	★ ★	+ 3 months
Teaching assistants	£ £ £ £	★ ★	0 months

Similarly, with a popular approach such as 'ability grouping' very common as a practice in literacy teaching in the UK, the benefits are seen only for high attaining students. The impact over time on the learning of low attaining pupils as a result of ability grouping tends to be negative, particularly on pupils' beliefs about themselves as learners and their aspirations. If schools decide to use these kinds of grouping, you should think about how they can limit or overcome this likely detrimental impact. This might be by looking at other approaches in the list that are more effective, such as significantly reducing the size of lower attaining groups (to about 15) or by increasing the amount or the quality of feedback that learners get about their work. Overall the research shows that this is one of the most effective things that a teacher can do.

It is worth mentioning that even the term 'ability grouping' may be part of the problem. We can group pupils by how well they are doing, or by their current level of performance or attainment. As the research on summer-born children indicates, this may not be a good measure of their actual ability, which is typically not shown by their current level of attainment. The term 'ability' implies something fixed that will not change. This is not supported by the evidence as children make progress at different rates at different times. If you think of a child as having low ability you do not think they can change. If you think of them as having low attainment, you believe that this will improve,

The good news is that many of the things that are highly effective are relatively inexpensive: improving the quality of feedback to pupils about their learning or supporting them in planning, monitoring, reviewing and evaluating their learning ('meta-cognition') can all be tackled through professional development and professional inquiry, such as by working in small teams to implement strategies and tracking the impact of any new initiative.

The most effective approaches, such as effective feedback, developing learners' strategic thinking about their learning (meta-cognition and self-regulation), and pupil-to-pupil tutoring, directly and positively influence teaching and learning interactions in the classroom. Pupil-to-pupil tutoring involves pupils about two years older than those needing help tutoring the younger learners in reading. Both in the pair benefit, but surprisingly the older tutor often learns more than the younger pupil. This is probably because the tutor learns to be more strategic and aware of their own reading skills as a result of teaching a younger pupil.

Some of the research, such as the impact of phonics interventions, also deserves closer inspection. (The 'Toolkit' contains a useful reference list for each of the areas it summarises and key references are provided at the end of this chapter.) The evidence (for example, Torgerson *et al.*, 2008) shows that phonics is clearly effective as an approach and can be an important strategy in helping the development of early reading skills, particularly for children from disadvantaged backgrounds. However, it is not a panacea, and it is also important that children are successful in making progress in all aspects of reading, including vocabulary development, comprehension and spelling, which should be taught separately and explicitly. We should also be aware that as schools spend more time on phonics-based approaches, support for those who are not making good progress may need to draw on other strategies, as giving children more of what they have failed with (and know that they have failed with) may not be a successful intervention strategy.

Overall, the approaches that are less effective focus on organisational or managerial issues, such as ability grouping, changing the timetable or performance pay. This emphasises the importance of concentrating on research-based approaches that can directly influence pupils' learning. School uniforms, for example, may be identified as one of the features associated with an improving school, particularly one where behaviour and the development of a positive school ethos were an important focus. Just asking or requiring children to wear a school uniform, however, will not directly improve their reading skills, though it may be part of a process that creates more effective conditions for learning.

Using research evidence

There are, of course, no guarantees when drawing lessons from the research evidence. The Toolkit summarises approaches that have been effective in the past. It is not a summary of 'what works', but what *has* worked, for other teachers, with other pupils, in other schools. The quality of the evidence, even with the strict inclusion criteria adopted for the Toolkit, is still variable. This means that the potential gain identified will not be automatically achieved in a new context. Each school and each teacher will still need to work out what is likely to be the most effective approach for their particular school and their pupils, and then monitor the impact to ensure that any new approach or any spending of additional funding is effective in actually improving the learning of the disadvantaged students it seeks to help. What the Toolkit aims to do is to provide information about how different approaches have (and have not) been successful in other contexts, as a guide to where there is likely to be potential benefit as a 'good bet' or more of a risky choice. The evidence suggests that this is not always straightforward, as many of the approaches we intuitively believe will be beneficial for attainment, such as smaller classes or additional adult support, are not the best bets to improve learning that we think they are.

Conclusion

Using research and being able to interpret and apply research evidence is one of the hallmarks of a professional teacher. We should not accept the argument that experience is suf ficient to improve practice. Experience alone will lead to blind spots in both our individual teaching and the kinds of practice we accept as 'effective' in the UK.

In the review of international evidence, you had the chance to see four areas of research that are relevant to your practice in primary schools. The overall international comparisons indicate literacy teaching in the UK reaches the highest standards internationally, but that we do not do so well with our lower attaining pupils, who fall further behind than in other countries. Gender is a regular issue in the news in terms of the differences in attainment between boys and girls. We are perhaps right to worry in the UK, as the gender gap is a little larger than in other countries, but the problem is not as great as the larger gap between our lowest and highest attaining children. A further area reviewed was that of the way the timing of the school year affects the youngest pupils in schools. This area receives relatively little interest in the media or in staffrooms, and yet the data suggest it is a very real problem for children born in the summer months in the UK. The final area summarised in this section concerned the school starting age for children and the learning of early literacy. Here the evidence is less clear and it appears that it is the kind of literacy experiences that children have that affects their success in early literacy, rather than the specific age at which they start school. Overall, it is unlikely that starting school at a younger age is a feature of the success, as children in a number of highly successful countries start later than children in the UK.

The evidence from research on interventions has investigated how to improve learning also has some surprises. Some of the things that we assume are effective may not actually improve children's learning. They may help to make a classroom run more smoothly, or make things easier to manage for the teacher, or may even engage and motivate pupils and make them more enthusiastic in school, but what we learn from research is that this may not be enough to improve learning. Better-behaved pupils may be easier to manage and to involve in tasks and activities in school, but unless this helps them to work harder, or for longer or more efficiently at their learning, it will not help their attainment.

Critical points

» *International comparisons help us understand our curriculum and the teaching and learning of literacy in the UK. It lets us know what is working well overall, but also where there are things we do less well.*

» *Rigorous research can inform our classroom practice, giving us 'good bets' for changing and improving our practice.*

» *Some of the practices we think are effective may not actually be 'working' for us.*

» *Research-based practice will always need to be considered in terms of its applicability to a new context, and then evaluated to ensure it is still effective.*

Critical reflection

» *How can you use research evidence to inform your practice as a teacher?*

Taking it further

Hattie, J. (2011). *Visible Learning for Teachers: Maximizing Impact on Learning*. London: Routledge Pages.

Marzano, R. J., Pickering, D. J., & Pollock, J. E. (2001). *Classroom Instruction That Works: Research-Based Strategies for Increasing Student Achievement*. Alexandria, VA: ASCD.

Taber, K. (2007). *Classroom-Based Research and Evidence-Based Practice: A Guide for Teachers*. SAGE Publications Limited.

References

Crawford, C., Dearden, L. and Meghir, C. (2007). *When You Are Born Matters: The Impact of Date of Birth on Child Cognitive Outcomes in England*. Centre for the Economics of Education, London School of Economics and Political Science. http://eprints.lse.ac.uk/19374/1/When_you_are_born_matters.pdf (accessed 20 June 2012).

Daniels, S., Shorrocks-Taylor, D. and Redfern, E. (2000). Can Starting Summer-Born Children Earlier at Infant School Improve their National Curriculum Results? *Oxford Review of Education*, 26:2.

Ehri, C.L., Nunes, S.R., Stahl, S.A. and Willows, D.M. (2001). Systematic Phonics Instruction Helps Students Learn to Read: Evidence from the National Reading Panel's Meta-Analysis. *Review of Educational Research*, 71:3.

Mullis, I.V.S., Martin, M.O., Foy, P. and Drucker, K.T. (2012). *The PIRLS 2011 International Results in Reading*. Chestnut Hill, MA: TIMSS and PIRLS International Study Center, Boston College. http://timss.bc.edu/pirls2011/downloads/P11_IR_FullBook.pdf (accessed 20 June 2012).

Slavin, R. E., Lake, C., Davis, S. and Madden, N. A. (2011). Effective Programs For Struggling Readers: A Best-Evidence Synthesis. *Educational Research Review*, 6:1.

Torgerson C.J., Brooks, G. and Hall, J. (2008). *A Systematic Review of the Research Literature on the use of Phonics in the Teaching of Reading and Spelling*. Research Report, No.711. London: DfEE.

Twist, L., Sizmur, J., Bartlett, S. and Lynn, L. (2012). *PIRLS 2011: Reading Achievement in England*. Slough: NFER. www.nfer.ac.uk/publications/PRTZ01 (accessed 20 June 2012).

Tymms, P., Merrell, C., Thurston, A., Andor, J., Topping, K. and Miller, D. (2011). Improving Attainment Across a Whole District: School Reform Through Peer Tutoring in a Randomized Controlled Trial. *School Effectiveness and School Improvement*, 22:3.

Verachtert, P., De Fraine, B., Onghena, P. and Ghesquière, P. (2010). Season of Birth and School Success in the Early Years of Primary Education. *Oxford Review of Education*, 36:3.

2 Developing vocabulary

DAVID WAUGH

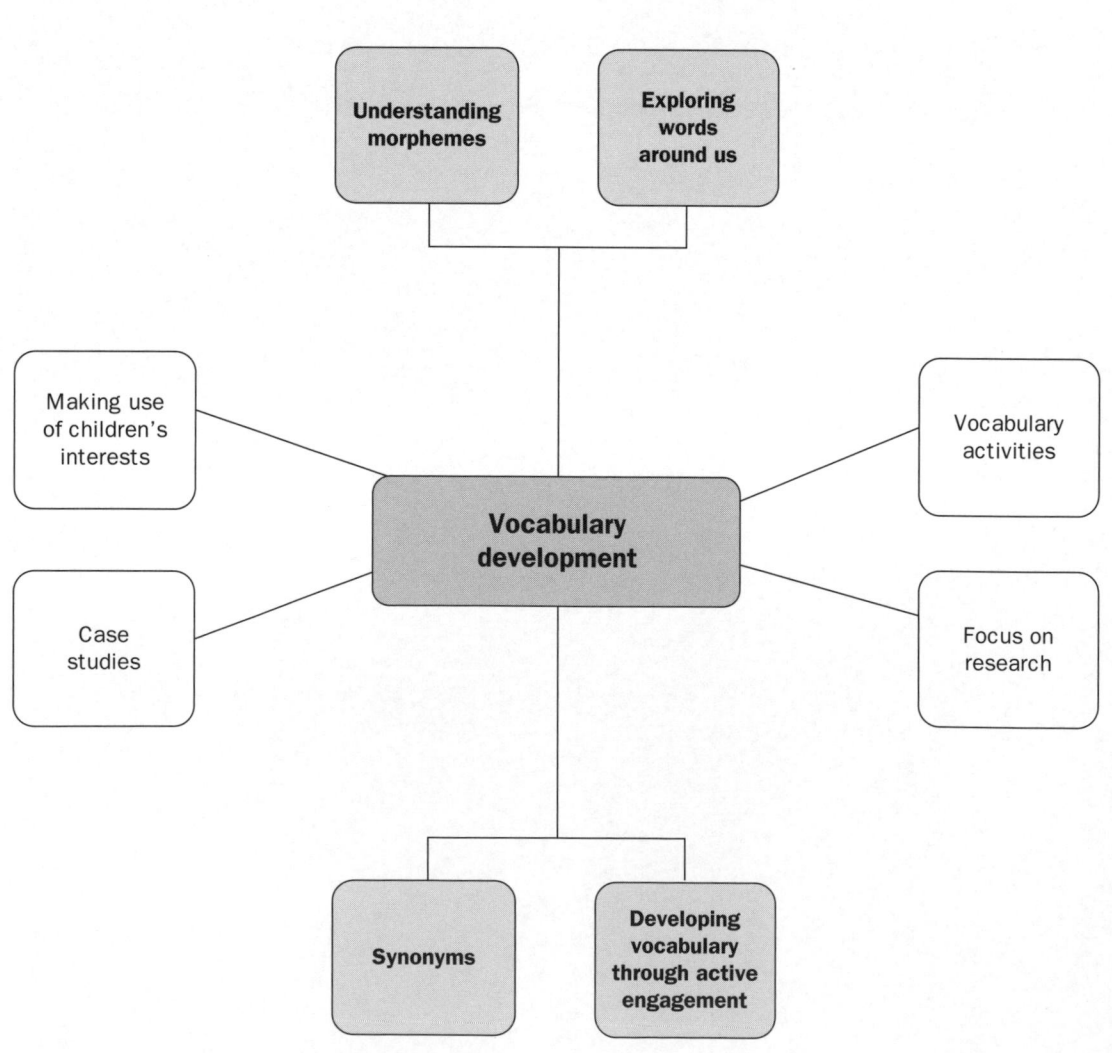

Teachers' standards

3 Demonstrate good subject and curriculum knowledge

*   have a secure knowledge of the relevant subject(s) and curriculum areas, foster and maintain pupils' interest in the subject, and address misunderstandings

*   demonstrate an understanding of and take responsibility for promoting high standards of literacy, articulacy and the correct use of standard English, whatever the teacher's specialist subject

*   if teaching early reading, demonstrate a clear understanding of systematic synthetic phonics

Critical questions

»   *How can we develop children's interest in words and extend their vocabularies?*

»   *How can we engage children's interest in the texts that surround them?*

»   *How can we use environmental print?*

»   *How can we help children to use their growing understanding of words to extrapolate when they meet unfamiliar words?*

Introduction

Imagine you have some coloured paints – a tray of five colours just as you might find in a primary classroom: white, black, yellow, blue and red. Does this mean you only have five colours to use as you paint a picture? Of course it doesn't. You can mix black and white in different proportions to make various shades of grey; blue and yellow to create a range of greens; blue and red to make purples; yellow and red to make oranges etc. Our vocabularies are rather like the tray of paints. We may know some basic words, but if we understand these words and what we can do with them to create new words, then our vocabularies are significantly enhanced. Thus, if we understand the word *like* and know that it can mean both *similar* and *agreeable*, we can begin to understand or work out meanings for a wealth of other words, including: *likely, likeable, alike, unlike, likeness, dislike* and *unlikely.*

To understand, read and use words successfully, it is important to develop an understanding of the roles and meanings of different parts of words and of the origins of words. In this chapter, you will explore *morphemes, etymology* and *neologisms* to see how you can develop both your pupils' and your own vocabulary. It is through being able to understand how words are created that we can enhance our vocabularies and work out what unfamiliar words might mean. All of this contributes to *automaticity* in reading: when we are able to read quickly and understand what we are reading. In this chapter, you will find examples of research that emphasises the importance of vocabulary development and offers strategies for this, and will see examples of activities in classrooms which have supported vocabulary development.

Exploring words around us

Next time you are in a classroom, look around at the many examples of texts that adorn the walls, furniture and even the doors and windows. Indeed, Brien (2012, 152) has argued that *a school should be a place where a love of language oozes out of the woodwork*. Children are surrounded by text both in school and in the street. Some of this text has no direct interest for them, but some will be highly relevant and will help them to find things they need, discover information and support their learning. It is important to recognise not only that children need to understand the nature and function of environmental print, but that they also recognise that it has relevance for them. As you can see elsewhere in this book, most children learn to read and can cope with simple texts by the time they leave Key Stage 1, but too many do not go on to be readers who view reading as an essential part of their everyday lives. The development of a wide vocabulary and an understanding of ways to approach unfamiliar words will help make a wide range of texts more accessible to them.

What do children see as they look at notices, shop signs, street signs and traffic signs? They see that some of the rules they have been taught in school, such as capital letters at the beginnings of names, use of lower case for words, and words appearing in sentences, do not necessarily apply. They find that businesses use wordplay in their names and sometimes deliberately spell them in phonically highly regular but technically incorrect ways (eg *Kleenex*, *Kwik Fit*). Hairdressers and fish and chip shops seem to be a rich source for clever plays on words such as: *Curl up and dye*, *Hair force*, *Clippity Do Da* and *Oh My Cod!*, *Battersea Cod's Home* and, from South Wales, *A Fish Called Rhondda*! Children find that there are advertising hoardings and sides of vehicles with pithy statements about the services they provide. A favourite was seen on the side of a van in Leicester driven by an Asian builder: *Patel and Patel: You've tried the cowboys. Now try the Indians!*

Clever wordplay can also be found in newspapers. Many children may look at sports pages, for example, to find football news and scores. They will often find headlines that they are able to read, but which may have little meaning for them because puns have been used. So *Roo Beauty!* might head a report in which Wayne Rooney has scored a winning goal, but young readers may not understand the play on words (*You* beauty!). Similarly, a late goal for Spurs' Gareth Bale might be reported as *Gareth Bales Spurs Out!* with the player's homophonic name having a second meaning. Collections of (appropriate!) tabloid headlines could promote interesting discussions, not only about double meanings, but also about different phoneme-grapheme correspondences. And those children who are especially interested in football will also know of many foreign players whose names often do not correspond closely to the English phonic system (Modric, Dzeko, Mignolet, Tchoyi, etc.).

Bunting (2000, 101) maintained that engaging children in activities that require close attention to language may *contribute to their interest in and ability to use language*. However, she cautions that this alone is not a justification for exploring language: *language is interesting in its own right and looking at language should be an everyday part of the work of the classroom* (101). Indeed, such work can also be done outside the classroom on literacy walks and language trails. A starting point could be work on maps, particularly of an area within easy walking distance of the school, as in the case study below.

CASE STUDY

Year 4 researching their locality

National Curriculum (2013): Pupils should spell words as accurately as possible using their phonic knowledge and other knowledge of spelling, such as morphology and etymology.

Liam, a third-year BA QTS student working with a Y4 class from a school in a small town wanted to combine work in geography and on the local area with vocabulary development in literacy lessons. He prepared by taking digital photographs of streets that surrounded the school and then creating a PowerPoint presentation. Some names of shops and streets were hidden or partly hidden in the presentation and children were quick to identify them. Liam asked for help with spelling the names and wrote the children's various suggestions on the board, discussing which letter combinations were likely. The children learned various names for streets, such as *road, avenue, crescent, close, lane, garth, way* and *gate*, and went on to create maps with streets named. Many looked at websites such as Googlemap, RAC and AA for ideas. Some investigated the origins of the street names.

Liam discussed some of the conventions attached to writing street names, such as using capital letters at the beginning of words when writing an address in a letter (eg Oak Road), but using uppercase letters only on street signs (eg OAK ROAD).

The class went on to discuss the fact that many estates' streets have names that follow a theme and that all the streets might, for instance, be named after birds or trees or flowers or towns or villages, and children were asked to investigate such themes in their locality. They used A to Z books and the internet and discovered themes such as battles (*Alma, Ladysmith, Waterloo*, etc.); cities (*London, York, Bristol,* etc.); musicians (*Mozart, Elgar, Handel,* etc.) and even, in Leicester, nuts (*Filbert, Hazel, Walnut,* and *Brazil*)!

Some children went on to look at maps of their locality or of nearby towns and devised alternative names for some of the streets. Some even thought of new names for the streets in the game of Monopoly.

Activity 1

» *Consider Liam's work with his Y4 class. How could he develop this to develop children's vocabularies further?*

Lessons such as the one described above not only enhance children's vocabularies, but also foster an interest in words and spellings. If you take the time to find out more about the names of the places children encounter, you will also help them to understand the origins and pronunciation of other less familiar places when they meet them. For example, if they know that *Doncaster* is a place on the River Don that had a castle or fort, they will be able to pronounce and understand other names such as Lancaster, Tadcaster and Ancaster. They can learn, too, that places with *chester* or *cester* in their names also had castles or forts (Manchester, Winchester, Leicester, Worcester).

FOCUS ON RESEARCH

Biemiller (2003) found that, when starting school, those children who performed well knew an average of 7100 root words, while those who performed less well knew only around 3000 words. This had implications for children's reading comprehension, since those with limited vocabularies could understand less of what they read (Chall *et al.*, 1990). Indeed, Fisher and Blachnowicz (2005) argued that a low vocabulary could trap children in a vicious circle, as they would not be able to read texts that might have extended their vocabularies and they would also be less able to use strategies to learn new words. It is, therefore, important to develop strategies for enhancing children's vocabularies. Fisher and Blachnowicz (2005) recommended:

- *ensuring the learning environment is word-rich;*
- *addressing vocabulary learning as a distinct area in the curriculum;*
- *careful selection of appropriate words for planned teaching and reinforcement (for example, words that have parts found in many other words, such as medicine/medical/medicate).* (DCSF, 2008, 7)

Making use of children's interests

Much of the vocabulary work you engage in with your class will involve particular topics and subjects as part of the curriculum. For example, in mathematics they might look at the names of shapes such as *triangle*, *heptagon*, *hexagon*, *pentagon* and *octagon*, learning as they do so about the prefixes, which tell them about the numbers of sides and angles in the shapes. In geography they might look at terms including: *town, city, region, country, continent* and *hemisphere*; while in history words such as *era, century, millennium, age* and *epoch* could feature. The words could be displayed with definitions in alphabetical order, both as an aid to spelling and to understanding. Links can also be made between the vocabulary of different subjects, for example, the *mille* beginning of *millennium* can also be found in units of measurement such as *millimetres* and *millilitres*.

Subject-specific vocabulary has, then, an important place in the classroom, but it is also important that children have opportunities to consider and share vocabulary that relates to their particular hobbies and interests, each of which will have its own meta-language (terminology specific to something), sometimes with words taking on new or slightly different meanings from those used in everyday activities. For example, *run, maiden, over* and *bowler* in cricket are all nouns, but *run* is a verb in *I run home*, *over* is a preposition in *Somewhere Over the Rainbow* and *bowler* can also be the name of a hat! *Maiden*, meanwhile, is a rather antiquated name for a single woman, but in cricket refers to a bowler bowling six balls without the batsman scoring any runs. Cricket gives us some other wonderfully odd uses of common words, including a batsman being *out* when he has to go *in* to the pavilion and *in* when he is *out* on the field batting. No wonder some foreigners are *stumped* by cricketing terminology!

Children could, then, collect terms for horses and horse-riding, dinosaurs, pets, sports, music, computers, computer games and so on. You can add your own lists, including football, cricket and rugby league tables; music charts; TV listings; lists of best-selling children's books; lists of popular boys' and girls' names in different periods; and lists of cities, countries and planets. The lists could be displayed and discussed and will provide opportunities for considering spelling, etymology and morphology.

More cryptic vocabulary activities

Crosswords, quizzes, trails and treasure hunts can engage children's interest and might even involve a competitive element for groups: something which many children enjoy.

Crosswords

Simple crosswords can be created using vocabulary relevant to a particular topic. Keep them simple at first and model strategies for solving them before asking children to work independently. This will need to include explaining how the numbering system works and how the number of letters in an answer is shown, as well as looking at anagrams and showing how these are sometimes indicated.

Solving a puzzle can reinforce children's knowledge of word definitions and spelling, so you might include clues for a mathematics crossword such as:

- five-sided shape (8);
- triangle with equal sides (11);
- take away (8);
- I dived (anag) (6).

If some children in your class are ready to be challenged by more cryptic clues you might include those such as:

- it sounds as if a corner has been badly damaged in this four-sided shape (9).

(Answer at the end of the chapter.)

You might also make use of word searches and partially completed crosswords, perhaps with some missing words or letters.

Treasure trails

Treasure trails are popular and need not involve children leaving the classroom, especially if they are done by two or three children at a time. Clues can be simple or cryptic and might be written in simple rhymes. For example, if the clue was hidden in Shirley Hughes' book *Dogger*:

> *To find the next clue won't take an age.*
> *Look in Dogger – there's an extra page!*

If a clue was stuck on a door:

> *You've found this clue, now look for more.*
> *There's something you need on a blue cupboard door.*

For younger children or those whose reading is not strong, treasure trails can be done with support from a classroom assistant or older children. Once children understand how these work, they often enjoy creating treasure trails for their classmates or, if they are in upper Key Stage 2, for Key Stage 1 or lower Key Stage 1 children.

Developing vocabulary through active engagement

International perspective

The activities described above involve developing vocabulary through active engagement and through incidental learning. They offer a range of different ways to draw children's attention to vocabulary, just as those described later in the chapter do. Consider the findings of the National Reading Panel in the USA as you reflect on them and read about further classroom activities. The Panel summed up research on vocabulary development by citing nine implications for reading instruction.

1 *Vocabulary should be taught both directly and indirectly.*

2 *Repetition and multiple exposures to vocabulary items are important.*

3 *Learning in rich contexts is valuable for vocabulary learning.*

4 *Vocabulary tasks should be restructured when necessary.*

5 *Vocabulary learning should entail active engagement in learning tasks.*

6 *Computer technology can be used to help teach vocabulary.*

7 *Vocabulary can be acquired through incidental learning.*

8 *How vocabulary is assessed and evaluated can have differential effects on instruction.*

9 *Dependence on a single vocabulary instruction method will not result in optimal learning.*

(National Reading Panel, 2000, 4–27)

Activity 2

» *Focus, in particular, on the fifth point in the panel's findings above. What kind of activities might engage children's interest? How might some of the other points be drawn upon to enable this to happen; for example through use of computer technology?*

Bunting (2000) makes numerous suggestions for activities and word games that have the potential to engage children's interest and develop their vocabularies. These include exploring words from other languages that have become part of the English lexicon such as *yoghurt*, *tobacco*, *menu*, *bungalow*, *anorak* and *mosquito*. To these we might add a number of words that are so commonly used now that many won't be aware that they were unheard of by some of our grandparents. Names of foods from other countries, in particular, become common parlance and include *pizza*, *pasta*, *spaghetti*, *masala*, *paella*, *tacos*, *fajitas*, *kebab* and *sushi*. By exploring such words, children can begin to understand that grapheme–phoneme correspondences vary around the world and that when learning another language they need to be aware of this.

Bunting also suggests word games such as inventing onomatopoeic words for everyday sounds, giving the example of the noise a shower makes as it starts. We might add our own ideas such as creating words for the sounds of the following:

- windscreen wipers going back and forth;
- a mobile phone ringing;
- a glass breaking;
- an aircraft flying overhead;
- children on the playground.

Another of Bunting's ideas that may appeal to children who have watched programmes like *Eastenders, The Only Way is Essex* and *Only Fools and Horses*, is the creation of new rhyming slang. Cockney rhyming slang, which was originally used so that locals could disguise their (sometimes dishonest) activities from outsiders, has spread as people outside London have watched films and television. Phrases include:

- *bread* for money (bread and honey – money);
- *donkey's* for years (donkey's ears – years);
- *loaf* for head (loaf of bread – head);
- *rabbit* for talk (rabbit and pork – talk).

Rhyming slang is not restricted to east London: it can be found around the world. Children could create their own rhyming slang and in doing so explore rhyme and vocabulary.

FOCUS ON RESEARCH

It is important that, when working with children to expand their vocabulary, we set this within a wider context. Dombey (2009) argues that semantic knowledge is particularly powerful.

The context in which a text sits, shapes our reading of its words, while the context provided by the text itself orients us towards particular vocabulary items. We construct patterns of expectation that prime us to recognise particular words and disambiguate homographs. So if we are scanning a train timetable, we immediately see 'Reading' as a place, not a process, and pronounce it accordingly. If we are reading about an accident, we are primed to recognise a word such as 'wound', without even considering the possibility that it may be the phonically regular past participle of 'wind'. (6)

Consider Dombey's views on the importance of context and then look at the activity below.

Activity 3

» *Consider the following words and how you would say them and what they mean. What would you need to know to ensure that you pronounced them correctly and understood their meanings?*

read   bear

'sow   lead

close   rebel

record   desert

minute   present

»   *A Heteronym is a word that has the same spelling as another word but with a different pronunciation and meaning. These words are sometimes also called homographs, although homographs is a wider term including words that are spelled the same and pronounced the same but have different meanings, for example* set, book, fine. *So for* read *we would pronounce the word as in* red *if we were talking about having read a book, but to rhyme with* reed *if we were going to read the book.*

Synonyms

Synonyms are words that mean exactly the same or something very similar to other words. So in English we have different words for small, such as *tiny, minute, minuscule* and even *petite*, imported from the French. For *big* we use words like *large, huge, massive, grand* and *great*. A thesaurus is a book or electronic text that provides groups of synonyms and can be invaluable when exploring vocabulary variations.

CASE STUDY

Year 6 looking at alternatives to using said in formal speech and writing

The new National Curriculum states that in Year 6 children should learn: The difference between vocabulary typical of informal speech and vocabulary appropriate for formal speech and writing (eg said versus reported, alleged, or claimed in formal speech or writing). Among the terminology they should recognise and use is synonyms

Richard, a second year undergraduate trainee, planned a series of lessons to explore synonyms with his Y6 class. He began by looking at some of the adjectives that children overused, such as *good* and *nice* and challenged them to find as many alternatives as they could for different situations. For example, they found synonyms for *nice* and *good* to describe food, weather and feelings.

Richard wanted the children to look at the way in which dialogue is presented, and in particular at alternatives to using *said*. Children worked in pairs to look at examples of dialogue in their books, and noted these on mini whiteboards before sharing them with the whole class. Many found that *said* was actually the verb most frequently used by authors, but they also found many alternatives, including *asked, added, retorted, cried, whispered, claimed* and *exclaimed*. Richard wrote each of the verbs on a piece of card and then asked children to create a chart on the wall, *Alternatives to said*, which could be added to as children discovered new verbs.

In a subsequent lesson, the class looked again at the words and discussed which would probably only be found in fiction and which might be used in more formal situations such as the reporting of dialogue in a newspaper. The class then conducted a similar investigation using a range of newspapers.

This activity could be developed for a range of other commonly-used words to encourage children to vary their vocabularies and be more adventurous when choosing words. For example, they could explore synonyms for the following:

happy/happiness   pleasant sounds

rain/raining   unpleasant sounds

being afraid

The work can incorporate or lead into use of a thesaurus, either a book or an online version.

Morphemes

One of the challenges we face when attempting to enhance children's vocabulary is that there are simply so many words in the English language that it would be impossible to teach children all that they need. Indeed, the English lexicon (the vocabulary of the language) is growing constantly, with new words being added to every edition of our major dictionaries. Consider the following words that have appeared in the *Oxford English Dictionary* (http:// public.oed.com/the-oed-today/recent-updates-to-the-oed/previous-updates/june-2012/ new-words-list/, accessed 5 October 2012) in recent years:

screenager   cyberslacking   muggle   superbad

subsign   photobomb   oh   e-learning

urbanscape

Take a few moments to try to define each of them. Some you will no doubt already know and perhaps use, but others, while they may be unfamiliar, may also be quite simple to define. This is often because new words are made up of morphemes that are already in use in other words; so *photobomb* is made up of *photo* and *bomb* and means *to get into other people's photographs by suddenly appearing as they are taken*. We know that *urban* is connected with cities and we also know words such as *landscape*, so when a new word is created using *urban* and *scape* we can work out that it has something to do with what we can see in cities. Similarly, the meaning of *screenager* (*a teenager who spends a lot of time using IT equipment*) can be deduced easily, and we might make an informed guess that *cyberslacking* (a phrase that was unheard of only a few years ago) means *using computers at work to surf the net for your own purposes rather than for work*.

Morphemes are the minimum units of meaning within our language and can be complete words in themselves (*free morphemes*) or parts of words that change meaning but cannot stand alone (*bound morphemes*). In many of the examples above, the words are compound, in that they are made up of two free morphemes. More established compound words include *football*, *hairbrush*, *handrail* and *network*, while *unusual*, *disquiet*, *lively* and *jumped* include a bound morpheme and a free morpheme (because *usual*, *quiet*, *live* and *jump* can each stand alone, while *un-*, *dis-*, *-ly* and *-ed* cannot and are only used to change meanings or grammatical status).

New words can also be created from abbreviations, some of which are often long forgotten. *Nylon*, for example, is often said to be an abbreviation of New York (NY) and London (Lon) while *radar* is short for *radio detection and ranging* and *laser* was created from *light amplification by stimulated emission of radiation* (it's hardly surprising that the terms were shortened!). Consider, too, some of the words that are derived from TV programmes and social networking, such as *TOWIE* (*The Only Way is Essex*) *HIGNFY* (*Have I Got News For You*) and *OH* in textspeak (another recent addition) which means *Other Half* (one's partner). We also routinely talk about *apps*, *tweets*, *googling* and being *online* – all terms that have emerged in the last few years and to anyone hearing them ten or 20 years ago would have either meant nothing, or something very different from their present meanings. Now, however, we use shortened versions of words often without knowing what their extended, original versions were (for example, *pram* for *perambulator, bus* for *omnibus*).

The language is changing and although it may be hard to accept that new words and different uses of old words should become commonplace, you might reflect that this has always been the case. Shakespeare is said to have introduced around 1700 new words into the language (including *submerge*, *outbreak*, *watchdog*, *moonbeam*, *eventful* and *eyesore*) and we have constantly acquired new vocabulary from other languages and new inventions. In any case, whatever your feelings about language changes, if you are to work with young people you need to be aware of the vocabulary they know and use and be able to discuss its origins and meanings.

Consider some of the words that are said to have been invented and first used by Shakespeare. Each of those cited above is made up of two morphemes or units of meaning. Shakespeare did what people still do today and took existing morphemes and then combined them in new ways to create words that summed up exactly what he wanted to say more precisely than already-available words.

An interesting way for children to explore and understand the meanings of morphemes is to discuss a range of words they already know and that use prefix morphemes such as *sub-*, *in-*, *dis-* and *super-*, and then provide them with cards with common prefixes and ask them to work together to create as many words as they can that include the prefixes. They can use dictionaries to check if the words they have created already exist, and where they do not they can create their own definitions. This kind of word and language play is invaluable in helping children to understand the functions of morphemes and their meanings. However, you may need to justify working in this way to people who may not appreciate its value, as the trainee teacher in the case study described below discovered.

CASE STUDY

Experimenting with morphemes in Year 3

The New National Curriculum states that in Year 3 children should learn:

formation of **nouns** using a range of **prefixes**, such as super-, anti-, auto-. In Year Two, among the words they should learn to recognise and use … through discussion and practice … is suffix, while prefix only appears for Year Three.

DfE, 2013

Louise, a *Teach First* trainee, provided cards with common morphemes for groups of children to create words. Many groups created already-established words such as *unlike*, *replace* and *display*, but some created new words such as *relike*, *unplace* and *disway*, which they defined respectively as: to like someone again who [sic] you used to like but fell out with; nowhere; and not a path.

A parent, whose child had taken part in the activity and had been especially enthusiastic about creating new words, complained that the activity was *a waste of time* and *would just confuse the children*. However, Louise asked her to look with her child at some words that included the various morphemes the children had used, and which were already in established dictionaries, to see if the child knew or could work out their meanings. A week later the parent returned to the school to say that she had been very impressed not only by her child's knowledge and understanding, but also by her willingness to speculate about meanings of words she had never seen before such as *substandard, dissatisfied* and *dispossess*. She even admitted that she and her husband had enjoyed inventing words and had *fallen about laughing* at some of those they had created and defined (sadly, mostly ones which could not be repeated here).

Further extending vocabulary

Take a look at the words below, which appear in the National Curriculum (DfE, 2013) list of words that Y5/6 should be able to spell.

develop   familiar   identify   accommodate

In learning these words, it is important that children understand that most words provide us with several other words that are derived from them. For example, *accommodate* can become *accommodation, accommodated* and *accommodating*; *develop* can become *develops, developing, undeveloped* etc; *familiar* can become *familiarity, familiarise, unfamiliar* etc; and *identify* can become *identified, unidentified, identifies* and *identification*. Once they begin to appreciate how words work, children often do not need to learn how to spell many new words, since they can use the knowledge they have of the root words, and their understanding of some general rules about adding prefixes and suffixes, to work out spellings for themselves. To illustrate this, look at the invented words below and change each to a plural.

vib   runch   ravy   fobey

You probably decided that the plurals should be:

vibs   runches   ravies   fobeys

Why is this? You draw on what you already know about words and apply it to new ones, so you know that one-syllable words with a short vowel sound like *pen, bit, pin, dog* and *cat* simply add an s for the plural. You also know that words that end in the digraphs *ch* and *sh* tend to add -es for their plurals. Words that end in *y* and are preceded by a vowel such as *lady, baby* and *body* tend to drop the *y* and add -*ies*, while those that end in a *y* preceded by a vowel, such as *monkey, donkey* and *boy,* simply add an s.

Activity 4

»   *Look at four more words form the National Curriculum spelling list for Y5/6. How many words can you create by adding prefixes and suffixes?*

   occupy   recognise   available   occur

   See the end of the chapter for some suggestions.

Of course, not all words can be used to create others, so children could use dictionaries, including more advanced ones, to check that words they create actually exist. But as you have already seen, people are constantly creating words from other words which go on to become common usage.

Duke and Moses (2003) maintained that, when deciding which words we should teach explicitly, it is important to consider how related the words are to those children already know, and also to evaluate how helpful knowing the words will be as they meet new texts in the future. They argue that it is important to raise word consciousness through games and songs and through wordplay, and that children can be encouraged to notice particular characteristics of words. Wordplay is a central feature of this and there are many opportunities you can take to focus attention on morphemes and ways of modifying words through their use.

Activity 5

»   Look at the words from the National Curriculum, which are to be learnt in Y3/4. Some have been presented in the curriculum with modified versions (eg though/although, woman/women) but most have not. How many could **not** be added to or modified to create new words? Remember, you can make the words into plurals (eg accidents), change nouns to verbs (eg answered), change verbs to nouns (eg appear to appearance), change adjectives to nouns (eg difficult to difficulty) etc.

   accident, actually, address, answer, appear, arrive, believe, bicycle, breath, breathe, build, busy/business, calendar, caught, centre, century, certain, circle, complete, consider, continue, decide, describe, different, difficult, disappear, early, earth, eight/eighth, enough, exercise, experience, experiment, extreme, famous, favourite,

February, forward, fruit, grammar, group, guard, guide, heard, heart, height, history, imagine, increase, important, interest, island, knowledge, learn, length, library, material, medicine, mention, minute, natural, naughty, notice, occasion(ally), often, opposite, ordinary, particular, peculiar, perhaps, popular, position, possess(ion), possible, potatoes, pressure, probably, promise, purpose, quarter, question, recent, regular, reign, remember, sentence, separate, special, straight, strange, strength, suppose, surprise, therefore, though/although, thought, various, weight, woman/women

» You probably found that hardly any of the words could not be modified. In fact, only *caught, enough, perhaps, potatoes* (which has already been made plural) and *therefore* cannot be modified. Most words can be modified, and if children understand the conventions for modifying them they are on their way to being both good readers and good spellers. An interesting development of Activity 5 would be to see how many words a group of people could create from those listed. You could try this with colleagues and with children. The activity can be developed to focus on spelling rules and conventions. Investigations might include:

– which words can be made into plurals?

– which can be made into plurals simply by adding an S?

– which form plurals in other ways (eg century becomes centuries)?

– which nouns can be changed to adjectives with the addition of morphemes (eg accident to accidental)?

– which verbs can be changed to nouns (eg believe to believer)?

Developing children's understanding of words

If children are to read fluently and with enjoyment, an appreciation of how words are made up, allied to an expanding vocabulary, is vital. As we have seen, this might be developed through looking at the morphemes that form the constituent parts of words and should also involve exploring the names of things they find around them. The latter might be extended to include a focus on how words and names came about, and could include a study of place names and personal names. This might be developed into an investigation into place names and people's names in fiction. Charles Dickens, in particular, tended to give characters names that reflected their personalities (*Scrooge, Sowerberry, Bumble, Slyme, Slowboy* and *Sloppy,* for example). Although children will probably find reading original versions of Dickens' works challenging, there are abridged versions that are more accessible. They might also look at names in more modern works, including the Harry Potter series where *Severus Snape* is head of *Slytherin,* the house that values ambition, cunning, leadership and resourcefulness, while the rather less threateningly named *Pomona Sprout* is head of *Hufflepuff,* the house in which hard work, patience, justice and loyalty are prized. A further area to study could be the origins of the names of some of Rowling's characters, since many are connected to classical mythology, for example, the caretaker is *Argus Filch* and *Argus* was the watchman of the Greek gods.

Conclusion

Dombey (2009) maintains that if children are to succeed as readers we need, among other things, to alert them to *the morphological and orthographic patterning of English words* and *help them adopt 'flexible unit size strategies'*. Crucially, she asserts that this should be done in:

> a rich environment of meaning-making, where children are helped to draw on their developing understanding of a text to aid in the identification of its words, and to look at those words in close detail to refine their comprehension and avoid misinterpretation. (10)

This chapter set out to explore ways in which children's vocabularies and understanding of words can be developed. Dombey's words are particularly appropriate at a time when prescribed lists of words are being presented for children to learn and spell. Explored and investigated through meaningful contexts, the words will add to children's understanding of their language and help them to extrapolate meaning from other words. However, if words are learned in isolation and out of context, and if they are not considered as building blocks for other words, learning them may prove a chore and a disincentive to vocabulary development. Through engaging children with some of the activities suggested in this chapter and by some of the authors cited below, you will encourage an interest in and an understanding of words which will benefit your pupils long after they leave school.

Critical points

»   *There are many interesting activities in which children can engage to develop their vocabularies.*

»   *It is important that children develop an understanding of how words are created using affixes and morphemes, since this will enable them to understand new words.*

»   *It is important that children experience a language-rich environment and that vocabulary development is set within meaningful contexts.*

Critical reflections

»   *Consider your own vocabulary development. What have you learned from reading this chapter that you could apply when meeting unfamiliar words? How can you develop your understanding of the way in which English words are formed so that you can help enhance children's vocabularies in an engaging and interesting way?*

Taking it further

Crystal, D. (2005) *How Language Works*. London: Penguin.

Like so much of David Crystal's work, this is a very readable and entertaining book, which explains things clearly without avoiding technical language.

References

Biemiller, A. (2003) Vocabulary: Needed if More Children are to Read Well. *Reading Psychology*, 24.

Blachnowicz, C. and Fisher, P. (2000) *Teaching Vocabulary in all Classrooms*. Columbus, OH: Merrill Prentice Hall.

Brien, J. (2012) *Teaching Primary English*. London: Sage.

Bunting, R. (2000) *Teaching About Language in the Primary Years* (2nd edn). London: David Fulton.

Chall, J.S., Jacobs, V.A. and Baldwin, L.E. (1990) *The Reading Crisis: Why Poor Children Fall Behind.* Cambridge, MA: Harvard University Press.

DCSF (2008) *Teaching Effective Vocabulary: What Can Teachers do to Increase the Vocabulary of Children who Start Education with a Limited Vocabulary?* Nottingham: DCSF.

Dombey, H. (2009) *ITE English: Readings for Discussion December 2009.*

www.ite.org.uk/ite_readings/simple_view_reading.pdf

Duke, N. and Moses, A. (2003) *10 Research Tested Ways to Build Children's Vocabulary.* New York: Scholastic Inc.

Horner, C. and Ryf, V. (2007) *Creative Teaching: English in the Early Years and Primary Classroom.* London: David Fulton.

National Institute of Child Health and Human Development (2000) *Report of the National Reading Panel. Teaching Children to Read: An Evidence-Based Assessment of the Scientific Research Literature on Reading and its Implications for Reading Instruction* (NIH Publication No. 00–4769). Washington, DC: U.S. Government Printing Office.

National Reading Panel (2000) *Teaching Children to Read: An Evidence-Based Assessment of the Scientific Research Literature on Reading and its Implications for Reading Instruction. Reports of Subgroups.* NICHD.

Answers

Activity 4: possible answers

For occupy you might have chosen: occupies, occupation, occupied, unoccupied, occupancy.

For recognise: recognises, recognition, recognisable unrecognisable.

For available: availability, unavailable, unavailability.

For occur: occurrence, occurring, occurred.

Crossword clue (page 23)

It sounds like a corner has been badly damaged in this four-sided shape (9)

Answer: rectangle (sounds like *wrecked angle*)

3 Proficient readers: what next?

EVE ENGLISH

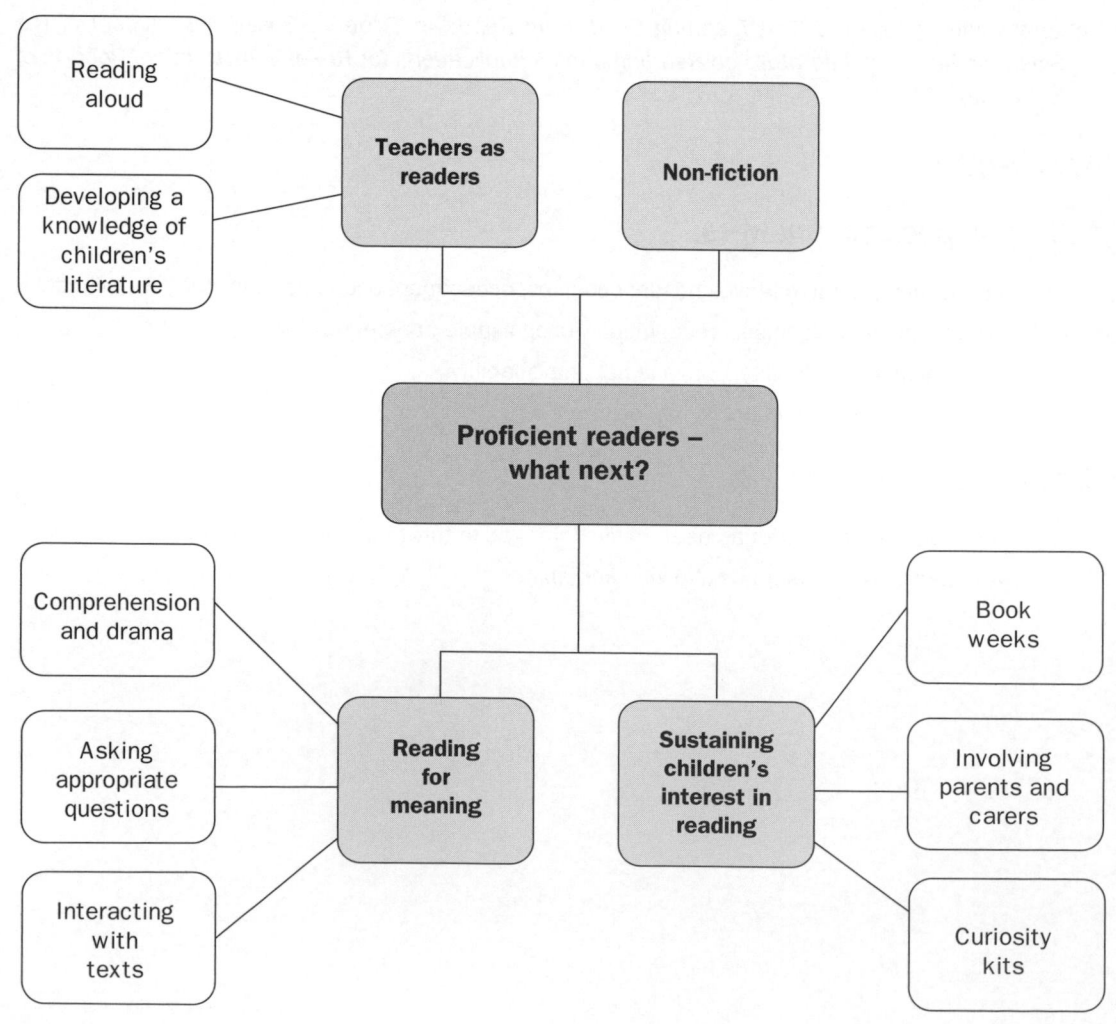

Teachers' standards

3 Demonstrate good subject and curriculum knowledge

- have a secure knowledge of the relevant subject(s) and curriculum areas, foster and maintain pupils' interest in the subject

- demonstrate an understanding of and take responsibility for promoting high standards of literacy and articulacy.

Critical questions

» *How can we encourage children to read and enjoy fiction and non-fiction once they are able to decode?*

» *How can we ensure that children fully understand and interact with the texts that they read?*

Introduction

> *So she was considering in her own mind (as well as she could, for the hot day made her feel very sleepy and stupid), whether the pleasure of making a daisy-chain would be worth the trouble of getting up and picking daisies, when suddenly a White Rabbit with pink eyes ran close by her.*

So the White Rabbit leads Alice into a wonderful world of fantasy and the imagination. Lewis Carroll's *Alice's Adventures in Wonderland* has enthralled readers for decades, along with books that have taken children into secret and midnight gardens, under kitchen floorboards and into Neverland. More recently, young readers have gone on bear hunts and have been accompanied to railway stations, to be whisked away to worlds where good and evil battle it out.

The title of this chapter might suggest that what is going to be discussed is what happens when children have mastered the basic decoding skills, but, in fact, the process begins much earlier than this. To ensure that children become lifelong readers, teachers and other adults involved in children's learning need to engage children in literature as soon as they become aware of books.

You will be well aware that there is concern, often voiced by successive governments and the media, that children are not reaching the required level of reading (eg Ofsted 2010, and see Chapter 1 in this book). However, many upper primary and secondary teachers are more worried about those pupils who can read but do not. These are the children who are just not interested in reading and are missing out both on fictitious worlds and also on the wealth of information provided by reference books. So, how do we engage children with books from an early age and ensure that their interest is maintained?

FOCUS ON RESEARCH

One of Alexander's aims of education is to excite the imagination of children, to:

advance beyond present understanding, extend the boundaries of their lives, contemplate worlds possible as well as actual, understand cause and consequence, develop the capacity for empathy, and reflect on and regulate their behaviour ... [W]e assert the need to emphasise the intrinsic value of exciting children's imagination. To experience the delights – and pains – of imagining, and of entering into the imaginative world of others, is to become a more rounded person.

(Alexander, 2010, 199 cited in Cliff Hodges, 2010, 62)

While Cliff Hodges recognises that Alexander is talking about education generally, she claims that this is a rationale for reading literature.

A project carried out by The Centre for Literacy in Primary Education (CLPE) (O'Sullivan and McGonigle, 2010) showed that *if children are given extended opportunities to explore texts in depth, they develop a deeper engagement, particularly in their empathy with characters and dilemmas* (58). The project provided many examples of changes in children's motivation as readers and looked at the importance of the quality of illustrations, humour, links with popular culture, important themes and significant characters.

Fletcher *et al.* (2012) looked at a project carried out in New Zealand that sought to discover what motivated children to read and improved attitudes to reading. Their findings included the importance of reading aloud to pupils and questioning them, promoting books that might interest them (this included encouraging the pupils to recommend books to each other), working on a one-to-one basis with the children to discuss their reading preferences and involving the parents.

Teachers as readers

The importance of teachers having a good knowledge of children's literature has been highlighted in terms of encouraging children to read. O'Sullivan and McGonigle (2010) argue that if teachers have extensive knowledge of literature then they are more likely to engage and motivate children as readers. They report how, at conferences organised by the Centre for Literacy in Primary Education (CLPE), teachers seemed to be unfamiliar with many books written for children.

Cremin *et al.* (2008a) undertook research that looked at teachers as readers. They sought information on primary teachers' personal reading, their knowledge of children's literature, their use of literature in the classroom and their involvement in school library services. When choosing their most important book (Cremin *et al.*, 2008a, 15), those books that teachers mentioned over ten times included books that were probably studied at school. When asked to name six good children's authors, 64 per cent of the teachers named the same six writers. Cremin *et al.* suggest that their findings show that teachers' *breadth of knowledge is limited and that they are drawing upon a very narrow range for use in the classroom* (15).

Teachers, then, need to be familiar with a wide range of children's literature if they are to induce their pupils to read widely and well. This range should extend from those texts considered classic to high quality modern literature, some of which will surely acquire classic status. Carter (2000) discusses the importance of teaching modern children's fiction.

> *Much of modern children's literature offers children the possibility of being specta-*
> *tors of and participants in lives they can clearly identify with. This is a most import-*
> *ant contribution both to children's self-knowledge and to their literary development.*
> *However, modern children's literature offers more than the possibility of psycho-*
> *logical development ... Children need to read stories not only in the language regis-*
> *ters of previous eras but also in those of the present. A classical heritage approach*
> *to the teaching of literature to children, used exclusively, would alienate. The lan-*
> *guage of literature would always appear as problematic, maybe even intimidating.*
>
> (109)

Children need literature that reflects their own world, with characters and situations they can identify with. They will still want to read about the past and read fantasy, but told from a modern perspective. This does not mean that children will be reading only about 'issues', about bereavement, divorce and hospital visits, however useful such texts might be. They will still be presented with magic, with wizards and witches, but in a language and modern context that they recognise. George English (English and Williamson, 2005) describes the heroic Mildred Hubble in Jill Murphy's *Worst Witch*, a determined young witch who fights against the repression of Miss Cackle's witches' academy. Mildred is very much a witch, a fantasy character, but with modern goals with which children will identify: a wonderful role model.

Children's literature helps children explore their own feelings and those of others. In a modern multi-cultural society, today's children will learn through the stories they read that there are many different cultures with different traditions, but that within these traditions there are many, many similarities. Ian Wallace's *Chin Chiang and the Dragon's Dance* tells the story of a young Chinese boy who has longed, for as long as he can remember, to dance the dragon's dance. However, when the time comes for him to take part, he is terrified. This big event in the Chinese calendar might not be familiar to all children, but the feelings of terror certainly will be.

Acting on the research

The research described above gives us plenty to think about. The CLPE project (O'Sullivan and McGonigle, 2010) and Cremin *et al.*'s (2008a) research highlighted the importance of teachers' knowledge of children's books. The Times Educational Supplement (www.tes.co.uk, 5 April 2013) has published a list of teachers' favourite (adult) books. Very few of the top ten books were recent and many were probably read as exam texts. It is likely that had the teachers been asked to name their favourite children's book, the list would have contained similar old favourites. It is important that as a teacher you keep up to date with children's literature if you want children to be motivated to read. This certainly does not mean that the classic tried and tested books should be ignored (after all, they are classics for a reason), but discovering new books can be exciting both for teacher and pupil. Reading reviews of children's books, visiting libraries and bookshops and enjoying reading new children's books can be very stimulating both for teachers and for the children to whom the new books are introduced. As Cremin *et al.* maintain:

If teachers' enjoyment of reading can be extended to a wider range of authors, then this can only be beneficial for future readers whose diverse interests and reading preferences deserve to be both honoured and extended.

(Cremin *et al.*, 2008a, 19)

Cremin *et al.* discuss the fact that there is no statutory requirement for trainee teachers to read and study children's literature and claim that:

To become effective reading professionals, student teachers arguably need to understand the significance of their knowledge about and pleasure in literature and need to become well acquainted with the widest possible range of children's authors.

(Cremin *et al.*, 2008b, 459)

Developing a knowledge of children's literature

One of the ways in which English specialists on the BA (Hons) Primary course at Durham University have kept up with recently published children's books is by reviewing them for *Primary Teacher Update* (markallengroup.com). Reading new books to review has extended the trainee teachers' knowledge of recent literature and also promoted new books in a professional journal. The two reviews below illustrate the depth of knowledge of texts which the students developed, and their ability to see how the books might stimulate purposeful classroom activities:

Fizzlebert Stump: The Boy Who Ran Away From The Circus (And Joined a Library)

A.F. Harold

ISBN 978 1 4088 3003 1

Published by Bloomsbury

Reviewed by Kristina Cuthbert

Cost: £5.99 (paperback)

The hero in this book is just like any other young boy … apart from the fact that his name is Fizzlebert and he wears an old red ringmaster's coat and you can often find him with his head inside a lion's mouth. So really he's not like any other young boy at all, but wouldn't it be exciting if we could all live in a travelling circus?

This is the story of Fizzlebert Stump, who one day decides to leave the circus and join a library where he encounters a toad-like receptionist and two crazed pensioners. Will the simple act of filling out a library card application form mean he may never make it back to the circus?

This fantastically funny book is a must have for any classroom bookcase. It would be suitable for shared reading or independent reading and with its gripping story line it will keep the whole class begging to hear more.

Link the book to classroom activities by turning your classroom into a circus. Ask the children if they have ever been to a circus, or if they have seen one on TV, and to note down all the constituent parts – animals and their handlers, clowns, acrobats. Then you could make coloured paper cut-outs or even make and design a circus tent.

The children could write an alternative ending to the story prompting ideas with questions such as; What would have happened if the children weren't found? Could the children have escaped by themselves?

Reproduced from *Primary Teacher Update*, (March 2013, 56) with permission of the publishers.

Mister Whistler

Margaret Mahy

ISBN: 9781877467912

Published by: Gecko Press

Cost: £10.99 (Hardback)

Reviewed by Joanne Willis

Absentminded Mister Whistler always has a song in his head and a dance in his feet. In a rush to catch the train, he is so distracted he loses his ticket.

Is it in the bottom pockets of his big coat or the top pockets of his jacket? Perhaps he slipped it into his waistcoat ...

This book is one of Mahy's last and has all of her vim and vigour. It is the kind of book where children can predict what will happen next and laugh together at Mister Whistler's antics.

Mahy's clever use of figurative language, onomatopoeia and alliteration help readers young and old piece together an image and become involved in the narrative.

The book is geared towards readers aged 5–8 but due to the quality of language it could be enjoyed by all readers. The attractive and intriguing illustrations burst with the joy and energy of the always smiling Mister Whistler.

You could base an activity around the idea of personality. What is Mister Whistler like? Do the children like the character? Why/why not? Write a character study on him. In pairs or groups create role plays that demonstrate feelings, expressions and how Mister Whistler's character performs in the story.

Reproduced from *Primary Teacher Update*, (May 2013, 56) with permission of the publishers.

Many journals review new books: look out for *Books for Keeps* (6 Brightfield Road, Lee, London SE12 8QF), *Carousel* (7 Carrs Lane, Birmingham BA 7TG) and *Primary Teacher Update* (Mark Allen Education, St. Jude's Church, Dulwich Road, London SE24 OP8, www.primaryteacherupdate.co.uk).

Seeking out and reviewing new books yourself will both increase your knowledge of children's literature and encourage your pupils to do the same. Sharing new titles and authors can be very pleasurable. Children often write to pupils in different schools; one of the things they can write about is a new book they have discovered.

Reading for meaning

Asking appropriate questions

Reading is about getting meaning from text. While children need to be taught the basic skills of decoding words, they also need, from the very beginning, to understand what they are reading. If children are getting nothing from their books, they will quickly become demotivated.

The research carried out by O'Sullivan and McGonigle (2010), described earlier, showed how important it is to give children opportunities to explore texts in depth and develop empathy. In fact, children need to be challenged to look for quite sophisticated meanings even before they can read. Skills, often referred to as *higher order comprehension* (English *et al.*, 2005), can and should be introduced when children are listening to stories before they can recognise words for themselves. Consider, for example, prediction and projection. On hearing the story of *Goldilocks and the Three Bears*, preschool children can be asked to imagine what might happen next from a certain point in the story or project themselves into the story by being asked, *What would you do if you were Baby Bear?* When children begin to read for themselves, and right through their education, they should be asked the questions that will ensure that they have understood and can engage with the text.

English *et al.* (2005) and Gamble and Yates (2002) refer to Barratt's taxonomy of comprehension as a way of categorising levels of understanding. Barratt (Clymer, 1972) listed the following:

*   literal comprehension where information is given in a straight forward way;

*   reorganisation, requiring the synthesis of information found in different parts of the text and summarising;

*   inferential comprehension (including projection and prediction);

*   evaluation where judgements are made;

*   appreciation, where an emotional response is required.

Activity 1

» *Choose a book that you know well and devise some questions that will elicit responses and demonstrate that the children can use the skills listed above. For example, when Cinderella cannot go to the ball children could be asked,* What do you think is going to happen next? *or* How would you feel if you were told you couldn't go to the ball? *(Inferential comprehension).*

Comprehension and drama

FOCUS ON RESEARCH

Arzu Güngör (2008) makes a strong case for the use of drama in developing comprehension skills. She brings together research that claims that:

As a learning tool, drama is beneficial to students of all age groups, because it provides them with the opportunity to develop more effective learning techniques, strategies and solutions ... it helps them to comprehend the world they live in and construct their knowledge and increases the chances for children to express themselves independently in any subject are including reading.

[The] link between drama and reading comprehension is a strong one ... drama helps students to develop skills embedded in the reading process, such as contextualizing what they read in a text to their own experience, feelings, attitudes, ideas, values and life situations.

(Güngör, 2008, 1–2)

Some drama techniques are very simple and yet very effective. 'Hot-seating' is one of the easiest to master. A child (or teacher) is asked to sit in the hot seat as a particular character, while the other children (often in role themselves) ask questions of the character. So, for example, in the poem *The Pied Piper of Hamelin* the mayor of Hamelin could be hot-seated by the rest of the class, as villagers of Hamelin, who demand that something is done to rid the village of rats. Note that no child in this drama scenario is required to run around the classroom and yet the children are in role and are really thinking about the poem, about motivation, about projection and about prediction. In the poem *The Highwayman* by Alfred Noyes, the ostler could be hot-seated by the press (the rest of the class) to find out what he knew about the events that unfurled.

The 'freeze frame' or tableau is also easy to manage. Here, the children form a still tableau from the scene of a story or poem. For young children, this could be the point in the story of *Goldilocks and the Three Bears* where the bears return from their walk and see the scene of destruction in front of them, with broken chairs and missing porridge. This tableau could then be extended to what is called 'thought tracking' which is best explained by thinking of 'thought bubbles'. What are the characters thinking of as they are frozen in a particular moment in time? In a recent thought tracking depiction of the Goldilocks story, Mummy Bear (a six-year-old), when asked what she was thinking, said, *Daddy Bear never remembers to lock the door!* This is such a good example of a child relating an aspect of a story to her own experience (see Güngör, above).

Using *The Highwayman* as a basis for creating tableaux the children, in threes, could create an image from the poem where Bess, the landlord's daughter, the highwayman and Tim, the ostler, all interact. This could easily then move on to thought tracking. What is the highwayman thinking as he prepares to go off and hold up a stage coach? What does Bess think about the highwayman, and what does the ostler think about the scene he has just witnessed?

There are many other drama techniques that can be used to help children delve more deeply into texts. The 'mantle of expert' is a term for a drama technique devised by Dorothy Heathcote (Clipson-Boyles, 1998) where the teacher, in role, manages the drama and the children's place in the drama. If you think back to *The Pied Piper of Hamelin*, the mayor (teacher as expert) could walk into the village hall (classroom) and say to the villagers (children) *So you've dragged me into this meeting, when I'm very busy, to talk to me about rats. What's going on?* Immediately, the children will become villagers (there's no need to say *let's pretend*) and their knowledge and understanding of the narrative poem will become much deeper than if they had just read it.

Sustaining children's interest in reading

Reading aloud to pupils

There have been times in recent years when reading aloud to children in the classroom seemed to all but disappear. Beginnings and endings of novels were considered along with characterisation and description, but whole books were just not being read. Fortunately, teachers now seem to recognise how important it is for children to let loose their imaginations in whole stories and not just use books as teaching points for the children's own writing. Graham, in the more recent edition of her chapter (in Goodwin, 2005), maintains that teachers and academics are now more convinced of the importance of reading aloud. Indeed, the draft National Curriculum (DfE, 2013, 43) makes it clear that this is expected at Y5–6, as well as earlier, stating:

> Even though pupils can now read independently, reading aloud to them should include whole books so that they are introduced to books and authors that they might not select themselves.

Reading to a group or class of children needs, however, to be planned as carefully as everything else. Choose your book carefully and not just because it has some tenuous link with the term's topic. Ensure that you have read the book before you read it to the children. Trelease (1982, 73–5) offers more tips.

* Remember that the art of listening is an acquired one. It must be taught.

* Avoid long, descriptive passages until the children's imagination and attention span are capable of handling them.

* Remember that reading aloud comes naturally to very few people. To do it successfully and with ease you must practise.

- Use plenty of expression when reading. If possible, change your tone of voice to fit the dialogue.

- Adjust your pace to fit the story. Slow down during an exciting part, draw out your words, bring your listeners to the edge of their chairs.

- The most common mistake in reading aloud is reading too fast.

- Don't read stories that you don't enjoy yourself.

Activity 2

» *Bearing in mind the advice given above, read a story to an appreciative audience. Ensure that you practise well beforehand, perhaps recording your reading and thinking about how you could improve it. Reflect afterwards on what went well and what you could do better next time. When was your audience most engaged and when did attention flag? Did you involve the audience in any way? Did you ask questions or promote discussion?*

Gamble and Yates (2002) describe how *the level at which children can understand written text is much higher when the text is read aloud by a skilled adult reader than when read alone by the child* (122). This is because gaps in the child's understanding can be filled by the way in which the words are spoken, as well as from the gestures, facial expressions and body language the reader uses.

Working with parents and carers

FOCUS ON RESEARCH

It has been well documented over the years that children are more successful in their reading if they are supported by parents and carers. Desforges (2003, 86), for example, states:

Research … establishes that parental involvement has a significant effect on children's achievement and adjustment even after all other factors (such as social class, maternal education and poverty) have been taken out of the equation between children's aptitudes and their achievement.

Differences in parental involvement have a much bigger impact on achievement than differences associated with the effects of school in the primary age range. Parental involvement continues to have a significant effect through the age range although the impact for older children becomes more evident in staying on rates and educational aspirations than as measured achievement.

As teachers it is, therefore, important to engage with parents and carers as much as possible. Not all parents can or want to become involved in the classroom, but they all need to be informed of what is going on in school. So how can that be done?

- Booklets in straightforward language should tell parents how they can encourage their children to read.

- Workshops for parents can be organised where information is given about how the school teaches children to read. (See Case Study below.)

CASE STUDY

Emily's presentation

Emily was lucky enough on her final school placement to join a workshop for parents organised by the school's literacy co-ordinator. Over a number of weeks the group:

- were introduced to the phonics scheme used by the school;

- were shown a number of fiction and non-fiction books and discussed what to look for in a book;

- wrote their own stories and information books for children;

- created Story Sacks and Curiosity Kits*;

- helped to organise a book week.

The literacy coordinator produced a leaflet for parents and carers, detailing some of the things they might do at home with their children. A few weeks later, Emily was called for interview at another school and was told to prepare a presentation for parents, carers and governors on ways in which parents and carers might support their children's reading. Emily created her own leaflet, together with a short PowerPoint presentation and confidently delivered a fifteen-minute presentation to her audience, observed by the interviewing panel. When told after interview that the school would like to offer Emily the post, Emily was delighted to hear that her presentation had really impressed and had been a key factor in her being appointed.

*See p 48 for more details of Curiosity Kits.

Activity 3

» *Create a booklet that will give information to parents and carers to help to support their children with reading at home.*

– *Language used should not be too technical (eg avoid terms such as syntactic cues, phonemes, miscues, etc.).*

– *The style should be friendly and personal.*

– *The tone should not be patronising.*

– *Insert children's drawings and statements at various points.*

- *Do not assume that each home will have the same opportunities for reading (don't make generalised statements such as, 'Read to your child before they go to sleep'. Some parents may work at night; others may be too exhausted to read before bedtime; they may be single parents who have other children to see to).*

- *Many children have opportunities for interacting with texts written in a variety of languages at home and in places of worship. It is important to acknowledge this in the booklet.*

- *Ensure that the booklet is concise and appealing (you need to both inform and interest parents).*

- *The booklet will address both decoding and comprehension. Make suggestions as to the type of questions parents should ask children.*

Book week

Book weeks were mentioned above in the case study that looked at the parents' workshops. Many schools now have book weeks where the focus of a week's work is related to a particular book, author or book theme. The purpose of these book weeks is to motivate children to read and, if possible, even meet authors who will inspire and encourage children. Cross-curricular work related to the chosen book or theme can also be part of a book week. This will be a time when children (and teachers) can dress up as story characters, get involved in drama activities, create plays and visit places of interest associated with the stories. Below are a few suggestions for book-related activities that could be part of a book week. Look at the activity and see if you could plan a book week.

Activity 4

» *Take a book or an author that you know well and then consider the following generic activities. Could any of the activities be applied to your book? Give some details.*

- *Take the characters and invent new stories for them – give them a life beyond the page.*

- *Make a 'radio play' of a story, using a tape recorder and sound effects.*

- *Make puppets and use them to retell the story.*

- *Make story sacks.*

- *Design book jackets. Extend this with older children so that they are acting as advertising agencies or a publisher's publicity department to decide how they would promote the book. Draw or paint individual characters or incidents. Perhaps children could do this in the style of a favourite illustrator. Encourage them to use the same media that the author/illustrator has used, (eg pen and ink washes or crayon resists for Charles Keeping books, or crayon for John Burningham's). Where stories are told in cartoon strip format use that format to create their own stories in a similar style.*

- *Link art work with a reading activity by giving the child a card on which is written a particularly descriptive passage from a book, and asking him/her to illustrate it. This will give them some insight into how illustrators work from other people's writing.*

- *Present stories in frieze form.*

- Let the children develop the story through play – turn part of the classroom into a spaceship, a desert island, etc.

- Stage a 'phone-in' or a TV or radio interview with the character/s or author being asked about motives, actions or intentions.

- Write in diary form a day/week in the life of one character. Write letters in role, as a character explaining or justifying actions to other characters or readers.

- Make a board game based on the story (a version of Snakes and Ladders always works).

- Report the major events in the story in the form of a newspaper report.

- Predict what will happen next and write the next scene, conversation or chapter. Write an alternative ending or write what might happen after the end of the book.

- Make a collection of artefacts from the period of the book.

- If there are people in the community whose lifestyle, jobs or experiences are similar to those in the book invite them in to talk to the children.

- Write letters to the appropriate tourist boards asking for posters and information on the areas studied.

- Write book reviews. Young children may use symbols to indicate whether or not they liked the book. Older children may organise a 'book programme' – a live or taped programme with chairperson and reviewers offering their views of the book.

- Write letters to another class, perhaps in another school, explaining why they would recommend the book.

The suggested activities (above) were used by some PGCE students as a basis for planning book weeks in their schools. The main aim of the book week was to motivate children to read and capitalise on their enjoyment.

CASE STUDY

Book week

PGCE students in a north-eastern university planned book weeks, using some of the suggestions above. They came up with some very interesting ideas. Lewis Carroll's *Alice's Adventures in Wonderland* was turned into a Snakes and Ladders game, with Alice falling down the hole and making her way through Wonderland meeting different characters on the way; some encouraged her to climb up ladders while others pushed her down snakes. *The BFG*, by Roald Dahl, for another student, was used as the basis of a week of activities. One idea was to create poems using the same sort of made-up words that the BFG is famous for. It was also suggested that children could draw maps of Giant Country showing key locations such as the BFG's cave. Another student was inspired by *The Iron Man* by Ted Hughes. She suggested that during a book week the children could use the book to create a musical story relating to different scenes.

All the students reported that they and the children had thoroughly enjoyed the week. Focusing most of the week's activities on one book had stretched their (the students') imaginations in terms of planning and given them ideas that they would continue to use.

Non-fiction

Research has shown that teachers must make themselves aware of what interests pupils and provide them with a wide range of literature to match that interest. Merisuo-Storm maintained:

> *Pupils are very different as readers, and they are motivated to read very different books and texts. The reader should find the topic of the text interesting and possess enough previous knowledge related to its subject matter. Therefore it is crucial to offer pupils a wide variety of reading material. In other words, an array of books representing a variety of topics, levels of difficulty and genres of literature is necessary.*
>
> Merisuo-Storm, 2006, 112

One of the ways in which teachers can find out about their pupils' reading preferences is through reading conferences. On an informal, one-to-one basis, teacher and pupil can discuss books that the child has enjoyed (at home or at school) and what he or she thinks about the books provided in the classroom. Children who do not enjoy reading are given the opportunity to think about why this might be the case. They can also talk about their interests and pastimes, and this can give the teacher an insight into what else the child might like to find out about. Reading conferences can be very time-consuming, but very worthwhile.

Reference books are essential in the classroom, not only because they are the reading of choice for many children, but also because they give pupils the information they need to find out about the world. When we talk about the reading of non-fiction, it is often in the context of boys' reading because it has been suggested that boys prefer reading reference books. Merisuo-Storm stated:

> *Boys prefer texts that have a purpose: getting information, making things and helping others. In order to encourage boys to read, schools should expand their view of what is worthwhile reading and connect literacy instruction to boys' interests.*
>
> Merisuo-Storm, 2006, 113

Lewis *et al.* (2001) carried out an interesting piece of research that sought to explore the impact of 'Curiosity Kits' on the reading behaviours of reluctant boy readers. The kits consisted of sports bags that contained:

*   non-fiction book(s) selected on a topic likely to appeal to boys. The range included topic such as planes, trucks, comets, black holes, skateboarding, mountain bikes, reptiles, dinosaurs, the Internet, the body, volcanoes and hurricanes;

*   a related toy or artefact (eg an airport play map and some toy planes, racing gloves and puncture repair kit, plastic reptiles and a video tape on reptiles);

*   a wipe-clean word search related to the book;

*   a magazine on the same topic aimed at adults;

- comment stickers;
- a comments notebook.

(Adapted from Lewis *et al.*, 2001, 1–2)

The researchers found that the boys were very positive about the book bags and that family members were also enjoying the books and the activities.

> *My Dad likes reading them himself, because he comes home from work really tired but reads all the things I've got in the Curiosity Kits.*

Lewis *et al.*, 2001, 5

All the teachers reported improved attitudes and enthusiasm.

CASE STUDY

Story sack

BA students, Jess and Hayley, used the list set out above (from Lewis *et al.*, 2001, 1–2) to create their own story sack.

The Story of Everything

Neal Layton

ISBN: 0764159852

Published 2006 by Barron's Educational Series

Topics covered the big bang, dinosaurs, evolution to modern life.

Included in the Curiosity Kit:

- the book;
- a magnifying glass;
- dinosaur figures;
- fossils;
- an inflatable globe;
- a jigsaw of the world;
- *National Geographic* magazine (www.national-geographic-magazine.co.uk) for parents;
- *National Geographic Kids* magazine (www.nationalgeographic-kids.co.uk).

The Curiosity Kits were designed to encourage reluctant boy readers, but it is important that girls are encouraged to read non-fiction too, just as it is essential that boys read fiction. Equally important is the fact that children have to be explicitly taught how to read non-fiction.

Narrative is still the dominant genre in a pupil's reading diet (Wray and Lewis, 1997) and reading a story, where we start at the beginning and read to the end, is very different from accessing information from reference books. Wray and Medwell have been successful in addressing this problem in schools and have given us a model for interacting with non-fiction text. Their Extending Interactions with Texts (EXIT) model describes how teachers can enable pupils to read and write non-fiction in a meaningful way. The model consists of:

- elicitation of previous knowledge;

- establishing purposes;

- locating information;

- adopting an appropriate strategy;

- interacting with text;

- monitoring understanding;

- making a record;

- evaluating information;

- assisting memory;

- communicating information.

Adapted from Wray and Medwell (1997, 7–8).

The above model ensures that children build on what they already know and read purposefully to find answers to questions that they have been set. The model will help the children avoid reading vaguely, not sure what they are looking for and not knowing when they should stop looking. By recording their findings in different ways and communicating those findings, the children will remember what they have learned and, subsequently, add to that knowledge and understanding.

So, for example, if you want your pupils to research 'life in Victorian England' you need to find out what they already know and then establish what you and they want to find out. With specific questions in mind, the children will look at the contents pages and the indexes of books to see if they will give them the answers they want. This is the way we, as adults, read reference books; we don't read telephone directories from beginning to end to find the number of a Mr J. Smith. Think about Wray and Medwell's EXIT model, described above, and attempt the next activity. The case study that follows will help.

Activity 5

» *Plan, briefly, a series of lessons on a topic of your choice.*

   How will you:

- *find out what the children already know about the topic;*

- *find out what the children want to know;*

- *explicitly teach the children how to get the information they want;*

- *help them interact with the relevant points and ignore those facts that are not immediately relevant to them;*

- *assist them to find out more about passages they perhaps don't understand;*
- *show the children how to record what they have discovered;*
- *help them evaluate the information;*
- *ensure that the children remember what they have read;*
- *help them communicate what they have learned and in doing so reinforce their own learning?*

The case study below demonstrates how a trainee teacher used the EXIT model to develop her pupils' knowledge, teaching them how to read for a purpose and assisting them in remembering what they had learned.

CASE STUDY

A half-term topic

Salma, a second year trainee teacher, introduced a topic on 'Animals' to her Year 4 class. In a whole-class shared reading session she and the children compiled a concept map that included everything they knew about animals. They then decided they wanted to find out, first of all, about wild animals in particular. Pairs of children (talk partners) discussed what they would like to know about wild animals. This part of the process is very important to the next stage in the enquiry. Instead of simply reading anything and everything about animals, reading is directed to finding out specific information.

The children decided, as a class, that they wanted to find out about habitats and animals' homes: where do wild animals live? In groups they looked at different animals.

Salma then took time to remind the children of how to locate information; they looked at contents pages, the indexes (with a bit of a detour into alphabetical order) and book blurbs.

The children, armed with specific questions, then looked for the answers to their queries. They reported back their findings to the whole class and discussed whether or not the books had been useful and had, in fact, delivered what they said they would do in the book blurb.

Salma helped the children with information they were able to tell her they didn't quite understand, often by pointing them in the direction of another book.

The children then made their own books about animal homes, one group even creating a book suitable for Reception-age children.

Over the half term Salma continually asked the children what they had found out, ensuring that the information was revisited.

The trainee teacher reported how satisfying the process had been and was delighted to find that the children could still remember what they had learned some weeks later. Particularly successful were the books that some of the children made for younger pupils.

Conclusion

This chapter began with the concern that many children seem to give up on reading after they have acquired the basic skills. Research, examining ways in which children can be motivated to read, has been described, and practical activities, addressing research findings, have been suggested. Case studies have shown how successful the activities can be in the hands of motivated teachers.

Critical points

»   *By sharing good quality literature with children and through developing our own knowledge of texts, we can encourage children to read and enjoy fiction and non-fiction once they are able to decode.*

»   *Through a range of meaningful activities, we can ensure that children fully understand and interact with the texts that they read.*

Critical reflections

»   *Identify children whom you teach who are proficient readers. Consider the ways in which you currently extend their reading, and what else you might now do to enable further development.*

Taking it further

Waugh, D., Neaum, S. and Waugh, R. (2013) Transforming Primary QTS, in *Children's Literature in Primary Schools*. London: Sage/Learning Matters.

References

Carter, D. (2000) *Teaching Fiction in the Primary School. Classroom Approaches to Narratives*. London: David Fulton.

Cliff Hodges, G. (2009) Children As Readers: What We Learn From Their Conversations About Reading. *Education 3–13*, 37:2.

Cliff Hodges, G. (2010) Reasons For Reading: Why Literature Matters. *Literacy*, 44:2.

Clymer, T. (1972) What is Reading? Some Current Concepts, in Melnick, A. and Merritt, J. (eds) *Reading Today and Tomorrow*. London: University of London Press.

Clipson-Boyles, S. (1998) *Drama in Primary English Teaching*. London: David Fulton.

Cremin, T., Bearne, E., Mottram, M. and Goodwin, P. (2008a) Primary Teachers as Readers. *English in Education*, 42:1.

Cremin, T., Mottram, M., Bearne, E. and Goodwin, P. (2008b) Exploring Teachers' Knowledge Of Children's Literature. *Cambridge Journal of Education*, 38:4.

Desforges, C. with Abouchaar, A. (2003) *The Impact of Parental Involvement, Parental Support and Family Education on Pupil Achievement and Adjustment*. London: DfES.

DfE (2013) *The National Curriculum in England: Framework document*. London: DfE.

English, E. and Williamson, J. (eds) (2005) *Meeting the Standards in Primary English*. London: RoutledgeFalmer.

Fletcher, J., Grimley, M., Greenwood, J. and Parkhill, F. (2012) Motivating and Improving Attitudes to Reading in the Final Years of Primary Schooling in Five New Zealand Schools. *Literacy*, 46:1.

Gamble, N. and Yates, S. (2002) *Exploring Children's Literature: Teaching the Language and Reading of Fiction*. London: Paul Chapman.

Grainger, T. (2003) Creative Teachers and the Language Arts: Possibilities and Potential. *Education 3–13*, 31:1.

Güngör, A. (2008) Effects of Drama on the Use of Reading Comprehension Strategies and on Attitudes Towards Reading. *Journal for Learning Through the Arts*, 4:1.

Lewis, M., Fisher, R., Grainger, T., Harrison, C. and Hulme, P. (2001) Curiosity Kits: the Impact of Non-Fiction Book Bags on Boys' Reading at Home. *Topic Action*, Spring 2001, Issue 25.

Merisuo-Storm, T. (2006) Girls and Boys Like to Read and Write Different Texts. *Scandinavian Journal of Educational Research*, 50:2.

Ofsted (2010) *Reading by Six*. London: Ofsted.

O'Sullivan, O. and McGonigle, S. (2010) Transforming Readers: Teachers and Children in The Centre For Literacy In Primary Education Power of Reading Project. *Literacy*, 44:2.

Trelease, J. (1982) *The Read Aloud Handbook*. Harmondsworth: Penguin.

Wallace, I. (1984) *Chin Chiang and the Dragon's Dance*. London: Methuen.

Wray, D. and Medwell, J. (1997) *Extending Literacy: Children Reading and Writing Non-Fiction*. London: Routledge.

4 Learning to comprehend

CLAIRE WARNER

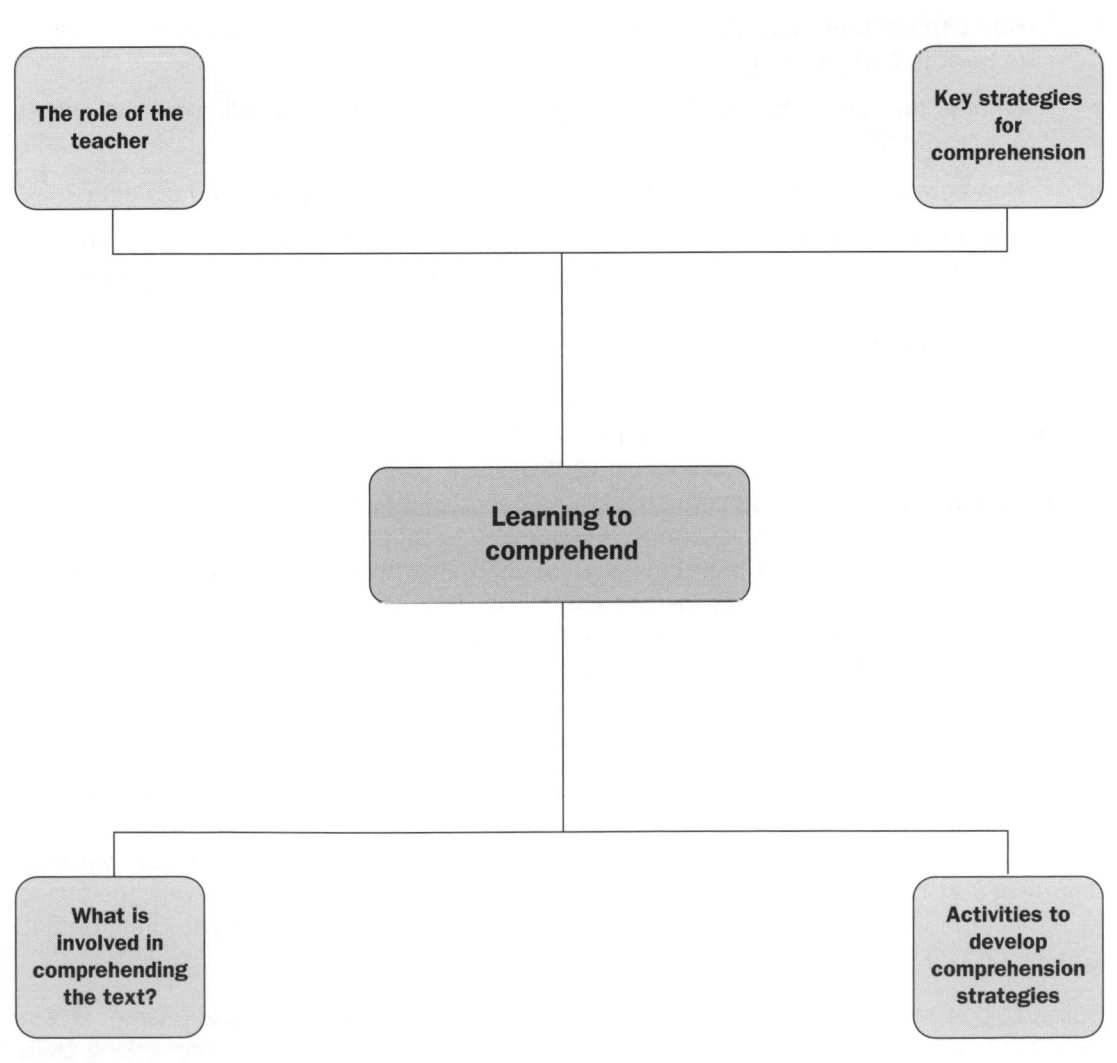

Teachers' standards

3 Demonstrate good subject and curriculum knowledge

- have a secure knowledge of the relevant subject(s) and curriculum areas, foster and maintain pupils' interest in the subject, and address misunderstandings

- demonstrate a critical understanding of developments in the subject and curriculum areas, and promote the value of scholarship

4 Plan and teach well-structured lessons

- contribute to the design and provision of an engaging curriculum within the relevant subject area(s).

Critical questions

» *How can we develop a range of strategies to help children engage actively with text?*

» *How can we make use of authentic contexts and high quality texts to motivate children to want to find meaning?*

» *What is the role of the teacher in helping children to think and talk about what they are reading?*

» *How can we plan comprehension activities to involve investigation and dialogue?*

» *How can we encourage children to articulate the strategies they are using to help them develop understanding and derive greater enjoyment of the texts that they read?*

Introduction

Being a reader is powerful. It offers children pleasure and enjoyment, opens up imagined worlds and makes possible endless opportunities to explore new areas of learning, new thinking and ideas. Guthrie and Wigfield (2000) have commented that engaged readers provide themselves with self-generated learning opportunities that are equivalent to several years of education. The Organisation for Economic Co-operation and Development (OECD) demonstrated that, whatever their background, children who are enthusiastic readers and read widely obtain higher average reading scores than those who are poorly engaged in reading. This is more important for success than having well-educated parents. Reading makes such a significant difference to children's academic achievement and to their life chances that it is hardly surprising that stakeholders, whether parents and carers or teachers, government ministers or Ofsted, all have a view on how it should be taught.

There has been a relentless drive to ensure that children have the phonic knowledge to decode the words on the page. We know that this is an essential skill for young readers, and far too important to be left to chance. For many teachers, phonics has brought a welcome degree of certainty to teaching reading. Where it is taught systematically and well, the majority of children will be successful and be able to read the words on the page (Johnston and Watson, 2005).

Being able to read with automaticity and accuracy is important for comprehension. This is because fluency leaves greater cognitive resources for the high-level text processing skills involved in making meaning from the text (Cain and Oakhill, 2006). However, you may have observed that having age appropriate or even advanced word reading skill is no guarantee that good comprehension will follow. Comprehension does not necessarily develop automatically once word decoding is proficient (Nation and Angell, 2006). You may have noticed children who are quite satisfied not to engage with or comprehend what they are reading. They are unlikely to become avid readers or benefit from all the advantages that being a reader can bring (Clark and Rumbold, 2006). Traditional comprehension activities do not always help. Reading a passage and answering questions tests rather than teaches comprehension. These have limited use for children who have comprehension difficulties. Even oral question and answer sessions tend to focus on drawing out what children know rather than involving explicit teaching. If we accept that comprehension needs to be taught, then it is important to consider what it involves and the best ways of doing this.

Key factors for teaching comprehension

An analysis of 230 studies into teaching comprehension (National Reading Panel, 2000) identified three key factors as being significant for developing comprehension.

1   Learning about words – the development of vocabulary.

2   Having access to adults who make the reading process visible by explicitly modelling and teaching a range of strategies for comprehension.

3   Interacting with texts – being active readers.

Chapter 2 looks at the first factor, while Chapters 3, 6, 7 and 8 examine the third. This chapter focuses on the second: making the reading process visible through the explicit modelling and teaching of a number of key strategies for comprehension. Many of the approaches suggested will also support vocabulary development and help children become more active readers, although this has been discussed more fully in other chapters. It will also touch on, but not explicitly consider, the personal response of children, their emotional engagement, evaluation and critical reflection. This is not because these aspects of reading are unimportant. On the contrary, they are an essential part of being a reader, but they require good comprehension, and it is learning to make meaning that is the main concern here.

What comprehension involves

The comprehension processes children use to understand written texts are the same as those they use to understand oral language. The difference, of course, is that visual word identification processes need to be incorporated for reading (Rose, 2006). You may be aware that the traditional framework for thinking about comprehension identifies three progressive layers of understanding: understanding at the literal level, at an inferential level, and at a critical or personal level, although as a skilled reader you will do all of these. Pardo (2004, 272) provides a helpful definition, describing comprehension as *a cognitive process in which readers construct meaning by interacting with the text through a combination of prior knowledge and previous experience, information in the text, and the stance the reader takes in relationship to the text.*

This definition recognises that comprehension requires cognitive resources together with a high level of interaction between the reader and the text. Children will bring their background knowledge to the text, their personal and cultural life experiences and their knowledge of the world, and this will influence their understanding. They will need linguistic knowledge to understand vocabulary and grammar, and to be able to handle figurative language such as metaphor, simile and personification. They will have to cope with increasingly complex and lengthy sentences and varied language patterns. Their past literary experiences and wider reading will be important too and will help them to understand a range of text structures, know how different texts are written, and make links between the new reading they are engaged in and other texts they are familiar with. Pardo also hints at the importance of taking a positive stance towards the text. Children are far more likely to persevere to make sense of the text if they know something of the pleasure and enjoyment that reading can bring.

Some key aspects of comprehension

Good readers use a range of strategies to support their understanding of the text. Pressley's (2000) major research review of comprehension provides a helpful list, and more recent studies have refined, developed and added to this (Pardo, 2004; Lewis and Tregenza, 2007). There are some differences between researchers, but the key strategies addressed here are:

- activating prior knowledge;
- prediction;
- questioning and clarifying;
- visualisation and imagination;
- summarising;
- drawing inferences;
- monitoring understanding.

Activity 1: Activating your prior knowledge

» *To help your own comprehension of the rest of the chapter, look at the seven key strategies above and decide:*

– *what you already know about each of them;*

– *what you would like to find out about of them.*

In the following section, each of the strategies is taken in turn and explained. You will be offered ideas for developing and strengthening each element of comprehension with children in the classroom, drawn from research and guidance (Kispal, 2008; Lewis and Treganza, 2007; DfES, 2005) and the work of practitioners in the classroom. The aim is to exemplify how each strategy can be taught and developed collaboratively, but in a way that strengthens independence and also makes reading an enjoyable experience.

The importance of prior knowledge

You may have experienced times when you have not been able to 'connect' with a book. It may have been because you were not able to identify with the subject matter, perhaps the characters or setting didn't interest you, or, in the case of academic writing, the complexity of the text may have been off-putting, irrelevant or just plain boring. Graham (2011, 51) suggests that *if children do not make connections between the lives they live, both physically and emotionally, and the lives portrayed in books, the chances are that books will remain peripheral to their lives.* Think about the times you have not been able to put a book or magazine down; it may well have been when you were reading something that interested you, when there was a need or desire to know, or when your personal and cultural knowledge, your experience and knowledge of texts and your understanding of language connected with what you read.

One of the key advantages experienced readers have over inexperienced readers is knowledge of language and the world. Stanovich (1986) explains that children who *choose* to read become better at reading and comprehending than those who do not. We know that the more children read, the more helpful knowledge they build up about the world, story schemas and non-fiction text structures. This has particular implications for those who are not yet reading widely and independently. If a key strategy for building children's knowledge is reading, then carefully planning a read aloud programme matters, so that all children, whether or not they are fluent readers, have the opportunity to hear and discuss a wide range of quality texts read aloud.

The children's background knowledge shapes their understanding and interpretation of the text, so it makes sense to strengthen and activate this and bring to the fore what they already know. This will help them to make meaningful links with new information that they are encountering, whet their appetite and tempt them into reading. As they become more experienced, your discussions can help them to develop an understanding of how any interpretation of a text is shaped by context and their personal view of the world.

Practical approaches to activate prior knowledge

The following are examples of activities that can help to activate prior knowledge.

*   Before introducing the text or at a key point in the text, provide pairs or groups of children with two or three carefully selected objects or images that are related to the text. Give them a set time to discuss them and to decide what the text might be about. Collect ideas on post-it notes, a flip chart or IWB, or put into speech or thought bubbles to be added to the working wall. They will offer a rich resource for further discussion and exploration of resolutions found later within the text. Invite children to tell you a little more about the reasons for their suggestions and make explicit how we draw on what we already know and have experienced. Affirm the importance and validity of doing this. Images, video and sound files can also be used effectively to generate discussion and activate memories and responses.

*   Give children one minute to write down as many words as they can, no matter how simple or random, that are associated with the title, front cover, or an image from the text. Pick out some of the most interesting choices and invite children to tell you where their ideas came from.

*   Create a *feely box* to introduce a text. Invite children to describe what they can feel – for example, sand, pebbles and shells or crisp leaves, twigs and conkers – while the other children work out what they think the setting of the text might be.

Prediction

Skilled readers anticipate what the text will be about before and during reading, and continually compare what they think might happen with what the author has written. Children who predict are likely to pay greater attention to what they read (DfES, 2005). It helps children to focus on key information, actively look for cues to back up their ideas and organise their thinking. This supports reading fluency, deepens understanding and offers an important opportunity to preview and use the vocabulary of the text.

It is important to allow children to make tentative and provisional suggestions about possibilities. Martin (2010) suggests that we extend this further by asking what they would *like* to happen. A group of seven year-olds responded to this when reading *The Tunnel* by Anthony Browne with comments such as, *I hope [the children] make up and get on all the time after that ... I want them to get back home safely... for the boy to appreciate his sister.* This led to a rich, sophisticated discussion of the text; they drew on their own personal experiences and made links with other stories they had read.

Prediction is not the same as guesswork of course, and the children were encouraged to consider why they thought as they did by being asked to say a little more. Was there any evidence in the text? Did it remind them of something they have read before, or that may have happened to them? How did it relate to what they knew about the character(s) so far?

Practical approaches to strengthen prediction

The following are examples of activities that can help to encourage prediction before and during reading.

* Demonstrate how to read the text a section at a time, explain what is happening and predict what will happen next. Point out the explicit and implicit evidence that supports or contradicts your predictions. Demonstrate through talk how to revise your initial ideas in the light of new evidence.

* Stop at the point where a character faces a problem or dilemma. Invite children to generate a list of statements. Provide a framework with prompts such as 'I wonder whether ... because ...' to scaffold their talk. Collect their predictions on post-it notes and display them. Encourage children to look for evidence in the text and encourage them to revise their initial predictions whenever they want to. Consider the consequences of each suggestion, and ask the groups to arrive at a group decision or prediction before moving on. Have these on display as part of your working wall as you continue to read the text.

* Story bags can be useful for introducing texts and characters. Put together a collection of items belonging to a character and encourage children to speculate about the character's life. The children can check how closely their ideas match the text as they read on.

Questioning the text

When we think about questioning, we usually think about the questions teachers ask children to elicit understanding and response. Getting this right matters and is explored elsewhere (see Chapter 8). But we also need to consider how children can interrogate the text for them-selves while reading. This is a key part of being an active reader. Tolerating and resolving uncertainty is what good readers do. Of course, being unsure about what is happening in a story will often be part of the author's intent and does not necessarily mean there is a lack of understanding of the text. We can model questioning by using prompts such as: *There's something puzzling here … I can't see how this fits with what we've already read or already know. I wonder whether… ? Does this make sense?*

An important aspect of questioning concerns validity, accuracy and bias. Being able to interro-gate a range of texts critically is increasingly important. All texts will encompass the particular values of their authors to some extent (Gamble and Yates, 2008), but at a time when anyone can publish anything on the web, it is critical that children do not become passive consumers.

Practical approaches to help children question the text

The following are examples of activities that can help children to question the text for themselves.

- Visual texts lend themselves to discussion about authorial intent and layers of meaning, and are inclusive for all children. Invite the children to consider: why the illustrator has chosen to use particular colours; why characters are positioned in particular ways; the use of perspective; contrasts – light and dark; layout; and the contributory role of text.

- Provide children with an illustration or a section of written text from the text you are reading. Leave wide margins and invite the children to jot down what they think they know. Invite them to underline what they are not sure about – and then turn these uncertainties into questions to be answered together.

- Invite the children to 'question the author'. You could choose a novel, a persuasive text such as a television advert to raise money for a charity, or a historical source such as a pamphlet on evacuation from the 1930s. Model the kind of questions they might ask. *Who do you think wrote this? Why was it written? What kinds of discussion do you think might have been going on while it was being written? What might the author have missed out and why?* Children could work collaboratively to come up with possible answers, and you or one of the children could take on the role of the author to answer them.

Visualising and using other senses to respond

You may know the disappointment of seeing the film of a book you have enjoyed, particularly when it seems so different from the pictures you created in your mind as you read. Benton and Fox (1985) suggest that mental imagery is the main means through which reading is supported. Turning text into images is an important part of engaging with the characters, the setting and events. When we encourage children to do this consciously and articulate the imagery or picture brought to their minds they are sometimes surprised, but it helps to make this important strategy explicit. Explain how valuable this strategy is. You will notice how it can challenge and extend thinking in ways that generate vocabulary, support inference and develop empathy and deepen understanding.

Image construction also includes drawing and drama. Drawing is an important way of children representing their ideas about a text; drama strategies can lift the words off the page and bring them to life. Such visualisation techniques can help children to be right 'inside' the story, and appreciate how the language of the text can portray a character or a setting at a particular point in time. They are useful when interpreting and commenting on a writer's choice of language and grammatical and literary features, for developing empathy and strengthening inference skills.

Practical approaches to help children to visualise

The following are examples of activities that you can use to help children see how powerful visualisation can be for understanding the text.

*   While reading a text rich in sensory imagery, stop at a key point and ask children to re-read and then think about the picture they have in their minds. Invite them to articulate the view they have in pairs or groups. Encourage more experienced readers to explain any of the author's language choices that particularly helped with the visualisation process.

*   Explain that the illustrator has forgotten to include an illustration for one of the paragraphs in a text and invite the children to 'paint a picture' of it and sketch out an idea of what the picture might look like.

*   Use drama activities such as freeze-framing, where children work in groups to represent a still moment in time. Encourage them to use body language to represent how characters are feeling. Extend this through thought tracking – that is inviting children to explain their stance and thoughts at that moment (see Chapter 7).

Summarising

A PGCE trainee recently invited children to share their reading preferences with each other as part of raising the profile of reading in his class. One of the children was invited to tell others the main events in the book he was currently reading. *Oh it's quite long*, he explained, *and I've been reading it for ages so I don't really know*. He had quite literally lost the plot.

To be good at comprehension, children need to have a competent working memory. They need to keep active what has already been read as they process subsequent information. Being able to summarise helps children to construct an overall understanding of a text, chapter or paragraph. A key part of this is determining importance, that is, deciding which elements are most significant. If children can identify the key information in the text as they go along, and recall and arrange this in order, they are more likely to be able to relate one part of the text to another, which is a key part of inferencing, as we will see below.

Practical approaches to help children to summarise

The following are examples of activities that can help children to identify the most important events, information or themes in a text.

*   Use a range of organisers to help to summarise and represent story ideas. Invite children to construct story maps and story charts that summarise the key events (see

also Chapter 8), or *box up* the story by asking children to summarise the key elements of the story in a set number of points. Invite them to compare with another group, and justify the decisions they have made.

- Re-present information from non-fiction texts as flow charts or timelines. For example, recast a written description of a volcano as an annotated drawing, or draw the steps involved in mummification.

- Invite children to give a book a new title once it has been read. Explain that they are not able to use the most obvious words. This can challenge children to identify the key themes in the text.

Teaching children to monitor and repair

If comprehension is to develop to a high level, children need to know and to care whether or not the text makes sense. Kispal (2008) suggests that active adult readers have a zero tolerance of inconsistency. You are likely to check your understanding almost without thinking about it. However, poor comprehenders tend not to pay sufficient attention when they misread the text, even when it leads to glaring gaps or inconsistencies (Oakhill *et al.*, 2005). Children need to know that part of their job as a reader is to sort out difficulties and misunderstandings as they go along and not to be satisfied with not understanding. Pardo (2004) discusses this in terms of *repairing the meaning*. You can help children to do this as you read aloud. You might make a deliberate error and question whether you have read the sentence correctly, go back and re-read; deal with a troublesome word by clarifying what it means; or question an assumption that no longer seems to be right.

Practical approaches to help children monitor understanding

The following are examples of activities that can help children to read the words on the page carefully for meaning. They are collectively known as Directed Activities Related to Texts (DARTs).

DARTs are reading activities originating from Lunzer and Gardner (1984). They help children to pay close attention to the text itself. They can make the text more manageable to read, and group discussion plays a central part in the process. DARTs can be divided into two main groups: *reconstruction activities* and *analysis activities*.

Reconstruction activities use text that is modified. They include:

- *text completion* (cloze); children predict deleted words (cloze), sentences or phrases;

- *diagram completion*; children predict deleted labels on diagrams by referring to the text;

- *table completion*; children complete deleted parts of a table using text as sources of reference;

- *sequencing and grouping*; these include card sorting activities, categorising information and reconstructing a text previously divided into segments;

- *prediction*; children stop at chosen points in the text to predict what will come next.

Analysis activities use the text in its original form. They include:

*   *text-marking*: this includes underlining, annotating and numbering the text, and often involves skimming and scanning to find specific information;

*   *labelling*: children label segments of text;

*   segmenting: children segment paragraphs or text into units of information, which are then annotated;

*   *reconstructing* the text: this involves reading then remodelling the information in another format, for example, as a diagram, flow chart, concept map, table or chart, timeline or factfile.

DARTs actively encourage engagement with the words on the page as they always take readers back to the text rather than away from it. Children will need to check and confirm their ideas and look for additional evidence by returning to the text. DARTs can be particularly supportive for inexperienced readers and allow all children to engage in purposeful reading.

Making inferences

Being able to make inferences has been described as one of the most important processes that occur during comprehension (Pardo, 2004; Butcher and Kintsch, 2003). It is key to making sense of the text and involves what has been described as *gap-filling*; taking two or more pieces of information from a text in order to arrive at a third piece of information that is implicit (Kispal, 2008). There are broadly two types of inference, *coherence* and *elaborative.* Coherence inferences, as the name implies, provide coherence within the text and tend to happen automatically. Take the sentence 'Sarah told Simon that he was late'. We know that the pronoun 'he' refers to 'Simon'. Elaborative inferences usually involve the more conscious application of reasoning skills. They are likely to require us to make sense by considering the text in the light of our own knowledge and experience and can add significantly to the richness of the text. For example, 'Gladys looked up at the now derelict house and the piles of rubble wistfully, still clutching her gas mask. She had not had the courage to return until now.' We may all infer slightly different meanings from this; we know that something significant has happened and may have a view about what it was and where and when it is set, based on a range of information from our knowledge of history, the description and perhaps the character's name. Brien (2011) explains that every text lays down a range of cues that lead the reader to the author's meanings.

There are many factors involved in good inferencing. Kispal's study (2008) highlights a number of preconditions.

*   Having a competent working memory.

*   Being an active reader.

*   Monitoring comprehension and repairing inconsistencies.

*   Having a wide background knowledge.

*   Having a good vocabulary.

*   Sharing the same cultural background as that assumed by the text.

Cain and Oakhill (1999) demonstrated that the ability to draw inferences predetermines reading skills: that is, poor inferencing causes poor comprehension and not vice versa. This is important to know as the development of inference skills can take place in a range of contexts; inference-making is not just confined to reading. You will use inference all the time. You can tell when someone's words belie their true feelings from the tone of their voice and body language; you can work out that the gym will be busy from the number of cars in the car park. Many children can and do infer at sophisticated levels, even though their decoding skills may be limited. If they are given the opportunity to develop such skills with pictures or moving images, we can scaffold the move from the visual to print and back again and help children develop deeper levels of understanding during reading. Many of the activities already described above will support the development of inferencing skills, but it is important to make what is involved explicit. As you explain and demonstrate that some things in the text will not be explained directly, you can encourage them to use information from elsewhere in the text, their own experience and their world knowledge to make sense of what they read. Try asking relevant questions aloud of yourself during shared reading, and answer them by thinking your thoughts aloud to show how you arrive at an inference. You could ask 'How do you know?' whenever an inference is generated as part of making this explicit.

Interestingly, research (Kispal, 2008) suggests that inferences are often made more consciously when reading information texts, particularly when these are about themes children know a lot about. This is because it is easier to see how using facts from the text, plus background knowledge, can lead to new knowledge.

In the case study below, you will see how Natalie, a Year 3 teacher, is developing children's inference skills on and beyond the page by using a carefully chosen picture book.

CASE STUDY

Teaching inferences

Natalie had chosen a high quality picture book with a well written and emotionally powerful storyline to be the focus for PSHE work on belonging. She also wanted to strengthen the children's understanding of making inferences. She had carefully chosen the text to engage the class, stimulate their ideas and feelings, and to be sufficiently challenging to promote discussion and debate. Natalie decided to bring the children's prior knowledge to the fore by leaving a basket of props related to the text on the carpet. This raised the children's curiosity and Natalie carefully generated discussion about who the items belong to. Natalie modelled and encouraged 'I wonder' questions. *Who might have left these things here, and why? What clues might they give about their owner?* She asked them to justify their opinions: *how do you think you know?* and *tell (me) more about what gives you that idea.* This engaged the children who generated their own 'I wonder' statements.

The following day, the text was introduced, and the children discussed the title of the book, and thought about why it might have been chosen. To stimulate further tentative thinking, Natalie left a note/letter from the main character in the text in the basket for the children to 'find'. The children talked in pairs about what they now thought about the story/theme and what happened to the main character from the text. Natalie acted as scribe, recording the children's responses on a flip chart.

They discussed together what they were not sure about and devised questions that were written on thought bubbles and displayed on a working wall. The questions were recorded for future reference so that they could look at how their thinking and understanding had changed.

Natalie read the whole text aloud, stopping to model questioning and uncertainty, using words such as *I wonder...* and *maybe...* The children were encouraged to listen out for the answers to their own questions, and confirm or amend their judgments as the story was read. They were invited to explore the themes and characters in the story and find possible answers to the questions through a number of drama techniques, including freeze framing, thought tracking and conscience alley. Thought tracking, allowed them to explore the characters and their motivation. It stretched their ideas and vocabulary and encouraged them to develop their thinking and exploration of possibilities in response to the text. The next day, Natalie asked the children what they thought about the main character using the drama technique 'role on the wall'. She asked questions such as *How do you know? What gives us an indication that we're right? Are there any ideas that don't fit together* or *Is there any information that's missing?* to take the children back to the text. As the text was re-read Natalie modelled the process of looking for clues, testing and confirming hypotheses and responses that had emerged. She used text marking to indicate where/why inferences had been drawn.

Natalie's well-chosen text offered a rich context for children to use language as a tool for developing inferences. Her approach involved articulating her thinking, and letting the children into the secret of what went on inside her head as she read. The children were encouraged to explore and imagine, speculate and wonder, reason and interpret information. In this way she was able to bring the hidden aspects of the reading process – and inference-making in particular – out into the open.

Activity 2

» *Now that you have read descriptions of the key strategies and have looked at practical approaches to developing children's comprehension, look at the strategies again and note briefly what you have learned about each:*

– *activating prior knowledge;*

– *prediction;*

– *questioning and clarifying;*

– *visualisation and imagination;*

– *summarising;*

– *drawing inferences;*

– *monitoring understanding.*

The role of the teacher

The importance of your role in teaching comprehension has been stressed throughout this chapter. There is good evidence that children make better progress in their reading when they are provided with direct instruction and when contexts and activities enable them to practise and internalise key strategies for themselves (Palincsar and Brown, 1984; Lewis and Tregenza, 2007). This is why there has been a strong emphasis on modelling the processes involved in comprehending the text and the importance of making these explicit and articulating what successful readers do when they read. Other key elements to bear in mind when teaching are described below.

Choosing and using texts

Just as decodable texts need to be matched to the children's phonic knowledge, the texts we use to develop comprehension skills need to be carefully chosen. It is clearly crucial to consider the breadth and variety of texts that children will meet in their reading, so that they are able to apply their developing skills to a range of text types. Texts need to be sufficiently challenging and worth reading. Narrative is best read as a whole: there is limited merit in using discrete extracts. The text needs to have resonance with the children in your class, to engage them and have layers of meaning – there needs to be deep understanding for comprehension. Sophisticated picture books can provide excellent opportunities for all children to engage with the text without being held back by a lack of fluency. Remember that you do not have to confine yourself to texts that children can read for themselves. Reading aloud, as we have already seen, provides good opportunities to develop sophisticated understandings.

Asking the right questions

The approaches that we have discussed demand a lot of us as teachers, and require us to think carefully about our own talk. The way we frame our questions as we talk about texts can open up or close down thinking. We need to find ways of encouraging tentative and speculative talk, using genuinely open questions. Thinking that there must be one right answer can be inhibiting for children. They need to know that a text can have a range of meanings and interpretations – they will each bring a unique perspective to it. This makes collaboration powerful. Sharing and discussing responses opens up opportunities to develop important cognitive and interpretive skills. 'What do you think about ...?', or 'does anyone have a different idea?' are good starting points. Don't be afraid to ask children what makes them think that, and to take the children back to the text, re-read and look for clues, and to test and confirm hypotheses and responses that have emerged from the discussions.

Self-regulation

Modelling, while important, is not enough to transfer skills. The suggested activities will help to hand these over to the children, but we need to provide ample opportunities for them to practise these skills in authentic contexts so that they become learned approaches and ways of thinking. Self-regulation involves children taking control and using the right strategy at the right time, autonomously and independently of the teacher. It grows out of good metacognition, or 'learning to learn' as this is sometimes known. This requires teaching approaches that make children think about learning more explicitly. For example, children will benefit from articulating the skills they are drawing on to support their understanding of the text. Encourage them to think out loud, however tentatively, and always acknowledge the contribution children make. Without your reassurance, this can feel a risky business. If they can explain what has helped them to understand the text, and the strategies they have used, they are well on the way to self-regulation.

Shared and guided reading

This chapter has not focused on classroom organisation, but shared and group work are the obvious contexts for teaching comprehension. What has been modelled in a whole-class reading session can be practised and applied to a new text in group work. This provides a good opportunity to strengthen and develop skills in a more focused and precise way, so that you can tailor your teaching to the particular needs of groups of children in a structured but responsive way.

Critical points

»   *Good readers can draw on a range of strategies, engage actively with the text, and create and build an understanding of what the author means for themselves. Discrete off-the-peg exercises will not teach comprehension.*

»   *Comprehension is dynamic and iterative, and skills are best taught in authentic contexts while reading quality texts that will motivate children to want to make meaning.*

»   *The role of the teacher is to externalise some of the internal processes used by skilled readers, slow the reading process down to model and teach key aspects of comprehension, and help children to think and talk about what they are reading.*

»   *Comprehension activities need to be carefully planned and will almost always involve investigation and dialogue. It makes sense for children to discuss their reading together, to share their knowledge, ideas and perspectives, and engage with new thinking in a way they could not do if reading alone. They will also need to be able to articulate the strategies they are using to promote self-regulation.*

»   *In these ways, children will arrive at a fuller understanding of the reading process, and, equally importantly, a greater enjoyment of the texts that they read.*

Critical reflections

»   *Make sure that you understand the key strategies for comprehension. Where do you currently use them in your teaching? How could you broaden the range of strategies that you use to promote children's engagement with texts?*

Taking it further

Chambers, A. (1993) *Tell Me: Children, Reading and Talk.* Stroud: Thimble Press.

This short book shows how genuine discussion arises when appropriately framed questions are asked. It provides practical suggestions for encouraging talk about texts together with a range of open ended questions that invite a range of responses and a depth of discussion.

DfES (2007) *Understanding Reading Comprehension*. London: DfES.

Three booklets written by the Primary National Strategy and full of suggestions of activities to support comprehension. Free to download.

Lewis, M. and Tregenza, J. (2007) Beyond Simple Comprehension. *English Four to Eleven*, November (30) Summer.

This excellent article and the case study that goes alongside it show what teaching comprehension strategies looks like in practice and explains the benefits of this approach.

Warner, C. (2013) *Talk for Reading*. Leicester, United Kingdom: UKLA.

This mini book considers ways of deepening comprehension through talk. It considers the importance of teaching children how to talk together about their reading to strengthen engagement and understanding.

References

Benton, M. and Fox, G. (1985) *Teaching Literature Nine to Fourteen*. Oxford: Oxford University Press.

Brien, J. (2011). *Teaching Primary English*. London: Sage.

Butcher, K.R., and Kintsch, W. (2003) Text Comprehension and Discourse Processing, in Healy, A.F. and Proctor, R.W. (eds) *Handbook of Psychology*, Volume 4, Experimental Psychology. New York: Wiley.

Cain, K. and Oakhill, J. (1999) Inference Making Ability and its Relation to Comprehension Failure in Young Children. *Reading and Writing: An Interdisciplinary Journal*, 11:5–6.

Cain, K. and Oakhill, J. (2006) Profiles of Children with Specific Reading Comprehension Difficulties. *British Journal of Educational Psychology*, 76:4.

Clark, C. and Rumbold, K. (2006) *Reading for Pleasure*. London: National Literacy Trust.

DfES (2005) *Understanding Comprehension*. London: DfES.

Gamble, N. and Yates, S. (2008) *Exploring Children's Literature*. London: Sage.

Guthrie, J.T. and Wigfield, A. (2000) Engagement and Motivation in Reading, in Kamil, M.L., Mosenthal, P.B., Pearson, P.D. and Barr, R. (eds), *Handbook of Reading Research* (3rd edn). New York: Longman.

Graham, J. (2010) Small Children Talking Their Way Into Being Readers, in Goodwin, P. (2010) *The Literate Classroom* (3rd edn). London: Routledge.

Johnston, R.S. and Watson, J. (2005) *The Effects of Synthetic Phonics Teaching on Reading and Spelling Attainment: A Seven Year Longitudinal Study*. Available from www.scotland.gov.uk/ Publications/2005/02/20688/52449.

Kispal, A. (2008) *Effective Teaching of Inference Skills for Reading: Literature Review*. DCSF Research Report (031). London: DCSF.

Lewis, M. and Tregenza, J. (2007) Beyond Simple Comprehension. *English 4–11*, 30.

Lunzer, E. and Gardner, K. (1984) *Learning from the Written Word.*

Martin, T (2010) Readers Making Meaning: Responding to Narrative, in Goodwin, P. *The Literate Classroom* (3rd edn). London: Routledge.

Nation, K. and Angell, P. (2006) Learning to Read and Learning to Comprehend. *London Review of Education*, 4:1.

National Reading Panel (2000) *Report of The National Reading Panel, Washington, DC.* Available from: www.nationalreadingpanel.org (accessed 20 June 2013).

Oakhill, J., Hartt, J. and Samols, D. (2005) Levels of Comprehension Monitoring and Working Memory in Good and Poor Comprehenders. *Reading and Writing: An Interdisciplinary Journal*, 18.

OECD (2002) *Reading for Change: Performance and Engagement Across Countries.* Paris, France: Organisation for Economic Co-operation and Development.

Palincsar, A. and Brown, A. (1984) Reciprocal Teaching of Comprehension-Fostering and Comprehension-Monitoring Activities, *Cognition and Instruction*, 1:2.

Pressley, M. (2000) What Should Comprehension Instruction Be The Instruction Of? in Kamil, M. *et al.* (eds), *Handbook of Reading Research*, Hillsdale, NJ: Erlbaum.

Pardo, L. (2004) What Every Teacher Needs to Know About Comprehension. *The Reading Teacher*, 58:3.

Rose, J. (2006) *Independent Review of the Teaching of Early Reading.* London: DfES.

Stanovich, Keith E. (1986) Matthew Effects in Reading: Some Consequences of Individual Differences in the Acquisition of Literacy. *Reading Research Quarterly*, 21:4.

5 Beyond books

JOHN BENNETT

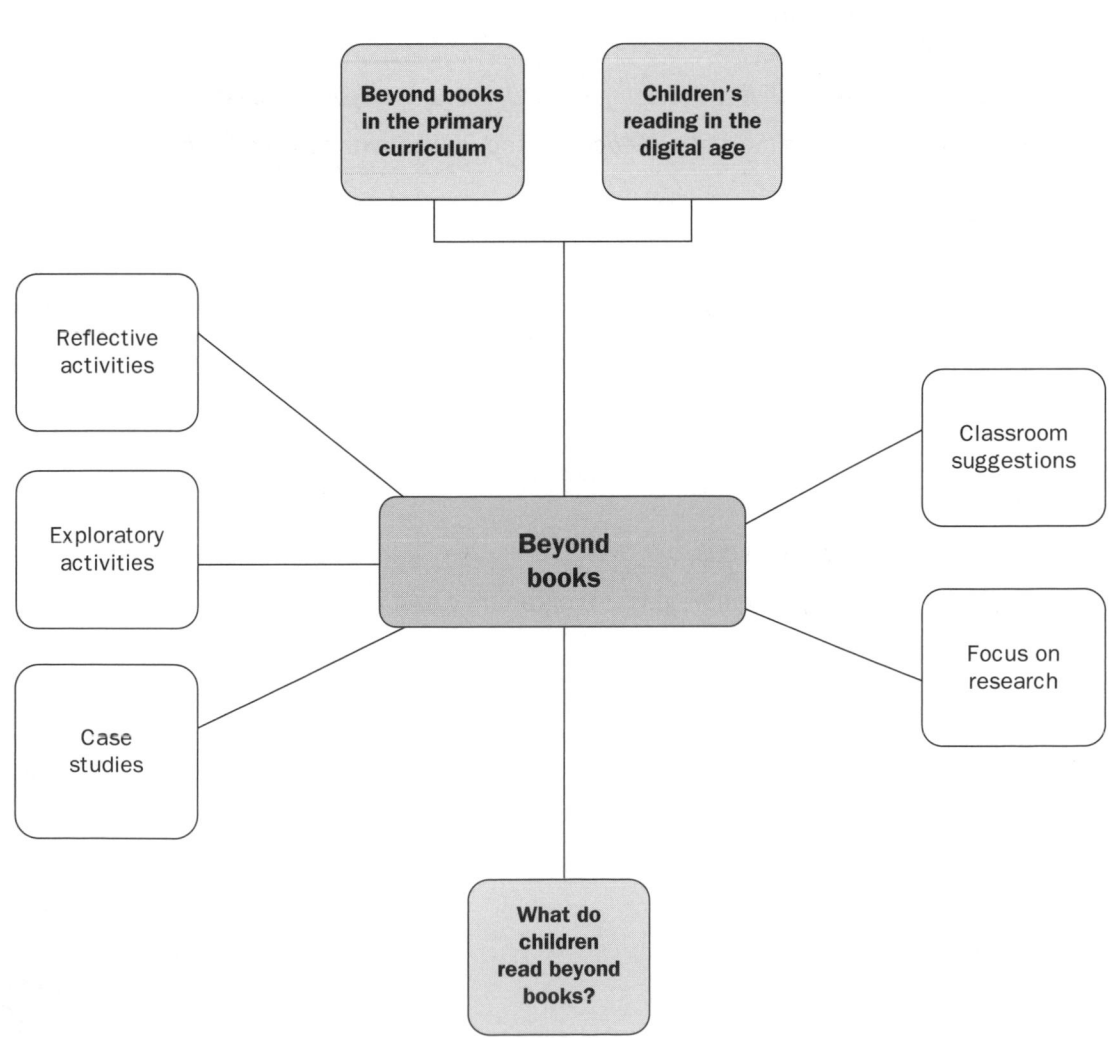

Teachers' standards

3 Demonstrate good subject and curriculum knowledge

- have a secure knowledge of the relevant subject(s) and curriculum areas, foster and maintain pupils' interest in the subject, and address misunderstandings

- demonstrate a critical understanding of developments in the subject and curriculum areas, and promote the value of scholarship

- demonstrate an understanding of and take responsibility for promoting high standards of literacy, articulacy and the correct use of standard English, whatever the teacher's specialist subject

Critical questions

» *What do children read beyond books?*

» *How can we ensure that the reading curriculum is relevant to twenty-first century readers?*

» *How can we ensure that the reading curriculum goes beyond books?*

» *How can we develop the skills needed to read digital texts as effectively as possible?*

Introduction

Consider what a 'typical' primary school child might read during a day. We know there is no such thing as a typical child and what follows would vary hugely, but we need to start somewhere, so let's start with a Key Stage 2 boy and his reading for a day.

Before school:

- comic;
- checking emails;
- computer game instructions;
- captions on the television breakfast programmes and adverts;
- road signs;
- adverts;
- shop signs.

In school:

- reading book;
- dictionary;
- maths textbook;
- workbook/worksheet;
- science investigation writing frame;

- a website to gain information about the geography topic on rainforests;

- lunch menu;

- lyrics for a song during collective worship;

- class blog;

- things on the interactive whiteboard;

- friend's work;

- displays and signs around the school.

After school

The same things as before school, plus:

- homework notes;

- reading book;

- text messages;

- websites about

  - rainforests for homework;

  - Star Wars LEGO®;

  - Manchester United;

- school learning platform, to upload homework.

That's a lot of different possible reading situations and many of them are certainly beyond books! Of course, for many children the above scenario is unlikely, due to a dearth of reading material at home, but some of the examples of incidental reading will be common to many children (see also Chapter 11).

Within this chapter there is no intention to explore every reading situation beyond books, but it should be immediately apparent that books are only a part of a child's reading repertoire and, with the growth in electronic texts, children now have access to more reading beyond books than ever before. This chapter will mainly be concerned with what children read beyond books in terms of electronic texts, rather than aspects of reading which do not require words, such as visual literacy (Stafford, 2011).

The rise in the use of electronic texts of various forms has led to the use of the phrase *digital literacy*, meaning the ability to use digital technology to access, find, create, use, evaluate and communicate information. For the purposes of this chapter, the focus will clearly be on digital literacy in relation to reading. The chapter therefore considers the emergence of new aspects or forms of literacy involving the reading of words, which need to be reflected in the approaches to literacy in school. It will explore what this means for classroom practice and look at ways of ensuring that the reading experience children have at school is more aligned to the reading experience outside school and what that experience may be like in the children's future.

What do children read beyond books?

Children's reading habits have changed over time, and whilst there is no doubt that we are in a period where the number of books that children can read and the range of different stories and themes covered is massive, the world of reading beyond books has changed considerably over the last decade. The digital age has moved the reading experience from page to screen for many adults and the same is true of children, particularly when not in school.

FOCUS ON RESEARCH

The national survey of children's reading conducted by The Literacy Trust in 2012 (Clarke, 2012) showed some interesting results about children's reading habits and it is worth considering these. The full survey includes comparisons over time, which show changes in children's views of reading, and also changes in what children read.

As a major survey, the results can be seen as giving a good overview of children's reading habits, with some interesting findings, particularly in terms of children's reading moving from paper books to other media and the reading of lyrics.

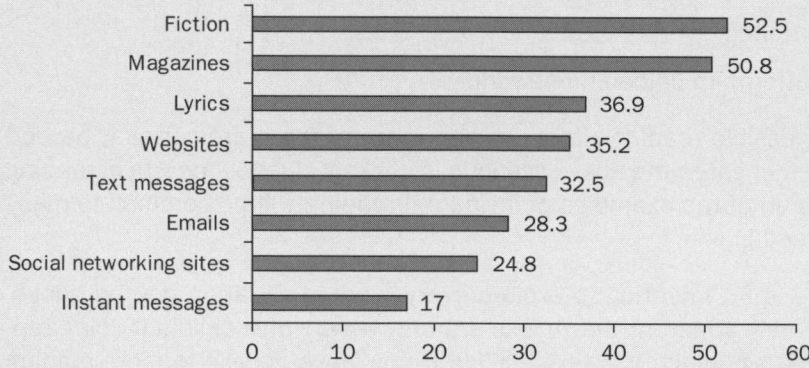

Figure 5.1 Key Stage 2 reading choices in terms of what children read outside of class at least once a month (percentages). Based on data from Clarke, 2012, 26.

Children, for a long time, have read beyond books. Although often frowned upon previously, it is now not uncommon to find comics and graphic novels in schools, especially since graphic texts are mentioned in the 2006 framework (DfES, 2006). There are many examples of comic books or graphic novels used in primary schools. Raymond Briggs' *The Snowman* uses a comic book frame approach, but without words, whereas books such as Neil Gaiman and Dave McKean's *The Wolves in the Walls* present a mix of graphics and text, mirroring earlier reading books, but akin to more sophisticated graphic novels aimed at older audiences. These are still books, of course. Comics, however, appear to be in decline, with the 2012 UK survey above showing that comic reading had almost halved over a 7-year period (Clarke,

2012). Recently, the classic comic *The Dandy*, a staple read for children of the 1950s and 1960s, became a digital only title (www.dandy.com/) and it is digital texts of one form or another that are likely to be the things that children will read.

For primary-age children, magazine reading may also feature, particularly associated with hobbies and interests, but as the 2012 survey notes, this is also declining. This may be because of the growth in websites devoted to children's hobbies and interests, previously explored through magazines. Why would a child (or parent) want to pay for a paper copy of *Doctor Who Adventures, Girl Talk* or *Match of the Day*, when so much of the content, with added interactivity and multimedia approaches, is available 'free' on the internet? The rise in KS2 children's web browsing could include a move from print to screen magazines for many children.

It is important for a primary school teacher to have an understanding of children's reading experiences and preferences outside school. Knowledge of these factors can help to personalise learning and can also help to ensure that what is offered, in terms of the media for reading, is both matched with and supplements what the children experience outside school. Short 'reading conferences' with children, on a few occasions in a year, can help the teacher gain an informed view of a child's reading, beyond what he or she has to do in school, beyond the reading books, and beyond books in general.

Activity 1: Reading conference or focus group

» *Ask a child or group of children what they read when they are not in school. They may start by only talking about print-based media, so may need prompting to think of more sources beyond those. Make a list and when it is complete, ask the children the following questions.*

Which of those types of reading:

- *do you do the most?*
- *do you never or hardly ever do at school?*
- *do you think are the most important and why?*
- *do you enjoy the most?*
- *Why do you enjoy that the most?*

In the following case study, a group of children give their descriptions of what and how they read outside school. From this, it should be clear that children's reading can certainly go beyond books in a variety of ways.

CASE STUDY

What do Year 5 children read beyond books?

A group of Year 5 children were asked to talk about what they read outside school. Their responses showed a real mixture of reading sources, ranging from traditional books to reading puzzles on handheld devices. The children talked enthusiastically about their favourite books and authors (Anthony Horowitz, Eoin Colfer, Anne Fine) and when asked if they ever read fiction books using any form of e-reader or electronic text, they said yes, but clearly expressed preferences for paper books. When it came to reading more broadly than fiction, it was clear that much of their reading of non-fiction was via electronic texts, although some of the children said they really enjoyed browsing 'big encyclopaedias'.

The children talked about using the internet to check on football and cricket scores, catch up with the news (www.bbc.co.uk/newsround), find recipes, find out about animals and a variety of other things, which they accessed via computers, tablets and mobile phones. The way in which they described how they used these devices demonstrated that they had developed a range of skills in finding, storing and bookmarking information. For example, one child talked about getting up in the morning, switching the tablet on and going straight to a 'favourite' page to check on the most up-to-date sports results.

In relation to social networking the children talked about parents sharing access to their social networking on the web (www.facebook.com) and reading the class blog online at home, via the school's extended virtual learning environment (www.learnanywhere.co.uk). Text messaging and email were features of the children's lives, with some using those more than others. Alongside books and web sources, the children talked about reading newspapers, but magazines and comics did not appear to feature, perhaps mirroring the decline noted in The Literacy Trust survey (Clarke, 2012).

As can be seen in the above case study, from even a brief discussion, it is clear that children's reading may go beyond books. The majority of the reading beyond books was for information purposes for the children in the case study, but there were indications that fiction was also read using electronic formats, just not as much.

Children's reading in the digital age

The media to be read has always been subject to change, but it is probably in the last 20 years that reading matter has changed the most. The growth of the internet, the rise in the number of people with access to computers or other devices that can carry digital text, and the migration of texts from paper to digital form, as well as the creation of much more digital content, has transformed the reading landscape. Arguably, the full impact of this has yet to be felt in schools, as the required technology may appear in school after its adoption by the general public. An example of this is the recent growth in ownership and use of tablet computers such as iPads. It still appears that many schools have not fully capitalised on the possibilities these kinds of devices can offer in the classroom, although some schools most certainly have, even to the point of assigning a tablet to each child (British Educational Suppliers Association, 2012).

The impact of the growth of digital text has raised some interesting questions and dilemmas for schools, not least of which is related to which technology to invest in. Beyond the hardware, there are also questions about what should be taught in school, the impact of children's digital reading experiences outside school, and how aspects of digital literacy can be effectively introduced and developed in the classroom. It is worth exploring some of the issues and opportunities, prior to considering what should and can be done.

Text messages and social networking

One of the most pervasive forms of reading beyond books today is text messages, and children today are almost inevitably learning the language of *textspeak*. There is no intention here to explore the arguments about the impact of textspeak on children's skills in English, which are numerous and ongoing, for example the investigation by a team at Coventry University (Wood *et al.*, 2011). However, the fact that texting has become a significant part of the way many people communicate, particularly young people, means that it must surely feature in some way in the education of children.

Textspeak, with its phonetic idiosyncrasies (w8, m8, cu l8ter) and its abbreviations (lol, btw, rofl), alongside its stoic refusal to require any form of punctuation at times, can be seen as a potential threat to the standard form of English, although the extent of the actual threat is debatable, as noted by Crystal (2008). With predictive text and fewer limits in the way in which text messages are presented, over time there are likely to be fewer abbreviated words. On smartphones, with sophisticated predictive text, you may be presented with three or more options for the word you are trying to input. This actually promotes reading and the practice of using all those phonics skills that children have learned, alongside sight vocabulary, to quickly decode the word options in order to select the correct one. Whilst there is little doubt that children will text in some form, the medium is changing so quickly and the text becoming much closer to Standard English, that perhaps the previous issues will not be as relevant in the future. Add to this the potential in the use of speech to text for creating messages and the whole future of textspeak does not feel assured.

Children in primary schools may also engage in various social networking practices, whether that is following tweeters on Twitter, becoming friends with people on Facebook, instant messaging in some form or myriad other opportunities to communicate and collaborate virtually. All of these require skills in reading, and in many cases those skills need to be quite refined in order to fully comprehend what is being read. For example, the brevity of a tweet often means that words are abbreviated or missing and, as with text messages, misinterpretation is possible. Only a good grounding in language can help with this and, critically, aspects of comprehension such as interpretation and knowing the author's intention are very important when reading such texts, to avoid misinterpretation.

Children play computer games on numerous devices. The evolution of video games has, unfortunately, moved the content from the text-based interaction of early adventure games, to limited use of text. The advent of console technology (Playstation, X-Box), designed specifically for gaming, has reduced the textual interaction to even lower levels, as many instructions are given verbally using sound files. The games most usually played by primary school children are unlikely to require a lot of reading. Although it is clear that many access and play games designed for older audiences (DCSF, 2008), which may contain more text, children may not need to read it, as the game can be played without that requirement.

Another aspect of computer games with potential to impact on children's reading habits and development is the narrative nature of many games. Although the more complex games tend to be aimed at older audiences, children in Key Stage 2 may access these, and even if they don't, they may still experience games that are story-led. These games can be immersive, drawing the player into new worlds and new identities. Whilst there is little doubt that written text can develop imagination and reading skills, these types of narrative games do have some place in creating an enthusiasm for story that goes beyond what has previously been available through radio, film and TV, because the added dimension is personal interaction with the environment, characters and plot – the player is in the story, in a way that almost no other medium offers. That is a powerful tool and one that, if educational software developers can capitalise on it, could be used to the benefit of reading development. The technology is now available to take children into virtual worlds (eg www.spaceheroes.com), and whilst these sometimes have limited textual content, the interest in plot and characters can help to develop a thirst for more of that, which other forms of reading can cater for.

There are, of course, some games designed to support the development of reading skills. Wordshark (www.wordshark.co.uk), for example, has been used in many schools for years. Such educational games and activities are available for home and school and a growing range is available for iPad and Android devices, although many are American in origin and therefore spelling and pronunciation can prove problematic for UK children learning to read. School computers have been populated by educational games for many years and these still have a part to play, which may grow as tablet computers become more commonplace in classrooms.

Beyond computer games there is a wealth of content creation software, through which children can create their own stories, web pages, blogs and other online text. The rise in Web 2.0 technology (Alexander, 2006) and ease of use, means that readers of websites, can also be authors and co-authors (Barber and Cooper, 2012; Davies and Merchant, 2009).

Some children may have e-readers, which offer them a growing range of texts to choose from. Books which have been transferred to e-readers, such as the Kindle or the Kobo, are read in similar ways to physical books and in many ways are designed to emulate the reading experience of a 'real' book. The more advanced features of e-readers certainly go beyond standard books, with sophisticated bookmarking, text-to-speech, dictionary and thesaurus options. We are now in a period of significant change in the market for electronic books, offering more ways for children to read electronically. As tablet computers become as affordable as the handheld games devices that children have played on for years, there are opportunities for these multifunction devices, through apps and web connectivity, to contain and access reading material aimed at children.

Interactive books have been a feature in many schools for some time. Within these the reading experience is considered to be enhanced through the addition of pictures, sound and interactive elements. These elements can be as simple as pictures that can be hovered over or clicked on to trigger an animation effect, or more complex and immersive, such as to start a small game that the reader can play, which relates to a part of the text. Talking books, where the story is read and often words are highlighted as they are heard, have also been a feature of early literacy. The interactive nature of such texts can draw children into the story, making the experience come to life more than just reading the words on the page. Music, sound effects, word reading, multiple languages and various forms of hyperlinking and animation add to the reading experience.

Many children already have access to new reading media (Clarke, 2012), and it seems likely that many more will in the not too distant future. The critical point here is that the education of our young people is not just for their present, but for their future, and even if they currently have limited experiences with the embedded and emerging technologies and the different forms of reading skills required to engage fully with them, in the future these digital literacy skills will be seen as essential to many, both socially and in the workplace. The current wave of social media has transformed the way many people communicate. It has led to significant changes to personal, social and business practices. This technology and these new media and reading practices are not going to go away. We must prepare children for their use and that is a role that schools must take, offering experiences and developing skills in approaching reading beyond books in the curriculum.

Activity 2: reading log

»   *Ask a class of children to think of all the things they read in a day. Ask them to think about all the different things they read and work out what form their reading takes most often. Are there differences between the boys and the girls? How much reading is on-screen, rather than on paper?*

»   *Children could complete a daily reading log, either from recall, or on an hour-by-hour basis, to analyse their own reading experiences. This could look at not only what they read, but why they read what they read.*

Beyond books in the primary curriculum

> *Many texts, including those enjoyed by children, now express meaning through both verbal and non-verbal or visual means. As technological changes multiply, therefore, each generation needs to rethink the concepts of literacy and reading.*
>
> Bell, 2005

Literacy is all about communication, and communication now is often done through digital media. Therefore, literacy should also be about understanding and using digital media in the best way possible. If it isn't, then it is not preparing children for their future.

As with any other aspect of the curriculum, a key approach to learning is to build on children's own interests and experiences. A school that fails to recognise both the impact and opportunities of this fact will not be capitalising on the motivation the children already have. All of the aspects of reading in the digital age that children are likely to experience in their home and future lives can have a place in the reading curriculum in school, and in most cases there are strong arguments why they must be there.

As previously noted, text beyond books in the form of media such as comics, graphic novels, magazines and newspapers can most certainly have a place in the reading experience of children in schools, but the growth in digital texts and the translation of these kinds of materials into electronic form, means that the digital versions of these can also appear in the curriculum, alongside all of the other forms of text that children will experience.

In the classroom, teachers have used texts beyond those on paper for some time to support teaching, via digital projectors, interactive whiteboards and visualisers (which use a camera system to project the image of a paper-based text onto a screen). These have made it possible easily to share texts with groups of children and have offered tools to highlight, edit, reorganise and annotate the electronic text, sharing key learning points with the children and enabling the children to take part in a shared learning experience. With digitally produced texts, the children can interact with the text on screen and can work in a collaborative way with sections, more easily than with paper versions. Projected images of paper-based texts can't be manipulated in the same way, but the advantage of using a visualiser comes with the opportunity to display any physical text for a class to see, including things the children have written themselves. This offers the opportunity for children to read, enjoy and evaluate the work of their peers immediately.

The use of laptops and, increasingly, tablet computers means that what is done on a large screen system with a whole class can also be more easily done with individuals and groups than previously in any classroom. With computer rooms being replaced by sets of devices for classes in many schools, the new media is becoming closer in its use to books and paper than ever before. The addition of schools' virtual learning environments and online storage, alongside systems that allow the children to take home devices such as tablets, makes the experience akin to carrying around reading and exercise books.

For children with specific learning needs, such as learning difficulties or those learning English as an additional language, electronic texts offer a significant range of enhancements to help develop reading skills.

- Electronic texts can be enlarged for visually impaired children and even read to the child using increasingly sophisticated text-to-speech software.

- For children with dyslexia, text can be reorganised into more manageable 'chunks', as well as being given a variety of colours and backgrounds to help alleviate some of the visual problems associated with reading black text on white backgrounds.

- The quality of text-to-speech software has improved significantly in recent years and whether it is reading single words, sentences or whole sections of text, the option to have a word 'read' by the digital device for the child will help the child who struggles with particular words.

Of course, no discussion of the reading of online texts would be complete without the mention of the essential area of e-safety. This is not the place to discuss this area in detail, but when teaching children how to read using digital texts, particularly when they are accessing those texts using the internet, it is incredibly important to be aware of the dangers and the ways that young people can be protected and taught to protect themselves. Schools' acceptable usage policies should be strictly enforced, children need explicit teaching in methods of online safety and school staff need to be vigilant in monitoring children's reading activities online. With all of these efforts in place, staff should feel secure in allowing children to engage with online texts in a variety of ways.

Developing reading skills for digital texts

There is a view that reading on screen is different from reading from conventional sources (Cull, 2011), but the basic skills of word recognition and reading comprehension are still fundamental. The development of phonic knowledge and the practice in reading for meaning applies equally to digital texts. Where the differences lie are in things such as the multimedia nature of digital texts, the potential interactivity and the way in which text may be presented. Reading skills in the use of non-fiction texts can readily be mapped to the use of websites and the now less commonly utilised information DVDs. For example, the basic skill of scanning for keywords, essential for working with non-fiction texts in KS2, becomes even more critical when dealing with sets of results from search engines. In order to make the best use of a set of results from a search engine, just like any aspect of literacy, children need guidance. They need to see this modelled in shared reading sessions and they need the opportunity to practice with support. There are a number of search engines available for children to use, which can make this an easier task to perform (see end of chapter).

Although the skills in reading electronic texts are considered separately within this chapter, in most cases it would be far more effective to teach them across the range of texts that children will encounter, not solely as 'traditional' or 'digital' literacy skills. There is so much common ground between the reading skills used that an approach that builds up understanding through practising the skills in both paper and electronic forms must help reinforce common concepts and build up that common understanding. In this section, a number of specific aspects of reading that relate significantly to digital texts of various forms will be considered and the skills to be developed to read those will be identified, alongside some possible teaching strategies. Much of this will be concerned with reading on the internet, as it is there where multimodal texts are most likely to be needed.

Advertising

One thing that children are unlikely to find in books (but would find in other texts such as magazines, newspapers and comics) is advertisements. Increasingly, websites include advertising and that may be tailored to match what appear to be the interests of the web user. Children need the skills to distinguish between information and advertisements. There are likely to be visual clues such as the changes in text, the use of banners and the use of any tricks to draw the reader's eye (and cursor) to the advertisement (flashing, zooming, glowing, pulsating, etc.) – enticing the reader to click on the hyperlink and away from the focus of what they were previously looking at. Those elements of web advertisement design should be explored, so children understand how on-screen advertising works. Within the advertisements there is also, of course, the use of persuasive language. Children are already taught to identify and use persuasive language as part of their work on persuasive texts, and therefore it is only the context that is different. As noted throughout this section, the key skills are much the same, but a school that only focuses on advertisements on paper is missing a significant element of children's current and future experience.

Hypertexts and non-linear approaches to reading

Web pages and websites can be considered to be hypertexts – texts that go beyond standard texts – but they are still texts and are still read basically in conventional ways, albeit with various enhancements.

Websites can provide children with much valuable information about topics they are studying and are an invaluable tool for developing knowledge and understanding. Information is available in a few key presses, mouse clicks or screen taps and so children need to be taught how to access that information in the most meaningful ways. Lessons on engaging with information texts may still have paper-based elements, but as often as possible children should be exploring information digitally. This can be done in much the same way as paper-based methods, but via the different media. For example, guided reading groups can use electronic texts as the basis for reading, questioning and discussion. As children progress through the development of their comprehension skills, the questions can become more complex and evaluative. Simple initial questions may be about the factual content and how to find the information required, whilst more appreciative and evaluative questions can focus on whether the children think the information provided is enough for their needs; whether the presentation helps or hinders their understanding; and whether they can identify any ways in which they believe the website could be improved. This should all go further than just the immediately apparent features such as basic layout, menus, use of graphics and text styles. Beyond these aspects, consideration should be given to the ways in which digital texts can be enhanced (see below). This all requires teachers to have an understanding of the structure and purpose of such elements and also to understand how text can be enhanced in a digital environment.

Enhancements available for digital texts

- Hyperlinks
- Mouseover/rollover effects
- Pop-ups
- Menus
- Animation
- Sound
- Video
- Easier searching
- Can be manipulated (copied, pasted, edited, annotated)

Activity 3: Analysing web pages

» *Choose a selection of information web pages for children (perhaps related to a topic you are going to teach) and analyse them in terms of:*

– *what features will appeal to children;*

– *is the language used suitable for the age of the children it is intended for;*

– *are there any items on the page which will detract from the key information;*

– *how are various types of graphics used to support the information;*

– *what is the balance like between the reading required and other ways of gaining information from the page (pictures, video, sound clips, etc.);*

–   *are all of the hyperlinks appropriate and useful;*

–   *how can you tell or find out how credible the web page is?*

The non-linear approach to web research or web browsing brings in skills that can be seen as extensions to the type of skills used when exploring non-fiction reference texts.

For many children, browsing the web will be nothing new. However, even if it appears that children have experience using websites and are able to navigate them, they may not have developed their skills fully. It is therefore important to teach the basic skills of reading a website, in much the same away as it is important to teach the skills of navigating a non-fiction text. This can be done effectively through similar approaches as with traditional texts in school.

The skills required in handling information on the web are multiple and many rely on literacy skills such as the following, for which classroom activities are suggested:

Skill	Possible activity
Generating key words for searching	Preparing for searching – key questions, key words, key places, key ideas, using structures such as KWFL and other grids.
Skimming (as part of browsing/exploring)	Skimming exercises. 5 minutes to find and bookmark a number of web pages for future use, via skimming them to ensure they are relevant to the topic.
Scanning (as part of browsing/exploring)	Scanning exercises. Playing word spotting games.
Note-taking	Avoiding the possibility of simply cutting and pasting, various note-taking frames can be used and the development of specific questions to be answered can help to ensure a more critical focus on what is being looked for. Another approach is to use text marking on text that has been copied and pasted, to highlight key points or use features such as the Comments feature in MS Word to personally annotate text (demonstrating a variety of comprehension skills).
Creating own web pages	Use simple software packages to model creating web pages that meet the requirements of non-fiction texts. Highlight possible enhancements on paper texts and how they are created. Discuss the impact on the reader of elements of web page design.
Identification of bias and authority	See below.
Evaluation of content	See below.

Web pages can be structured in many different ways and, like many children's non-fiction texts, the format is not simply 'title then text'. Menus may appear in various places on the screen and in many different forms, and text can be in columns or boxes or sections in a multitude of configurations. Pictures are frequently used in web pages and there may be logos, icons, videos, animations, word clouds and a whole range of other features that can either distract or direct the reader. The phrase 'browsing the web' can be interpreted as starting to look for one thing, but then getting drawn down unexpected pathways to other interesting and possibly unrelated content, simply by clicking on multiple hyperlinks. Whilst this can be helpful in unearthing further useful information and finding unexpected links, for children (and adults) it can lead to a lack of focus on the task at hand. Children need to learn the skills required to deal with this, such as the use of favourites and bookmarks, as well as scrolling and the 'back' button. These are new skills, but are analogous with turning down the corners of pages (not a recommended practice), putting slips of paper between pages, using actual physical bookmarks or sticky notes, and flicking backwards and forwards in paper books – all strategies and skills used by readers.

Identification of bias and authority

The bias or lack of authority within material on the internet is sometimes obvious due to the language used ('in my view') or a lack of evidence to support given facts. For readers in primary schools, the things they will be exploring online are unlikely to lead to significant difficulties with bias, authority and credibility, but a critical approach should still be encouraged as early as possible.

Wray and Lewis (1997) assert that when reading non-fiction texts effectively, children need to be able to:

- identify questions that the text needs to answer, prior to reading;

- find information from the text;

- tell the difference between what is presented as fact, what is an author's opinion and what is attempting to persuade;

- take full account of the authority of the author when writing on the subject.

The skills to do all of the above have to be directly taught, through example and practical application, in order to ensure that children are engaging with non-fiction in a critical way and with an understanding of the differences between fiction and non-fiction, fact and opinion, authority and lack of authority. In primary school we start to develop children's skills in these areas, but critical and evaluative reading continues to develop through the rest of an individual's education and beyond. Electronic texts, particularly websites, offer opportunities to develop these skills and also provide some interesting challenges.

Consider a class or group of children investigating an aspect of Roman life as part of their topic 'The Romans in Britain'. The class has been asked to find information from the web, but beforehand, the teacher wants to make sure that where the children look will provide credible information. The teacher wants the class to assess the credibility of the sources used and so a framework is devised to support that aim. During their exploration of the web sources, the children will complete a 'Credibility Grid', as shown below. Some guidance would need to be given here in relation to each investigative element and of course, good modelling of the approach would help, but even if definitive answers to the evaluative questions cannot be given, simply raising the questions teaches children the importance of thinking about the credibility, authority and value of what is being looked at online.

Credibility Grid

Source	Fact opinion	When was it created/ updated? Could the information be out of date?	Author known?	Well-informed writer (professional)	Less well-informed writer (amateur)	Poorly informed writer
Personal web page of an amateur archaeologist						
Wikipedia						
Encyclopaedia Britannica Online						
The website set up by the historical trust responsible for the Roman villa the children visited						
A web page on another local school's site						

Another strategy could be to ask children to answer some focused questions.

- Does it help answer your questions?
- Who wrote it?
- Is it from an 'official' site?
- Is it a site from a known publisher?
- Why was it written?
- Are there any clues to help answer the above?
- Can you be sure that this is true?
- How can you check if this is right?
- Can you spot any bias in what is written?

A way of supporting this learning could be to look at a deliberately fake website, such as allaboutexplorers.com. This can be an interesting and enlightening exercise with a group of KS2 children.

Evaluating content

Children need to use higher order thinking skills when evaluating the content of a website. Exercises can be developed which direct the children to websites to evaluate, with increasing complexity of focus questions.

Initially, children might be asked how easy it was to find the information they needed and what features of the web page or website were particularly useful (such as navigation buttons, text boxes, diagrams, pictures, etc.). As skills develop, the questions can become deeper, broader and more evaluative, asking how they have decided that a website is particularly useful or not, what criteria could they say they have used and asking them to compare websites in terms of their relative value to a given task. Alongside these questions, higher order skills like analysis and synthesis can be brought into the experience, as the children make suggestions about how the experience could be enhanced and how they can use the information they have gained in different contexts. The synthesis of information from a variety of web sources immediately requires children to be making judgements about what to use and how information is connected or can be connected. As Starkey (2012) notes, *Learning in the digital age is a process of mastering concepts and skills, exploring boundaries of these and creating knowledge through connections* (71).

The future of reading beyond books

For all of the benefits that electronic texts hold, there are arguments that they lack the permanence and emotional connections of traditional paper-based texts, making the reading experience a less personal one (Read *et al.*, 2010). To some degree this remains to be seen, as young people today may look back fondly on the immersive interactive books they encountered as children. However, with the media, formats and devices changing so quickly, keeping digital editions of well-loved texts is certainly harder than keeping a set of favourite books on a bookshelf.

The future of electronic texts appears assured, for the moment. However, exactly what form electronic texts will take in the future is unknown. Unless there is a major change made to the nature of text, reading skills will continue to be important, although text-to-speech facilities may impact on these skills. One of the latest technological innovations is the development of Google Glass, a pair of glasses that includes a projection linked to the internet, with a camera and voice controls. It is not a great step to imagine a pair of glasses that will track text as the eyes follow it on a page and then 'read' that text to be heard by the 'reader' through an earpiece that is part of the frame. Take a step further than that, into the realms of science fiction, and you have contact lenses or ocular implants, which might fulfil the same functions in the future. All this could be seen as the evolution of the human race (Kelly, 2010), and, of course, we must remember that yesterday's science fiction is often today's science fact. Who knows what the future will be for reading?

At the time this chapter was written, the National Curriculum (DfEE, 1999) was under review and programmes of study for English had been published (DfE, 2013). Curiously, those programmes of study made no mention of digital literacy or electronic forms of communication at all and were indicative of the kind of pre-screen world in which the children who would be taught using that curriculum would not be living. The development of skills in the use of information technology may be seen to permeate pedagogy in practice, but sometimes it is necessary to be more prescriptive in statutory documents in order to ensure that all teachers see something as an expected part of their job and in this case, given that for many teachers digital literacy is relatively new, having a clear national directive to educate for reading in the future could be easily argued to be essential. It remains to be seen whether a future version of the National Curriculum acknowledges a digital age and a digital future more, but whether it does or doesn't, it is hoped this chapter will have made it clear that a twenty-first century education in communicating in English must go beyond books.

Activity 4: The reading classroom of the future

» *Imagine the primary classroom of the future.*

   How do you think children will access text in five or ten years? What do you think reading media will be like then? Do you think portable devices like tablets and e-readers will have replaced traditional paper formats? Do you think all schools will have the technology required for children to start to prepare for their lives in the digital age as fully as possible? Might text-to-speech be so commonplace that the skills in reading we develop today will not be as critical?

Critical points

» *The reading curriculum must be designed to explore the broadest range of media used for reading.*

» *The reading curriculum must look towards future reading activities, not just those with which the majority of children will currently engage.*

» *Skills in reading digital or electronic texts must be developed, alongside their more traditional counterparts.*

» *Schools must resource and develop strategies for reading beyond books that will build on children's interests and experiences*

Critical reflections

» *Consider your own experience with reading beyond books. What have you learned from reading this chapter that has helped you identify any areas of a child's reading landscape you may need to develop further knowledge and understanding of yourself? How can you do that? What resources would you need? How could you incorporate a wider variety of texts into your classroom to support reading development in the context of digital literacy?*

Taking it further

Useful children's search engine sites:

www.safekids.co.uk/childfriendlysearchengines.html

www.kidsclick.org/

www.bbc.co.uk/webwise/guides/kids-search-engines

kids.yahoo.com/

www.askkids.com/

kids.aol.com/

www.searchbox.co.uk/kids.htm

References

Alexander, B. (2006) Web 2.0: A New Wave of Innovation for Teaching and Learning. *EDUCASE Review*, 41:2. www.educause.edu/ero/article/web-20-new-wave-innovation-teaching-and-learning.

Barber, D. and Cooper, L. (2012) *Using New Web Tools in the Primary Classroom*. London: Routledge.

Bell, D. (2005) Speech by David Bell, the then Chief Inspector, at the National Literacy Trust, on World Book Day, 2 March 2005, in Ofsted, *English at the Crossroads*. London: Ofsted, (2009).

British Educational Suppliers Association (2012) *Press release: BESA releases 'Future of tablets and apps in schools' research*. www.besa.org.uk/documents/besa-releases-future-of-tablets-and-apps-in-schools-research/.

Clark, C. (2012) *Children's Reading Today. Findings from the National Literacy Trust's Annual Survey*. London: National Literacy Trust. www.literacytrust.org.uk/assets/0001/4450/Young_people_s_reading_-_FINAL_REPORT.pdf

Crystal, D. (2008) *Txtng: The Gr8 Db8*. Oxford: Oxford University Press.

Davies, J. and Merchant, G. (2009) *Web 2.0 for Schools: Learning and Social Participation (New Literacies and Digital Epistemologies)*. Oxford: Peter Lang Publishing Inc.

DCSF (2008) *Safer Children in a Digital World: The Report of the Byron Review*. Nottingham: DCSF Publications.

DfE (2013) *English: Programmes of study for Key Stages 1–2*. London: DfE.

DfEE/QCA (1999) *The National Curriculum: Handbook for primary teachers in England*. Norwich: DfEE/QCA.

DfES (2006) *Primary Framework for Literacy and Mathematics*. London: DfES.

Kelly, K. (2010) *What Technology Wants*. London: Penguin.

Read, W., McQuilken, L. and Robertson, N. (2010) A Novel Romance : Conceptualising Emotional Attachment as a Barrier to Adoption, in *ANZMAC 2010 : Doing More With Less: Proceedings Of The 2010 Australian and New Zealand Marketing Academy Conference*. Christchurch, New Zealand: ANZMAC.

http://dro.deakin.edu.au/view/DU:30031976

Starkey, L. (2012) *Teaching and Learning in the Digital Age*. London: Routledge.

Wood, C., Jackson, E., Hart, L., Plester, B. and Wilde, L. (2011) The Effect Of Text Messaging on 9- and 10-Year-Old Children's Reading, Spelling and Phonological Processing Skills. *Journal of Computer Assisted Learning*, 27:1.

Wray, D. and Lewis, M. (1997) *Extending Literacy: Children Reading and Writing Non-Fiction*. London: Routledge.

6 Lessons from Hogwarts

MARTIN RICHARDSON

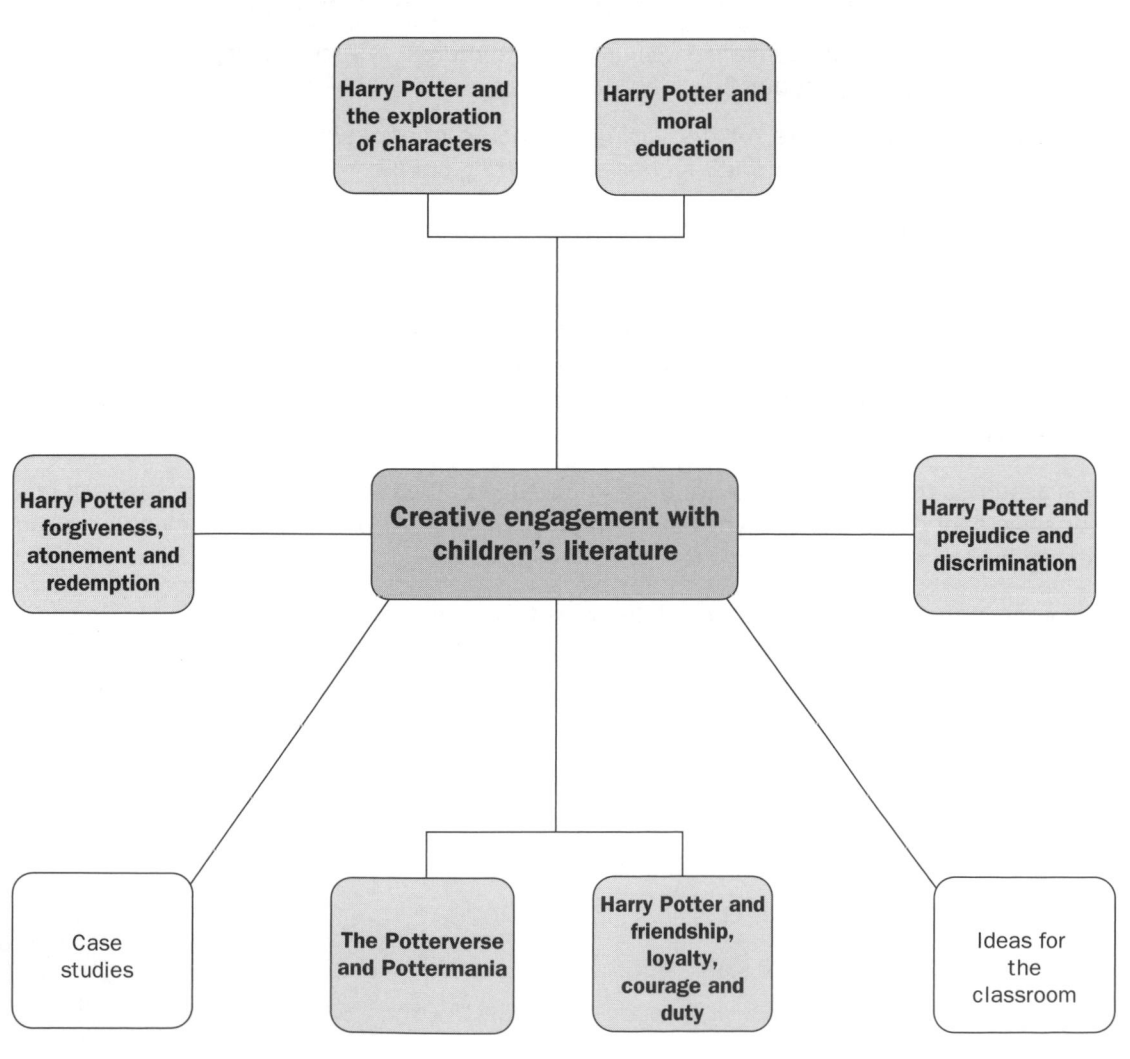

Teachers' standards

2 Promote good progress and outcomes by pupils

- demonstrate knowledge and understanding of how pupils learn and how this impacts on teaching

3 Demonstrate good subject and curriculum knowledge

- have a secure knowledge of the relevant subject(s) and curriculum areas, foster and maintain pupils' interest in the subject, and address misunderstandings

- demonstrate an understanding of and take responsibility for promoting high standards of literacy, articulacy and the correct use of standard English, whatever the teacher's specialist subject

Critical questions

» *What is the place of the Harry Potter series in children's reading experiences?*

» *How can teachers capitalise upon children's interest in Potter to engage them with a range of literary themes?*

» *What scope is there for discussing character, relationships and social and moral issues, using J.K. Rowling's stories as a starting point?*

Introduction

What follows in neither a précis of the Harry Potter series, nor an in-depth analysis either of J.K. Rowling as a writer or of the plot-lines. The chapter will place the Harry Potter stories in context and consider some of the issues raised by a study of the series; and incorporate suggestions for the classroom, including case studies of one teacher's success in introducing Potter-related material to her primary pupils.

It is assumed that readers will have a fair knowledge of the basic outline of the series. If not, you have a lot of reading to do by way of preparation, or you could watch the eight films – or ideally both.

For ease of reading, throughout the chapter the following abbreviations are used for the core texts; where I refer to the film version, I simply add film to the end of the book title (though note that the last book was split into two films). All page numbers refer to the British editions published by Bloomsbury.

Stone – Harry Potter and the Philosopher's Stone, June 1997

Chamber – Harry Potter and the Chamber of Secrets, July 1998

Prisoner – Harry Potter and the Prisoner of Azkaban, July 1999

Goblet – Harry Potter and the Goblet of Fire, July 2000

Order – Harry Potter and the Order of the Phoenix, June 2003

Prince – Harry Potter and the Half-Blood Prince, July 2005

Hallows – Harry Potter and the Deathly Hallows, July 2007

The Potterverse

Harry is of course famous for being the 'boy who lived'; but he could equally be famous for being the boy who *lives*. Harry, and the whole wizarding world created by J.K. Rowling, has managed something truly magical; he has crossed worlds. Harry is one of those fictional characters who has blurred the boundary between what is real and what is imagined. This blurring of boundaries has long been recognised, as too have its dangers. As Lucius Malfoy warns Harry when he enters the Ministry of Magic in the mistaken belief that his godfather Sirius Black is imprisoned there, *It's time you learned the difference between life and dreams* (*Order*, 690).

Activity 1

» *Consider other stories in which characters enter other worlds or time periods, such as Alice's Adventures in Wonderland, The Chronicles of Narnia and Tom's Midnight Garden.*

– *How do authors enable their characters to make the journey between worlds?*

– *Why are such books popular?*

Pottermania

How seriously should we take Harry Potter? Harry is certainly important and responsible for a unique global phenomenon, *Pottermania*. The books have been translated into more than 70 languages, including Latin and Ancient Greek; book sales are estimated to be around half a billion, much more if one takes the e-books into account. Then there are the films: at the cinema, the DVD sales, and on the television screen. There are people in China, Chile and Cheltenham who have views on the relative merits of Draco Malfoy and Neville Longbottom. Furthermore, the *Potterverse* is expanding, and not only via the pen – or more accurately the keyboard – of J.K. Rowling herself. *Pottermore*,[1] the web-based outlet through which J.K. Rowling gives further details of all things Potter, is frequently updated and still has a long way to go; so far, members are only up to the third book, *Prisoner of Azkaban*. Added to this is the proposed expansion of the Harry Potter Theme Park in Orlando, with another expected to be opened in Hollywood next year, as well as one in Japan, and rumours of more in Singapore and China.

There are also the regular Harry Potter exhibitions that tour the world; Platform 9¾ at King's Cross with its iconic luggage trolley embedded in the wall and from where the Hogwarts Express continues to steam around the countryside; and the wonderful Leavesden Studios where the films were made, which has rapidly become one of the UK's most popular tourist attractions. Furthermore, the timing of the books, coinciding as they have with an explosion in communication, has meant that there are currently in excess of 600,000 Harry Potter stories written by fans accessible online. For, it seems, J.K. Rowling is responsible not only for getting computer-game-obsessed children to read books, but also for an unprecedented outpouring of creativity, and not only in terms of writing: examples of fan art and fan videos emerge it seems on a daily basis.

Whilst the work of the fans lies outside this chapter, it is worth mentioning that a considerable number of fans re-work the stories, sometimes writing prequels or sequels, as well as placing the key characters in different situations. There is, then, an already established practice of rewriting the stories and this can provide both ideas and examples for teachers wishing to use the series as a starting point for their pupils' writing.

Activity 2

» *Unlike in many series in which the same characters appear in each book, Harry Potter and his friends grow older. Compare this with popular series such as Blyton's Famous Five and Secret Seven and Crompton's Just William. What are the advantages and disadvantages to authors and readers of characters being 'frozen' at a certain age, and being allowed to age as their adventures unfold?*

In terms of Harry's continued relevance, the series is part of the so-called *bildungsroman* genre which focuses on the moral and psychological development of its main characters. One appeal of J.K. Rowling's series is that she has created a parallel rather than an alternative universe, and this makes it far more relevant to the classroom. In so many respects, Hogwarts is a school like many others, and certainly some British children will relate to the notion of terms, prefects and house systems, although for most perhaps not until secondary school.

There are those who consider the whole of the *Potterverse* as a classic example of capitalist ideology at work; Harry as a global brand, literally the *product* of media hype and clever marketing. The most widely reported estimate of the monetary value of the Harry Potter franchise is an incomprehensible $15 billion. But Harry is much more than that. First and foremost, Harry Potter is a literary figure; and once the red carpet has been rolled up, the theme parks closed, the figures and toy wands broken, what will remain is the word. And as Dumbledore reminds us, *Words are our most inexhaustible source of magic* (Hallows Part II, Film, 2011).

Harry Potter and the exploration of characters

There are many reasons why J.K. Rowling's series has been so successful, one of the most important being that readers can relate to Harry and to his world. The Harry Potter series is a wonderful example of crossover fiction; it crosses the divide not only between adulthood and childhood, but also between an imaginary world and the real world. The fact that the magical world resonates with our own does not meet with universal approval. Thus, for Pennington (2002, 78), *the series is fundamentally failed fantasy.* Yet it is the fact that Rowling has created a world that is instantly recognisable that is one of the series' greatest strengths. While the adventures of the boy wizard are quintessentially British, albeit in a narrow time-locked sense, Harry Potter has become part of the world's cultural register. The key to understanding the *Potterverse* and its success is its relevance – the fact that at its heart the series is about the human condition; it is about all of us. It is about *our* identity and *our* relationships.

Sebastian Faulks (2011) reminds us just how important fictional characters are:

> *In fiction, we meet people whose inner lives we get to know so well that they're more familiar to us than our own families and friends, so much so that it's in the power of their experiences that we see our own lives in a new light. These characters live beyond their times, and beyond the page – in our imagination, in our memory; and*

on both the big screen and the small. The events that befall them shape them as people, but they affect us too. The lives of these characters help us to understand ourselves.

In the next part of this chapter, character will be explored with reference to moral education; friendship, loyalty, courage and duty; prejudice and discrimination; forgiveness; atonement and redemption are all topics that might be discussed using the Potter series as a starting point, and extended to an exploration of the themes in other stories.

In his chapter, 'Harry Potter and The Reinvention of the Past', Blake (2008) calls the series a *deliberately retrolutionary creation*; ie exploring the old yet dealing with new concerns. In the final analysis, the books are about the timeless and universal struggle between good and evil. However, it is the genius of J.K. Rowling that has revealed what appears on the surface to be a simple morality tale as something far more complex; just as in real life, in *our* life, things are not always as they seem, not black and white, but various changing shades of grey. The case study below describes a lesson that explores character, devised by Laura, a PGCE student, who had been reading *Harry Potter and the Philosopher's Stone* to a Year 5 literacy class, using each chapter to inspire a writing activity. For the chapter 'The Mirror of Erised', pupils were asked for their understanding of the characters' true desires before producing their own passages based on what they would see in the mirror.

CASE STUDY

The Mirror of Erised

After reading the chapter, hot-seating took place in which questions were aimed at pupils in the characters of Harry and Ron about what they saw in the mirror and why. Comparisons between the two main characters were made using evidence they had previously gleaned from the book in order to make sense of their different desires:

*   Harry: the orphaned baby, adopted into an unloving family, his past and his legacy kept a secret for more than 10 years, consequently sees his entire lost family in the mirror.

*   Ron: swamped by his talented older brothers and his famous friend, and desperate to prove himself, sees himself holding the House Cup as Quidditch Captain and Head Boy.

Children were then asked to look into a mirror and imagine what they would see, before writing their own scenes to replace the one in the book. They were asked to focus on their descriptive language, developing their ideas and creating a slow reveal as J.K. Rowling does in the book.

This was a lesson that could easily be adapted to PSHE, asking the children to think introspectively about themselves and find out what would truly make them happy. It used the book as a starting point, but could be developed into a broader examination of characterisation in stories.

Curricular links: Developing an understanding of character

The curriculum (DfE, 2013) requires children to explore various aspects of texts.

- *Y3–4: drawing inferences such as inferring characters' feelings, thoughts and motives from their actions and justifying inferences with evidence.* (36)

- *Y5–6: in writing narratives, considering how authors have developed characters and settings in what they have read, listened to or seen performed ... in narratives, describing settings, characters and atmosphere and integrating dialogue to convey character and advance the action.* (47)

Harry Potter and moral education

Pullman (2005) argued that stories can offer a moral education: *thus, we can all learn what's good and what's bad, what's generous and unselfish, what's cruel and mean, from fiction ... [they] show us human beings like ourselves acting in recognisably human ways, and they affect our emotions and our intelligence as life itself affects us ... And our moral understanding is deepened and enriched by the awakening of our imaginative sympathy.*

So much in the *Potterverse* is open to interpretation and re-interpretation. We see much of what goes on through Harry's eyes. Interestingly, one of the deleted scenes from *Deathly Hallows Part I* (the film) shows the death of Harry's mother from the point of view of her sister, Petunia Dursley. This adds a new dimension to our understanding; it is interesting to see other characters' points of view. For example, we know so little about Voldemort. Was he born evil? Is anyone? Was it the rejection by his mother that influenced the rest of his life? What does this tell *us* about the importance of family life or of forming relationships with other people? Why did Sirius Black reject his family? Is Sirius a *good* person? Are all Slytherins bad? Ambition is seen as a Slytherin virtue: is ambition therefore a *bad thing*? These are issues that might be discussed, both as part of personal, social and moral education and in relation to other stories. They can also promote consideration of ways for children to invent characters in their own writing, who have different dimensions to their personalities.

Harry Potter and friendship, loyalty, courage and duty

Friendship and friendship groups are essential elements in the *Potterverse*. The Death Eaters and the Order of the Phoenix, Dumbledore's Army, the Inquisitorial Squad and Draco's gang with Crabbe and Goyle are all friendship groups with their own memberships and codes of conduct. Of course, there is no stronger friendship group than that of the *golden trio*, Harry, Ron and Hermione. The trio was born after the *incident* in the girls' bathroom: *But from that moment on Hermione Granger became their friend. There are some things you can't share without ending up liking each other, and knocking out a twelve-foot mountain troll is one of them* (*Stone*, 132). Through shared experiences, trials and tribulations, their friendship deepens; until at the start of *Deathly Hallows*, its intensity is shown:

> *There was silence in the room, broken only by gentle thuds, as Hermione continued to throw books on to one pile or the other. Ron sat watching her, and Harry looked from one to the other, unable to say anything. The measures they had taken to protect their families made him realise, more than anything else could have done, that*

they really were going to come with him and that they knew exactly how dangerous that would be. He wanted to tell them what that meant to him, but he simply could not find words important enough.

(*Hallows*, 86)

The trio are brave and fiercely loyal, though they do have their differences from time to time. It would seem on the surface that the trio are all good role models, ideal citizens. As one has come to expect, however, there are faults and shortcomings: there is Harry's temper and recklessness; Ron's attitude to house elves, giants, werewolves and to Hermione; and Hermione's own attitude to house elves, centaurs and to Ron.

The characters, good and bad, often have demanding moral choices to make, and this tells us it really is *our choices … that show what we truly are far more than our abilities* (*Chamber*, 245).

For one particular lesson based on Chapter Nine – The Midnight Duel, the main focus was to understand the thoughts, feelings and motivations of Harry's arch-rival, Draco Malfoy, and to produce a letter from Draco's perspective based on a reading comprehension exercise.

CASE STUDY

Learning styles

To inspire the more reluctant readers of the class, a range of different learning styles was incorporated into the lesson. During the introduction of Malfoy in an earlier chapter, the children had used the 'whooshing' drama technique (a technique that gives all children the opportunity to act out a role within the story, whether it is a character or inanimate object, before calling out 'whoosh' and resuming their normal positions in the circle ready for new pupils to take on the roles), to focus on how the character was presented, particularly drawing attention to his behaviour and attitude towards other characters, both friends and foe. It was clear that during this activity, the children (including reluctant readers) were engaged and inspired to write, gaining an understanding of the newly introduced characters and an eagerness to share this knowledge during whole class discussion.

This understanding was reinforced by a reading comprehension activity, where the children investigated the presentation of Malfoy during his first conflict with Harry Potter at Hogwarts. The following areas were considered:

- Description of Malfoy – How did the description make them feel about Malfoy? Would they like him if they met him? Why? Why not?

- Dialogue – How does Malfoy feel about other characters?

- Action – What does the action tell them about Malfoy? What type of person do they think he is?

During whole class discussion and the task, the children were so engaged that they identified key aspects about the character, including why Rowling had named him Draco, and drew strong parallels with a character they already knew that was similar in the book, Dudley

Dursley. They even made tentative suggestions that touched upon the idea of Malfoy's status, based on his treatment of others, including 'friends'; why he was constantly referred to by his surname; and his relationship with one of the class teachers, in which he was considered by one child as teacher's pet! The children were then able to successfully translate this character-understanding into writing a letter to Professor Dumbledore from the viewpoint of Malfoy, stating his side of the story about the conflict (which is not explicitly touched upon in the book).

This shows that given the right story and inspiration, reading comprehension can be exciting (see also Chapter 4)

The advantages of this chapter were also clear for cross-curricular activities as Laura was then going to lead on to a PSHE topic, discussing Malfoy's relationship with his peers, and how they would feel if they were in the place of one of the other characters.

Activity 3

» *Think about relationships in other examples of children's literature. How are friendships portrayed? Are heroes always perfect or are they sometimes flawed? Can you think of examples of unpleasant characters who have some redeeming features or explanations for their character flaws?*

Harry Potter and prejudice and discrimination

Building on the earlier work of Gordon Allport, Karen Brown (2008) talked about four things that can lead to prejudice and discrimination: *ignorance, indifference, insecurity* and *intolerance*. On the surface, this theme is easy to explore and link to today's society with its emphasis on inclusion. Thus in multi-ethnic, multi-faith and multi-cultural Britain the separateness in the *Potterverse* is clear to all. At its most basic level, there is the split between the wizarding world and the Muggle world. Within the wizarding world there is the emphasis on blood status: as Aunt Marge says in *The Prisoner of Azkaban*, *It all comes down to blood, as I was saying the other day. Bad blood will out* (*Prisoner*, 26). Thus, the pure-bloods represent the wizarding aristocracy; the half-bloods are next in the pecking order (and it is interesting to note that each of the *Abandoned Boys* – Snape, Voldemort and Harry – are half-bloods); and at the bottom of the social hierarchy are the Muggle-born witches and wizards – infamously referred to as mud-bloods by the (seemingly) evil Draco Malfoy, and including the incomparable Hermione, *the cleverest witch of her age* (*Prisoner*, 253). Though what is *clever* about the series is the way J.K. Rowling portrays the notion of blood status and shows it up for what it is – meaningless.

In addition to the above, there are many other social gradations: squibs (non-magical folk born to magical parents); magical non-humans such as elves and goblins; magical creatures; and so on. As suggested above, these are easily described and the lessons learnt are readily outlined. Equally clear is the prejudice and discrimination of the Ministry of Magic, especially, though not exclusively, when under the control of Lord Voldemort. Here again the links with totalitarian régimes, most notably Nazi Germany, are easily made.

However, there are two interesting examples of just how complex the *Potterverse* can be; and how what appears at first glance commonplace is in fact far from it. Thus, in the fourth book, Hermione emerges as the champion of the oppressed house elves; so moved is she over their apparent (and probably real) slavery, that she forms SPEW, the Society for the Promotion of Elfish Welfare. This is clearly an act of compassion, and whilst the idea doesn't really catch on with most wizards nor, it has to be said, house elves either, one can nevertheless only admire Hermione's motives, until one is reminded of the similar motives of the more zealous missionaries who went to Africa in the last quarter of the nineteenth century, *to bring the heathen to the light of God* and to 'civilize' the *lesser breeds beyond the law* (Kipling, 1897).

In a similar vein, Arthur Weasley is *fascinated by Muggles*, and there is no doubt about his motives; throughout he is pro-Muggle and anti-pure-blood dominance. However, there is just the suspicion that he might find Muggles fascinating in the same way that lost Amazonian tribes might be seen as fascinating by some Western anthropologists.

Whilst these two examples don't discredit Arthur Weasley's and Hermione's motives, for one is certain that they are honourable, there is nevertheless clearly an alternative interpretation. Indeed, it is the very notion of alternative interpretations that makes studying the *Potterverse* so fascinating.

Harry Potter and forgiveness, atonement and redemption

Few people live blameless lives, and all of us at some point need to ask for forgiveness. This fact was recognised in the National Curriculum (DfEE, 1999) where it was acknowledged that children have to *learn* not only to forgive others, but to forgive themselves as well.

As suggested above, throughout the Harry Potter series J.K. Rowling proves herself a master at misdirection; so many things are not as they first appear. There are many themes that appear and reappear throughout the series, however, two of the most powerful are reserved for the final book, *The Deathly Hallows*, Rowling's 'Book of Revelation'. The whole notion of the Hallows is an interesting one, and it has clear links to the Arthurian quest, the most obvious being the search for the Holy Grail – though the two should not be seen as identical. Towards the end of the book, Harry has to decide whether to seek the Hallows, as others including Dumbledore had done before, or search for the Horcruxes, the objects in which Voldemort's soul had been hidden. Of course, in the end, Harry achieves both tasks.

For the first five books these goals might almost be viewed as adventures, and although in *reality*, as we find out later, such a view is rather limited, it does make each of these books stand-alone stories in their own right. Thus one sees each one at the end as a complete story. The sixth and seventh volumes are very different; just as the Harry Potter generation is in *reality* getting older and moving towards adulthood, so too do the books get older and life becomes more complex.

At the climax of the series much more is revealed about many of the key characters, though there is intriguingly much that is still unknown. Readers who stay to the end find they need to reassess feelings about many main characters such as Snape, Dumbledore and even

Voldemort, in the light of new information about the characters' histories and motivations. The twin themes of forgiveness and redemption are very powerful and speak directly to us all, and are yet another way in which the Harry Potter series sheds light on our own world.

Suggestions for classroom activities

As Marissa Davis and Pat Williams said about the impact of using Harry Potter in their primary classroom in Llandaff, *Harry Potter is a brilliant book which can be read and relished by anyone (yes, including adults) ... J.K. Rowling's portrayal of Harry's adventures at Hogwarts ... is utterly believable and takes the young mind into Harry's world in a totally convincing manner* (cited in Horn, 1999, 7). These two teachers then go on to describe how the series was used to inspire their children to analyse Harry and produce a This is Your Life documentary.

Additional activities might be centred on the qualities of each house.

*   Which house is the best and worst, and why? Debate your answers.

*   Design a poster to reflect your house's qualities.

*   Add a fifth house – what characteristics would it have?

Look at the whole notion of identity and belonging. Here the different houses and groups at Hogwarts and in the wider wizarding world, can easily be linked to current PSHE requirements at Key Stages 1 and 2: 'Preparing to play an active role as citizens'. Thus at Key Stage 1 pupils are taught that they belong to various groups and communities, and are encouraged to identify and respect the differences and similarities between people. Whilst at Key Stage 2 pupils build on this to develop good relationships and respect differences between people.

To what extent are Harry, Ron and Hermione good role models? There is a huge opportunity here to focus on Harry's *sensitive* side. Some, such as Ximena Gallardo-C and C. Jason Smith (2009), have talked of Harry as a *Cinderfella* figure. Hagrid too has his caring *feminine* traits – very interesting as a starting point for discussing gender issues. Do the boys have all the fun in the series? Is Hermione a good example of a modern empowered female figure, or as Heilman and Donaldson (2009) suggest, is she an example of yet another *helper female* who simply *enables* the boys to grab all the glory?

The whole series is, of course, full of interesting characters worthy of analysis. In addition to the golden trio, the other obvious candidates to explore are Dumbledore, Snape and Draco. Less obvious characters, but with huge potential, include Petunia Dursley.

*   How would you feel if your sister had been chosen to attend Hogwarts and you were left behind?

*   Does Dudley's handshake (*Hallows*, 40) change our opinion of him?

*   What must it feel like to be a squib like Argus Filch?

*   Why does Dumbledore trust Mundungus Fletcher?

The films are rich in discussion potential. From the obvious favourite character questions, to playing out scenes, or having discussions about the huge number of moral dilemmas.

- Should Hermione have left Ron?

- Should the trio break so many rules? (Hermione lies to teachers: McGonagall over the troll incident (*Stone*, 131), and Umbridge over Dumbledore's secret weapon (*Order*, 659))

- Is it right to lie to teachers if the circumstances demand it? What does this tell us about the moral universe of the school?

- What do the films add that the books lack, and vice versa?

There are also wonderful things to be explored in history centred on the real witch hunts, in mediaeval times, but especially in the sixteenth and seventeenth centuries. In geography there are the place names such as Godric's Hollow, Little Hangleton and Budleigh Babberton, as well as real places like King's Cross and the Forest of Dean to explore, and the locations for the films, such as Durham, Alnwick, Gloucester and London. Which locations would you choose? In English, there are the wonderful character names: Voldemort – the flight from death; Cornelius Fudge the politician; Sybill Trelawney the seer; the list is a long one. As is the list of characters with alliterative names: Severus Snape, Salazar Slytherin, Godric Gryffindor, Luna Lovegood, to name but four. And of course there are the spells! There is little doubt that the potential of Harry Potter to initiate teaching and learning activities is only as limited as a teacher's imagination.

Furthermore, as one might expect in this digital age, there are websites devoted to Harry Potter in the classroom, replete with ideas for teachers and pupils, though as with all such, they have to be modified to suit individual circumstances. One particularly useful one is from Scholastic, the series' US publishers: www.scholastic.com/teachers/lesson-plan/harry-potter-brings-magic-classroom.

CASE STUDY

Classroom activities

PGCE student, Laura, shares a brief synopsis of the activities that she devised based on *Harry Potter and the Philosopher's Stone*.

- Chapter One – The Boy who Lived: here the pupils wrote a letter to the Dursleys from Dumbledore (we don't get to read this in this book). Children are asked to persuade the Dursleys to take Harry in. There then followed a discussion about the loss of one's family and about orphans; the hidden powers of Harry – how could a baby manage to defeat a powerful dark wizard? What sort of sort of protection might Dumbledore offer Harry?

- Chapter Two – The Vanishing Glass: the children changed the setting from the zoo and imagined their own magical event.

- Chapter Three – The Letters from No One: the children wrote a diary entry with all of Harry's thoughts and feelings, eg being abandoned by the Dursleys, curiosity about who wants to get in touch with him so badly. The follow-up discussion centred on how and why the Dursleys treated Harry so badly.

- Chapter Four – The Keeper of the Keys: the children wrote another diary entry, this time centred on Harry's thoughts and feelings now he knows he is a wizard. Hot-seating was used for both this and the previous chapter, where children pretended to be Harry.

- Chapter Five – Diagon Alley: the children wrote an advertisement to be placed in a shop/magazine for a magical item of their choice.

- Chapter Six – The Journey from Platform Nine and Three-Quarters: we used a whooshing drama technique with this chapter based on what happens in the train compartment and the first run-in with Draco. Ideas of bullying, prejudice and status were discussed. Children then wrote a script based on the interaction of these characters.

- Chapter Seven – The Sorting Hat: after discussing the qualities of the houses as represented by the four animals, children were asked to sort themselves. This also included hot-seating, where the children not in the seat had to pretend to be the Sorting Hat's thoughts. They then wrote a poem for the Sorting Hat about the house that they had chosen.

- Chapter Eight – The Potions Master: this led to a discussion about Snape's treatment of certain pupils. The children also designed their own magical potions.

- Chapter Nine – The Midnight Duel: as discussed in the case study above (p 93).

- Chapter Ten – Hallowe'en: the children had to pretend to be newspaper reporters, and as they heard the chapter they had to find the answers to a series of questions; and they were encouraged to ask members of staff or magical experts on trolls. Questions included, who broke into the castle? Why did they break in? Where and when did they break in? Who are the suspects for letting the troll in? This was an assessed piece of writing and the children focused on getting quotes and speech marks in their writing. This lesson also focused on intrigue and mystery. Discussion followed about where Quirrell, Snape and Draco were at the time. There was also a discussion about Hermione and why she was upset, yet helped Harry and Ron in the end.

- Chapter Eleven – Quidditch: the children wrote instructions on how to play Quidditch.

- Chapter Twelve – The Mirror of Erised: the children had to imagine they were standing in front of the Mirror and had to see their true desires before writing a descriptive piece on what they had seen (see case study above, p 91). They were also asked to think about why Harry saw his family in the mirror, and why Ron was captain of Quidditch and holding the House Cup.

Critical points

» *In this chapter you have seen the potential for developing a range of reading experiences, using Harry Potter as a starting point.*

» *Teachers can capitalise upon children's interest in Potter to engage them in a range of literary themes. These might include looking at stories in which characters move between worlds, and the way in which friendship is portrayed.*

» *Character, relationships and social and moral issues are elements of J.K. Rowling's stories, which engage and interest children.*

» *By using the Potter series as a familiar starting point, you can involve children in discussion and debate, and help them to reflect on their own portrayal of these elements in their writing.*

Critical reflections

» *Consider another text that portrays character, relationships and social and moral issues. How could you use this text as a starting point for developing children's ability to analyse such features and incorporate them into their own writing?*

Taking it further

Texts devoted to the boy wizard are growing all the time; below is a selection of those that so far I have found valuable. There are, of course, the fan sites, of which the most popular are www.mugglenet.com and www.the-leakey-cauldron.org. There is also my own website Thepotterverse.com, which by the time this book goes to print will be live.

Anelli, M. (2008) *Harry, A History: The True Story of a Boy Wizard, His Fans, and Life Inside the Harry Potter Phenomenon*. London: Pocket Books.

Ark, S.V. et al. (2009) *The Lexicon: An Unauthorized Guide to Harry Potter Fiction and Related Materials*. Muskegon: RDR Books.

Baggett, D. and Klein, S.E. (eds) (2004) *Harry Potter and Philosophy: If Aristotle Ran Hogwarts*. Peru: Open Court.

Bassham, G. (ed) (2010) *The Ultimate Harry Potter and Philosophy: Hogwarts for Muggles*. New Jersey: John Wiley and Sons.

Blake, A. (2002) *The Irresistible Rise of Harry Potter*. London: Verso.

Duriez, C. (2007) *The Unauthorised Harry Potter Companion*. Stroud: Sutton Publishing.

Eliot, T.S. (1963) *A Choice of Kipling's Verse*. London: Faber and Faber.

Falconer, R. (2009) *The Crossover Novel: Contemporary Children's Fiction and Its Adult Readership*. London: Routledge.

Falaschi-Ray, S. (2011) *Harry Potter a Christian Chronicle*. Brighton: Book Guild Ltd.

Granger, J. (2007) *Unlocking Harry Potter: Five Keys for the Serious Reader*. Wayne, PA: Zossima Press.

Gupta, S. (2003) *Re-reading Harry Potter*. Basingstoke: Palgrave Macmillan.

Maybin, J. and Watson, N.J. (eds) (2009) *Children's Literature: Approaches and Territories*. Milton Keynes: Palgrave Macmillan and The Open University.

McCabe, B. (2011) *Harry Potter from Page to Screen: The Whole Film Making Journey*. London: Titan Books.

Nel, P. (2002) *J.K. Rowling's Harry Potter Novels: A Reader's Guide*. New York: Continuum.

Prinzi, T. (2009) *Harry Potter and Imagination: The Way Between Two Worlds*. Wayne, PA: Zossima Press.

Prinzi, T. (ed) (2011) *Hog's Head Conversations*, Vol. 1. Wayne, PA: Zossima Press.

Rowling, J.K. (2001) *Fantastic Beasts and Where to Find Them*. London: Bloomsbury.

Rowling, J.K. (2001) *Quidditch Through the Ages*. London: Bloomsbury.

Rowling, J.K. (2008) *The Tales of Beedle the Bard*. London: Bloomsbury.

Sims, J. (ed) (2012) *The Sociology of Harry Potter*. Wayne, PA: Zossima Press.

Whited, L.A. (2002) *The Ivory Tower and Harry Potter: Perspectives on a Literary Phenomenon*. Columbia, MO: University of Missouri Press.

Notes

1 Pottermore – opened April 2012; this refers to J.K. Rowling's website Pottermore.com where additional material and back stories about the characters and the wizarding world in general can be found. Children can join Pottermore, buy a wand at Ollivander's, and be sorted into their House!

References

Blake, A. (2008) Harry Potter and the Reinvention of the Past, in Montgomery, H. and Watson, N. (eds) *Children's Literature: Classic Texts and Contemporary Trends*. Milton Keynes: Palgrave Macmillan and The Open University.

Brown, K.A. (2008) *Prejudice in Harry Potter's World*. College Station, TX: Virtualbookworm.

DfE (2013) *The National Curriculum in England Framework document*. London: DfE.

DfEE (1999) *The National Curriculum: Handbook for primary teachers in England*. London: DfEE and QCA.

Faulks, S (2011) *Sebastian Faulks on Fiction*. London: BBC Books.

Gallardo-C, X. and Smith, C. Jason (2009) Cinderfella, in Anatol, G. L. (ed), *Reading Harry Potter Again: New Critical Essays*. Westport CT: Praeger.

Heilman, E. and Donaldson, T. (2009) From Sexist to (sort of) Feminist, in Heilman, E. (ed) *Critical Perspectives on Harry Potter* (2nd edn). London: Routledge.

Horn, C. (1999) The Harry Potter Phenomenon. *Books for Keeps: The Children's Book Magazine*, 177.

Pennington, J. (2002): From Elfland to Hogwarts, or the Aesthetic Trouble with Harry Potter. *The Lion and the Unicorn*, 26:1.

Pullman, P. (2005) Miss Goddard's Grave, available at www.philip-pullman.com/assets_cm/files/PDF/miss_goddards_grave.pdf

Rowling, J.K. (1997) *Harry Potter and the Philosopher's Stone*. London: Bloomsbury.

Rowling, J.K. (1998) *Harry Potter and the Chamber of Secrets*. London: Bloomsbury.

Rowling, J.K. (1999) *Harry Potter and the Prisoner of Azkaban*. London: Bloomsbury.

Rowling, J.K. (2000)*Harry Potter and the Goblet of Fire*. London: Bloomsbury.

Rowling, J.K. (2003) *Harry Potter and the Order of the Phoenix*. London: Bloomsbury.

Rowling, J.K. (2005) *Harry Potter and the Half-Blood Prince*. London: Bloomsbury.

Rowling, J.K. (2007) *Harry Potter and the Deathly Hallows*. London: Bloomsbury.

7 Creative engagement with children's literature

STAFF FROM SEVEN STORIES

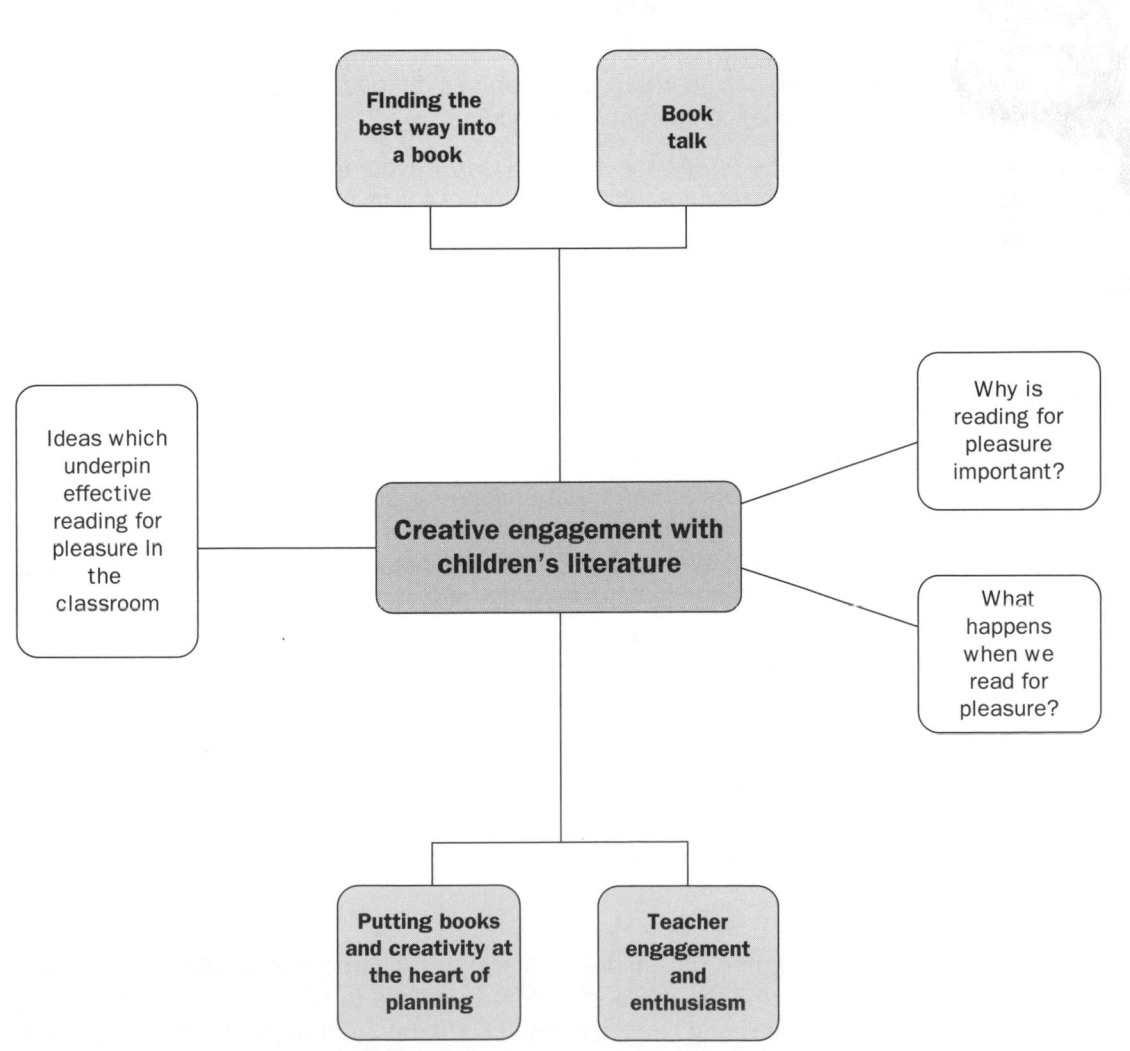

Teachers' standards

3 Demonstrate good subject and curriculum knowledge

- have a secure knowledge of the relevant subject(s) and curriculum areas, foster and maintain pupils' interest in the subject

- demonstrate an understanding of and take responsibility for promoting high standards of literacy and articulacy

4 Plan and teach well-structured lessons

- contribute to the design and provision of an engaging curriculum within the relevant subject area(s)

Critical questions

» How can reading for pleasure increase children's motivation to engage with language and meaning in books?

» How can you create rich learning opportunities by encouraging children to make personal and emotional connections with books?

» How can your practice bridge the gap between decoding what is on the page and personal motivation to read for pleasure?

» What criteria can we use for choosing children's books? How can we identify a 'good book'?

» How can you use the full potential of children's books in your planning and teaching?

Introduction

What was the last novel you bought or borrowed, and why did you decide to read it? Was it a personal recommendation from a friend that engaged your interest? An amazing review? A marketing campaign? An author you've enjoyed before? Or perhaps a cover illustration or title that appealed to you? Whatever it was, something motivated you to make that choice, to open the cover and have what was, hopefully, the pleasurable experience of discovering what was inside. Children too need to be motivated to read. They may be able to apply phonic knowledge and decode text, but without truly engaging with books, they may never progress to becoming *real* readers, who read for pleasure.

In this chapter we'll look at the *Seven Stories* approach to reading for pleasure, and explore different ways in which teachers can engage their children in books.

Seven Stories, The National Centre For Children's Books

Seven Stories is Britain's home for children's literature, where playful, immersive exhibitions and exciting events bring the world of children's books to life, celebrating the magic and power of books to spark young imaginations. It is the home of original manuscripts and illustrations of British children's literature, celebrating this cultural heritage and inspiring children, educators and artists. Seven Stories' inclusive learning and participation programme approaches reading as a creative and cultural experience.

FOCUS ON RESEARCH

The importance of reading for pleasure

Hooking young children into books and reading can have long-term benefits in terms of children's motivation to read. This motivation to read has a powerful effect on learning. If children are 'hooked on books' it follows that they are motivated to read, and therefore, able to reap all the rewards that come from books and literature. Conversely, children who don't enjoy reading are not motivated to read and thus cannot reap the benefits of books and reading. This is supported by research evidence.

Clark and Rumbold (2006), in their paper on reading for pleasure, explore the role of motivation to read. They acknowledge that becoming a lifetime reader is predicated on developing a love of reading, and that there is increasing evidence of the importance of reading for pleasure for both educational and personal development.

They conclude that motivation is one of the critical determinants of the success and quality of all learning, including reading. They cite research that concludes:

Motivation to read, and reading ability are synergistic, mutually reinforcing phenomena (Bauman and Duffy, 1997, 6).

Research also indicates that teachers acknowledge that a lack of motivation causes many of the problems that they face in teaching (O'Flahavan et al., 1992). Motivation to read also mediates the 'Mathew Effect' in reading (Stanovich, 1986), which refers to the circular relationship between practice and achievement: better readers read more, which leads to better reading, and so they read more. And, conversely, poorer readers read less and so don't improve, and so the gap widens.

What happens when we read for pleasure?

Think back for a moment to a book you really loved when you were a child; one which was very important to you. Think about the story; try to recall the way it made you feel and what was so special about reading or listening to it. How did it affect you? Could you sum it up in two or three words?

Responses to this task may vary widely, but very rarely do they include references to the mechanics of reading, focusing instead on escapism, emotional engagement, inspiration and learning in one of four main areas:

1   knowledge and understanding of the world;

2   language acquisition and development;

3   creativity and imaginative development;

4   social and emotional development.

Books and stories can have an extraordinary power to develop children and young people emotionally, creatively and intellectually, and there are thousands of them just waiting to work their magic on the children in your class. However, selection of the *best* books is vital in the process of engaging children and inspiring them to read, as are teacher role, attitude and approach.

Some fundamental ideas that underpin effective reading for pleasure in the classroom

Seven Stories' approach to reading a full text is based on the principle that the more creative, pleasurable and personal the child's experience of reading, the greater the impact on their attainment, social and emotional development, motivation to read further, and understanding of the world. There are four fundamental ideas which we focus on in order to achieve this:

1   finding the best way into a book;

2   book talk;

3   putting books and creativity at the heart of planning;

4   teacher engagement and enthusiasm.

Finding the best way into a book

Preparing a route into a book can build suspense and engagement before you even open it. At Seven Stories we refer to this as the 'key' or the 'way in' to the book. This usually entails active participation by the children and might involve props, music or sound effects to set a scene, or perhaps a game, drama exercise or other activity, which explores an issue raised by the story. For example, central to the story *Jack and the Flumflum Tree* (Donaldson, 2012), used in the case study below, is the inventive use of everyday items to solve fantastic problems faced by the hero and his friends. Setting sail with nothing but a bag full of strange objects, they encounter a range of perils that they overcome using the contents of the bag. You can introduce the idea by presenting children with just such a bag full of items and eliciting the children's ideas by playing the 'it's not a …, it's a …' circle game. One of the items in the bag is passed around, and each child has to invent new uses for it, saying *it's not a slipper, it's a … mobile phone/hat/cup* and so on. This can result in some very imaginative ideas, and exploration of the concept of 'amazing possibilities'. By the time the bag is empty, children are eager to hear the story, to find out about the potential of objects and ideas.

Providing these 'ways in' to books is an effective way to increase children's motivation to engage with the language and meaning in a book, be it in their mother tongue or a new language. In the case study below, you can see how working in this way can be especially effective when children are accessing language which is unfamiliar to them. In this example, the children were learning an unfamiliar modern foreign language. However, the approach is equally valuable with children who speak English as an additional language, including refugee or asylum-seeker children, and with children who have limited language or vocabulary in English where it is their first language.

CASE STUDY

Finding a way into a book

Working with books that are not written in the children's first language

Carey and Jackie work with English-speaking children in Years 3 to 7 in the north-east of England, and with French-speaking children in Epinay-sur-Seine, France, developing a 'Reading for Pleasure' approach to sharing books in a foreign language.

Their aims for the children were to:

- enjoy and be engaged with the books;

- play with language and ideas;

- explore what is meant by commonalities, differences and culture;

- develop their ability to think critically, communicate and create.

They did this by:

- exploring a specially-selected collection of picture books, the text of which the children were unlikely to fully understand;

- taking part in drama games that address the themes in the books;

- reading for pleasure and talking about their responses to the books.

The success of this work was fundamentally dependent on three things. The first was selecting the right books: books that were challenging, quirky, memorable and fun and, most importantly, books that were illustrated. The second was finding the right 'way in' to interest the children. The third was the role of the teacher. They found that when the presentation of the text was clear, engaging and had momentum, it did not matter if the vocabulary and grammar were unfamiliar.

Two of the seven books they chose were *Petite Beauté* (Browne and Duval, 2010) and *La Planete Bizarre* (Voutch, 1999).

Petite Beauté is a translation from the original English version by Anthony Browne, and is full of his superbly detailed illustrations. It was inspired, in part, by an experiment in the USA involving Coco, a captive gorilla taught to communicate in sign language. In Browne's version, after signing that he wants a friend, the gorilla is provided with a tiny kitten (Beauty) by the zookeepers to keep it company. The story of their relationship is beautiful and funny, with subtle references to *Beauty and the Beast*.

Before the children saw it, they were introduced to the ideas it contained via a drama exercise. Without introduction, Jackie spoke to them for a minute or so in gobbledygook! Using her own 'language' of invented sounds and noises, she welcomed them, told them about her journey to work, spoke about the weather, how she was feeling and so on. The children were hooked! Animated discussion showed that they had understood her and could explain that they had 'read' her gestures, facial expressions, body language and intonation. Did they want to have a go themselves? The answer was a resounding 'yes'.

In pairs, the class explored communicating with each other without using speech. They took turns to silently convey a series of emotions to their partners, and then to the whole class. When the book was finally introduced, with discussion around the question *What would it be like if you had to communicate with another species?*, almost everyone had an idea, and all were keen to hear the story.

The second book they chose was *La Planete Bizarre* (Voutch, 1999). This is a humorous and slightly eccentric little book, which was the most popular with almost all children involved, even though at first glance its board-book format might suggest a far younger age range.

Carey and Jackie asked the classes to imagine a place where everything is the opposite way around to the way we know it, or absurdly different from real life. Groups discussed what they might find there, and had a few minutes to plan a TV news report that introduced viewers to some of the more unusual aspects of life there. The task inspired the children to think imaginatively, and great hilarity ensued with the result that everyone was really immersed in the theme of the book and keen to explore and compare their ideas with those dreamt up by Voutch. Aided by the witty illustrations, the pupils were immediately drawn into a world where rabbits say 'quack' and cats lay eggs!

All the teachers involved in the project observed high levels of engagement. They reported that even the children who normally had difficulty concentrating were fully involved during the sessions. They also commented that many children were observed returning to the foreign-language books to look at them again, and compared words with ones that they found in the dictionary. The teachers were wonderfully enthusiastic about the project, commenting:

It's wonderful ... seeing how enthused the children are by stories and how it [this approach] really gets their imagination going.

The potential for using drama activities which link to the emotional content of the book is huge.

My style of teaching has completely changed [as a result].

Activity 1

»   *Choose a picture book that you know well. Read it again and identify the main themes within it. Now plan a short game or activity that explores one of the themes – those which focus on social or emotional issues are often the most effective. Consider how the activity can be used as a 'way in' to the book, which builds anticipation, engages children and aids their understanding of the story.*

Book talk

It is well known by marketing professionals that word-of-mouth recommendations are highly effective in promoting merchandise. The more our friends, family and acquaintances refer to a product, the more likely it is that we will want to buy it. A good example of this, within the world of children's books, is the first of J.K. Rowling's Harry Potter series (see also Chapter 6). After an initial print run of just 1000 copies, *Harry Potter and the Philosopher's Stone* (Rowling, 2001) became a global success story, originally, purely through word of mouth.

As teachers aiming to inspire children to read for pleasure, we can learn from this focus on communication, and use book talk as one tool to hook children into the joys of books. The more of a 'book buzz' you create, the more likely it is that your class will be motivated to read. Frequency is key to success.

Effective book talk is:

- informal and relaxed;

- involves personal, emotional responses which, because of their nature are not 'right' or 'wrong', so all opinions and contributions are considered and valued;

- a regular part of everyday life in school. Frequent, short bursts can be far more effective than a single lengthy discussion;

- something that adults participate in as readers, honestly and with passion;

- a way to assess children's comprehension in a relaxed and informal way;

- accessible for everyone;

- highly dependent upon the enthusiasm and commitment of the teacher;

- fun!

Book talk works by:

- building interest by immersing children in books without pressure to achieve;

- raising the profile and status of reading;

- modelling genuine interest and enthusiasm about books;

- encouraging children to consider choices and develop preferences;

- giving children a voice in relation to what they read, without fear of disapproval or failure;

- building children's self-image as readers and reviewers.

Despite the term, book talk doesn't always have to be verbal. It can include a wide range of communication about books. It does need to take place at a variety of levels so that it is inclusive. An example developed by Seven Stories is to build a bank of post-it notes inside the front cover of books. In their simplest form, these may be wordless, colour-coded labels to show whether each reader has liked or disliked a book, so that the next person to open it has an immediate visual representation of class opinion. They may record in a few words one aspect of that book that each reader has particularly enjoyed: a favourite word, character or page, or perhaps a score out of ten from each child or adult who has read the book. This sort of response is short, achievable (both in terms of time and inclusivity) and easy to refer to when choosing a book to read.

CASE STUDY

Introducing book talk

At the start of the year, many children in Beth's Y3 class did not read for pleasure. Few children had access to books at home, the local public library had closed and readers as role models were scarce in the community. It was a struggle to motivate them to read. When asked about favourite books, few could name recent reads, and many answered the question with the names of TV programmes and films.

To address this Beth aimed to:

* increase the children's exposure to a wide selection of children's books;

* empower the children to select and explore books;

* increase the children's love for books and motivation to read;

* create a reading for pleasure culture in her classroom.

She carefully selected a collection of high quality, illustrated children's fiction that represented a range of genres, interests and reading levels, and planned a lesson around exploring the books. Children were invited to move around the displayed books, looking for covers or titles that appealed to them in different ways, with a short time to 'dip into' several of them. Unusual and attractively illustrated books certainly created a level of interest, but key to the engagement of the children was the type of communication Beth encouraged during this exercise. This was designed to be achievable by all children, whatever their confidence or ability in reading. Asked to choose one word to sum up a book, to point to the book they thought looked the most interesting, to give the name of the person they would recommend a book to, or to show everyone the picture they liked the best in a book, children quickly gained confidence and enjoyed contributing. She asked them to decide which of the books they would like to have in their classroom during the following week, and a small selection was made.

With the chosen books displayed and accessible, Beth timetabled daily slots when she read them to the class, and when everyone (adults included) read them for their own enjoyment. These times always included informal chat about their responses to the books, with everyone's contribution valued.

Beth also prioritised times when she recommended a book she had particularly enjoyed, talking with enthusiasm and passion, modelling behaviour, vocabulary and different types of response. Each day she was seen reading for pleasure, and every day she made informal comments about something she had been reading for her own enjoyment.

At the end of each week the class voted for their favourite books from the selection and repeated the process.

As the term progressed, Beth introduced new ways of communicating about books, for example, giving children 'shelf shouters' to write a one-sentence recommendation about a book (much less daunting to create and more easily read than a book review) and setting up league tables of everyone's favourites. One day when she wasn't in school, she challenged a volunteer to champion a book in her absence, and thereafter encouraged children to do this, following her model. Other staff came to ask the children for advice about books and they recommended books for other classes (older as well as younger).

By the end of the term, book talk had become a natural part of every day, often instigated by children. Children readily used the vocabulary modelled by Beth to discuss and describe books, and there was genuine excitement at new books, and about book-browsing sessions to choose the classroom selection.

Books that Beth championed became the most frequently read and the most commented upon. Children asked to borrow them to take them home to share and were diligent about returning them. Beth's own reading and knowledge of children's books increased as she prepared for reading to the class and for championing book talks. It became obvious that her increased level of knowledge about, and passion for, specific books steered the children's excitement and motivation to read.

Children often chose to read during *Golden Time* (reward time of self-selected activity) and those who previously had struggled to participate in guided reading sessions were far more engaged and keen to participate.

Activity 2

» *List the ways in which Beth introduced short and achievable ways to increase communication about books in the classroom.*

» *Using these as a model, plan a series of informal book talk activities to use with a class in the school library, with the aim of enabling children to develop preferences and make informed choices about books they borrow. Activities should be short, varied, interesting and achievable for all children.*

Putting books and creativity at the heart of your planning

The best children's books are an art form, full of rich language, concepts, images and emotions. At Seven Stories we advocate that education practitioners harness this art form to enrich and contextualise learning, to allow imagination and creativity to lead learning, and to create a future generation of book lovers.

What follows is an example of how choosing one book can enable you to develop a topic that can lead you into literacy across the curriculum, including learning outside the classroom, family engagement and on into further reading. Learning contextualised by a book models the value of books and leads to children having a memorable shared story experience. This personal and emotional approach to learning can have a very positive impact on children's learning.

Central to the picture book in the case study below are the themes of choices, change and the environment, with a little magic, imagination and a lot of aspiration. In it we meet the exuberant Ruby Nettleship in the run-down park near her inner city home and find out how, with the help of a magic ice-lolly, her imagination transforms it into the most fabulous and fantastic playground!

This is a lovely book with a really upbeat and optimistic atmosphere, and a positive role model in Ruby. The lively illustrations have lots of detail and reflect the rich cultural and social mix of British cities. The story emphasises the importance of free play and imagination, as well as the power of children to influence change.

The themes and ideas of this story can inspire the aims, central questions and activities for a themed topic.

* Following the idea of citizenship and environmental design through into the local environment.

* Revisiting the book in different ways and on different levels, creating a long lasting relationship and experiential memories of the book.

* Using it to develop literacy and language; speaking and listening, vocabulary and story writing.

* Cross-curricular work on design in the environment.

* Developing learning outside the classroom.

* Encouraging family engagement and celebration.

Some books are rich, exciting and have depth enough to inspire a whole topic. Some books are not. Finding the book that can do this task for you is the hardest job. Once you've found it, the rest is easy. What follows is a case study of how a teacher used one book to do just that.

CASE STUDY

Putting children's literature at the heart of planning

Year 2 teacher Daniel's whole-school topic for the summer term was called 'My Place' and was all about the local environment, citizenship and belonging. The aim of the topic was to teach the term's work with a view to children having more pride in their local environment. The local area and school property had a history of vandalism and antisocial behaviour.

When Daniel read the synopsis below in the Seven Stories *Hooks into Books* pack, he felt inspired to read on and find out more about the potential of this intriguing sounding book called *Ruby Nettleship* (Docherty, 2011).

Plot synopsis: When the final, working swing at their dilapidated playground breaks, the waiting children head sadly for home. Everyone except Ruby, that is, who hangs around for a while thinking about how the playground really ought to be. Surprised by the arrival of an ice cream van, Ruby explains the problem to the lady behind the counter, who cheers her up with a free lolly with the words 'plant me' written on the stick. Following the instructions, Ruby is amazed to find that it springs to life, growing rapidly into an enormous vine which creates its own ever-changing, constantly expanding, play place. Gathering her friends on her way, Ruby is swept along on a dream-like adventure as this magical playground spills out into the city, taking children, zoo animals, shoppers and traffic along with it ... heading straight for the town hall and the Mayor's office door! Ruby takes a deep breath and heads into the office, where she finds a strangely familiar-looking Mayor, who works some more magic for Ruby and her friends in a slightly more practical way, changing their park play space for good.

Initially, Daniel sat and read the book at home with a cup of tea, showed it to his daughter, and began to scribble ideas for his class. At the end of the next day, he read it to the other Y2 teacher and the teaching assistants. The potential of the book had everyone very excited, and soon *Ruby Nettleship* was at the heart of everyone's planning. The first thing Daniel did was to send a letter to parents arranging two class trips to the local park: the first for the children to assess and redesign it; the second, at the end of the project, for children and families to celebrate the work. Then Daniel took his class on a journey into the world of Ruby Nettleship and beyond!

Daniel's aims were to:

* redesign the local playground with imagination and aspiration;
* increase the quality of children's story writing;
* introduce the children to a variety of quality books;
* develop a love of books, stories and reading.

Daniel did this by:

* introducing the children to their own imagination and aspiration, and the potential for change;
* choosing an enjoyable, enriching and inspirational book;
* visiting the local park;
* creating a dance piece;
* sharing lots more stories.

The children did this by:

* writing and illustrating a story about their local park after it has been imaginatively rebuilt;
* creating a class dance piece to perform in the local playground and in assembly;
* creating a display of their work for the rest of the school.

Ways in

Daniel began the project, before introducing the book, by making multi-coloured fruity ice-lollies with sticks that said 'plant me' on them. The children were invited to make up ideas about what might happen once the sticks were planted. They were really excited by this. There was a diverse range of ideas about what would grow from plants; from furniture to whole buildings and scary creatures. The children drew and labelled their ideas. When Daniel finally read *Ruby Nettleship* to the class, you could hear a pin drop, and the children gasped with amazement when they saw what Ruby's lolly stick grew into.

Stepping inside the story

The illustrations from the book were a gift. Daniel copied full spreads for various exercises and discussions. He let small groups and pairs have time to look at just one picture before asking them to feed back their ideas and reflections. For one of the exercises, he gave the whole class a copy of one of the full pages (the busy double-page spread in the centre of the town straight after the supermarket) and asked the class to *step in to the picture*, asking *What can you see? What can you hear? What can you touch? What would it feel like? What can you smell? How does it make you feel?* Children recorded their words to support the use of rich vocabulary in their story writing.

Visiting the local park

There were many different aspects to the visit to the park, including:

- developing a language and vocabulary to support story writing;
- redesigning the playground to contribute to the story writing;
- choreographing a dance piece.

Collecting words for writing

Daniel stood at the bottom of the slide and filmed children as they slid down. He challenged them to each think of different words (verb/adjective/adverb) to describe the experience and say it to camera. This was repeated at the swings, roundabout, etc. Back at school they reviewed the film, talking about the language and the experience, and adding new vocabulary. These ideas were part of the story-writing process.

Redesigning the playground

Daniel went into role and pretended to be chief executive of a playground design company. He gave the children the brief to design *the world's best playground*, with no limitations. They had at their disposal endless money, ideas and a little bit of magic. It was crucial that the designs were unique and had ideas that had never been seen before in a playground. The children were sent off with fresh, clean note books and pens. They met for small group critiques at different stations in the playground, with grown-up helpers acting as focus groups.

These ideas were then used back in the classroom to begin writing stories about finding or creating *the best playground in the world.* In character development, Daniel focused on how the new playgrounds made children feel before and after the changes, linking directly to the theme of *My Place.*

Dance

In PE the children had already started work on a piece of dance, telling part of the story, starting with the vine growing and ending as it shrinks back into the ground again. They had started by collecting movement words from the book. Using the pictures of tendrils and stems on vines, they had practised making curling, twisting, unfurling movements with hands, arms, legs and feet, and extended these into whole-body movements.

In the playground they introduced strips of ribbon and lightweight fabrics to emphasise the shapes, turns and patterns created by the vine, starting slowly as it sprouts from the lolly stick, and continuing with variation of speed and level, sometimes allowing the fabric shapes to lead the movement, sometimes letting the children's own movements lead. They practised freezing momentarily and using the slide and the different heights in the grassy mounds. They added in a larger piece of lightweight cloth (eg voile) to flap and roll under, to run with and float over other children. The end of the dance changed pace, and all the children slowly sank to the ground and curled up.

Further reading for pleasure

Daniel arranged small group story-reading and whole-class story times, using different books with similar themes, for example:

*   *Belonging* (Baker, 2008);
*   *A Child's Garden* (Foreman, 2010);
*   *Once Upon an Ordinary School Day* (McNaughton and Kitamura, 2005);
*   *Here Comes Frankie* (Hopgood, 2009).

The success of this topic depended upon the children's enthusiasm and commitment to the cause of environment and citizenship. The book was so imaginative that it gave the children *permission* to be inspired. The children loved the topic and this could be seen in the quality of their writing and illustrations. The impact on families was strong; there was such a buzz about the story and the ideas that more families than usual came to the celebration in the park, saw the dance and heard *Ruby Nettleship* read aloud. Families asked where they could buy a copy of the book.

Activity 3

» *Discover where you can find books with topic-based potential. Try the following:*

– *Seven Stories Hooks into Books packs (www.sevenstories.org.uk/learning/books-and-resources);*

- Carousel *(subscription magazine);*

- Books for Keeps *(subscription magazine);*

- *www.guardian.co.uk/childrens-books-site;*

- *librarians;*

- *colleagues;*

- *keep a notebook of books with potential;*

- *create a book collection around a particular topic. Seek out a high quality collection of books for your class, school and school library. Choose ones that are easy for your class, or a particular age range, to read, that can be read to the class, and that will inform your knowledge of books available and different subjects. These could include non-fiction, picture books and chapter books.*

The quality of the book

At Seven Stories our book collections are diverse and include perennial favourites, as well as lesser-known and more challenging titles. We recognise that children and young people need different books for different reasons at different times and we believe that they should have access to the best books currently available in the UK and beyond. We know that books that are loved will have the power to speak directly to young people's hearts and minds, and – ultimately – change their lives.

Types of books

Think about books in terms of the following characteristics.

Quality

A high quality book will:

- have consistent and believable characters and plot;

- have beautiful, rich and challenging illustrations;

- be distinctive;

- evoke questions and have the potential to be interpreted in different ways;

- use language in different ways: rich language, simple language, or none at all;

- be a springboard for activities and further learning.

Sharing

- Will it be good to share aloud?

- Will it extend children's experience of language, ideas and images?

Achieving

•   Is it accessible and does it have the potential to build confidence and skills with reading words, visual literacy and enjoyment?

Inspiring

A range of good quality books to explore can be as inspirational as a trip to the theatre or a good film. Do you have at your disposal a range of themes, genres, styles, characters, authors and illustrators?

Diverse range

Think about range when you are choosing books. Choose books that are different, challenging, familiar, appealing and unusual. Choose from a range of publishers' styles, different authors and illustrators.

Themes

When thinking about a topic or theme, the more books you have read, the easier it will be to link books together. It is best achieved by focusing on concepts rather than issues, eg friendship and fears rather than bullying.

Illustrations

Picture books are for everyone. There is a vast range of picture books that are for children from KS2 and beyond. They are rich, challenging and provide an excellent springboard for exploration and learning. Seek these out and learn about their potential for your class, through reading and exploring them together.

Enjoyment

Children have a wide range of interests. Think about your class and the features they would like, for example, humour, fear, silliness, being true to life, fantasy, science fiction.

Recommendations

Look for a small number of trusted sources of recommendations. Finding one or two new titles a month is more achievable and effective than trying to find twenty four new books at the beginning of the year. The links given earlier (pp 113–114) are a starting point. Choose independent recommendations where people have already trawled through different and diverse publishers for you. Keep a record/journal/note book/file of the books that you love.

Teacher engagement and enthusiasm

Teacher engagement with and enthusiasm for children's books is critical in all aspects of reading for pleasure. Children don't suddenly acquire the ability to read for pleasure as soon as they learn to decode; it's something they need to be introduced to, taught to do and see modelled, long before they can decode. A role model must love books, share the love of books and care about the children's enjoyment of books. Children need to be enticed, encouraged, guided and inspired by high quality children's books. Reading for pleasure needs to permeate every part of school life, not just as a special lesson. Reading for pleasure can underpin every curriculum area. As a teacher, any time you spend searching out new books for your classes is never wasted. The best books are an art form; they are an incredibly rich resource of meaning and questions, ready to take you and your class on a journey. Make the time, every month, to find and read children's books for pleasure and you will have everything you require to enable your classes to fulfil their potential as book lovers and readers for life.

Conclusion

Engaging children in books and reading for pleasure requires us, as teachers, to be pro-active in seeking out ways to open up the possibilities of books for children. As outlined in this chapter and illustrated in the case studies, there are many ways in which this can be achieved. Using a carefully chosen, active 'way in' to entice children into a book before reading will not only lead to heightened levels of engagement and interest, but will also enhance their understanding of concepts and language within the text. Communication about books is imperative in raising their status and in developing positive attitudes towards reading. The teacher's own commitment and interest are central to the success of 'Book Talk' as a means of encouraging reading for pleasure in the classroom. Putting books at the centre of your planning enables a rich and meaningful learning experience for children. But, perhaps most importantly, we, as teachers, need to be engaged and enthusiastic about books and reading, and to communicate this to children to hook them into books.

Critical points

» *Increasing children's pleasure in reading motivates them to read.*

» *Offering rich learning opportunities enables children to make personal and emotional connections with books and stories.*

» *Choosing and using good books enhances children's experience of books and stories.*

» *Children's literature is an excellent starting point for teaching and learning.*

» *Personal engagement and enthusiasm for books is fundamental to supporting children's love of, and engagement with, books.*

Critical reflections

» *Consider the role that books have in your life. What do you enjoy about books and reading? How can you communicate this to the children? What more do you need to know, and do, to familiarise yourself with children's books and literature so that you can put them at the heart of your teaching?*

References

Baker, J. (2008) *Belonging*. London: Walker Books.

Bauman, J.F. and Duffy, A.M. (1997) Engaged Reading for Pleasure and Learning: A Report From the National Reading Research Center. Athens, GA: NRRC.

Browne, A. and Duval, E. (2010) *Petite Beauté*. Paris: L'Ecole des Loisirs.

Clark, C. and Rumbold, K. (2006) *Reading for Pleasure: A Research Overview*. www.scholastic.com/teachers/article/collateral_resources/pdf/i/Reading_for_pleasure.pdf

Docherty, T. (2011) *Ruby Nettleship*. Dorking: Templar.

Donaldson, J, and Roberts, D. (2012) *Jack and the Flumflum Tree*. London: Macmillan Children's Books.

Foreman, M. (2010) *A Child's Garden. A Story of Hope*. London: Walker.

Hopgood, T. (2009) *Here Comes Frankie*. London: MacMillan Children's Books.

McNaughton, C. and Kitamura, S. (2005) *Once Upon an Ordinary School Day*. London: Anderson.

O'Flahavan, J., Gambrell, L.B., Guthrie, J.T., Stahl, S. and Alvermann, D. (1992) Poll Results Guide Activities of Research Center. *Reading Today*, 10:1.

Rowling, J.K. (2001) *Harry Potter and the Philosopher's Stone*. London: Bloomsbury.

Stanovich, K. (1986) Matthew Effects in Reading: Some Consequences of Individual Differences in the Acquisition of Literacy. *Reading Research Quarterly*, 21:4.

Voutch (1999) *La Planete Bizarre*. Paris: Thierry Magnier.

8 Active reading: its impact on writing

DAVID BOORMAN AND JEMMA RENNOCKS

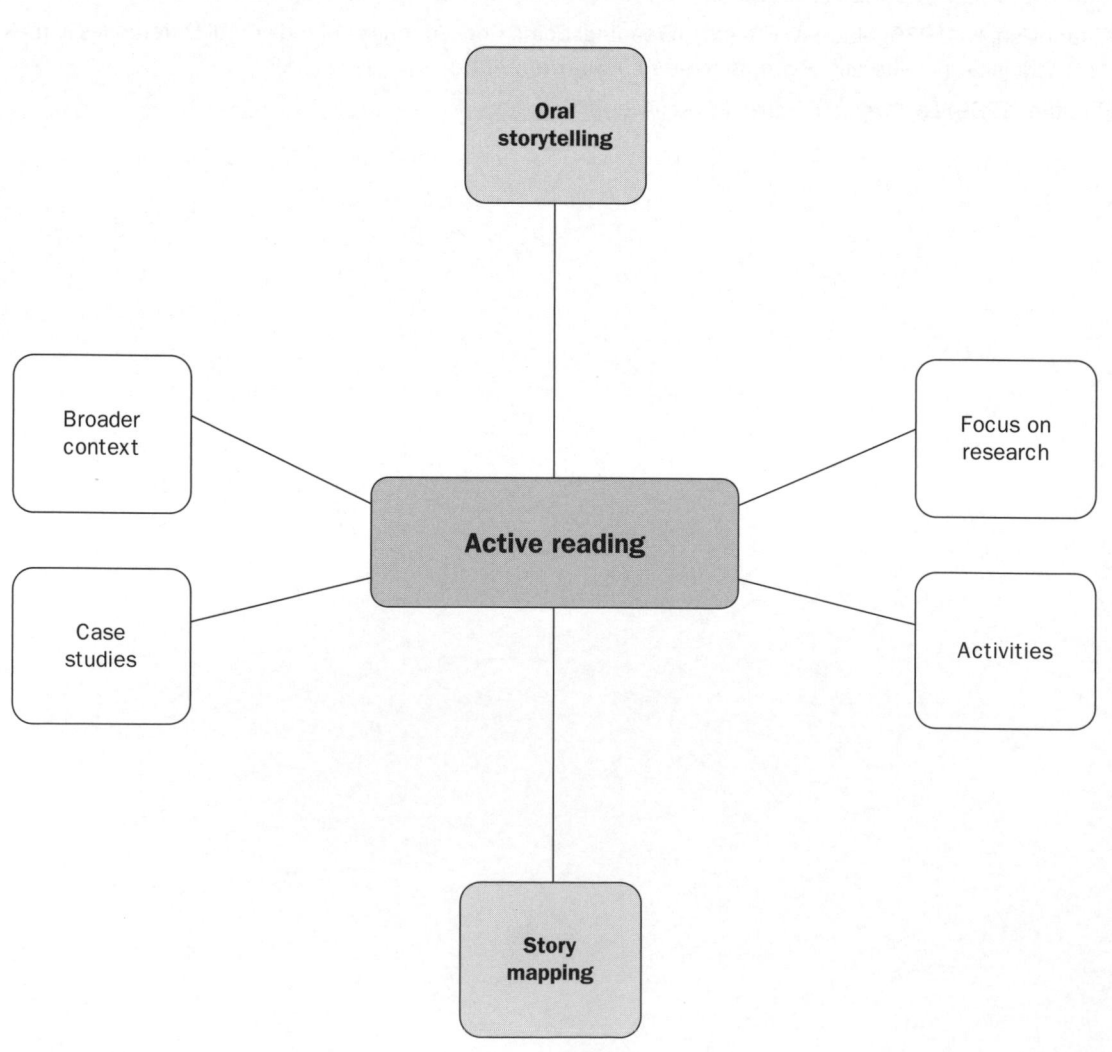

Teachers' standards

3 Demonstrate good subject and curriculum knowledge

* have a secure knowledge of the relevant subject(s) and curriculum areas, foster and maintain pupils' interest in the subject, and address misunderstandings

* demonstrate a critical understanding of developments in the subject and curriculum areas, and promote the value of scholarship

4 Plan and teach well-structured lessons

* contribute to the design and provision of an engaging curriculum within the relevant subject area(s).

Critical questions

» *How can reading be active rather than passive in order to appeal to more reluctant readers?*

» *How can we harness the power of talk to deepen children's understanding of texts and thereby develop children's proficiency in writing?*

» *How can we deepen children's knowledge of books to improve their writing?*

» *How can texts be used most effectively to improve children's knowledge and understanding of how to write at sentence and text level?*

Introduction

Children who engage in reading are more able to write texts that are suitable for their audience and purpose (Corbett, 2007; Millard, 2001). It follows that those children who do not engage with high quality texts will therefore struggle to compose effective texts themselves (Smith, 1994). So, how can we encourage those children who are not keen or proficient readers to engage with texts?

Without effective preparation for writing, most children will be left struggling even to know how to begin. In order to avoid the desperate refrain of 'I don't know what to write!' ringing around the classroom, it is necessary for the teacher to make sure the children have been 'filled with ideas' before they start. However, *ideas* does not only refer to content. Content is essential, but children also need to know how the text type in hand is constructed, as well as the vocabulary and the sentence structures necessary to compose it (Corbett, 2007; Smith, 1994). Unless we give children these tools, even the most able young writers are unlikely to be able to construct effective texts that suit both the audience and purpose of the task, let alone those children who have the additional barrier of poor secretarial skills to contend with.

It would be logical to assume that reading and interacting with high quality texts is an essential part of the preparation necessary for children to compose their own (Cremin, 2011). They provide a model, an example children can refer to that helps them to structure their own writing, sentence structure and vocabulary (Lewis, 2001). By extension, children who lack an accumulated knowledge of stories will be at a considerable disadvantage when they are asked to plan and write their own texts (Corbett, 2007). As an example, a child who has never heard a traditional tale would be unable to write using the conventions of a traditional tale, such as 'good vs evil', set in the countryside.

However, if children are merely *passively* listening to a story being read to them, this will not necessarily lead to engagement, and thus could leave many ill-equipped to write a text with the requisite features. Children must be encouraged to *actively* engage with a text in order to gain a deeper understanding of it (Cremin, 2011; Mandel-Morrow, 1989). Children (and adults) have an innate desire to tell and discuss narratives in order to construct meaning (Rosen, 1988) and so it is logical for this to be harnessed.

For example, children should be given opportunities to communicate orally, eg recounting a school trip. Can we reasonably expect children to write something that they cannot say? In addition, it could be argued that pupils who are superior storytellers are then able to write more engaging stories, thus providing their stories with verisimilitude.

The power of 'talk' has been identified by the New Literacy Framework, which produced the key document *Talk for Writing* (DCSF, 2008). Often, there can be a significant gap between pupils' spoken vocabulary and their competency in writing (Smith, 1994). Therefore, they need ample opportunities to rehearse and revise their own stories aloud, so their knowledge of the story they are composing is secure *before* they attempt to write (Corbett, 2007). However, it is clearly not sufficient to rely on reading stories to children and hope that eventually they will accumulate enough knowledge to be able to write them (Mandel-Morrow, 1989). As with all effective teaching, a multi-sensory approach is required to make the texts memorable for children (Corbett and Strong, 2011; Horner and Ryf, 2007).

In this chapter, you will explore reading activities that are *active*. The case studies that follow explore oral storytelling and the power of adapting learnt stories, and the development of quality talk based on texts. These techniques allow children to be active in their exploration of texts and promote the engagement necessary to improve their writing skills.

Oral storytelling and adapting known stories

The National Curriculum (2013) programme of study outlines the expectations for children's writing, stating that:

> *Effective composition involves articulating and communicating ideas, and then organising them coherently for a reader. This requires clarity, awareness of the audience, purpose and context, and an increasingly wide knowledge of vocabulary and grammar.* (15)

To enable children to make effective choices about composition, it is necessary to teach them to internalise the text type features.

When learning to write, children use texts they have read as models. Corbett (2007, xi) calls this the 'story storehouse', which involves enabling children to commit a range of texts to memory and then teaching them to adapt these models (Lewis, 2001) for new purposes, audiences and contexts. This is achieved by teaching children to retell the texts themselves. And it is not just for writing fiction that this method can be used; non-fiction texts can be learnt and 'innovated' on just as easily (Corbett and Strong, 2001, 20).

The quality of the text chosen as the model that the children will learn to imitate in the first stage of this process is vital. It is important that the text is not too long and that it exhibits the features the teacher wishes the children to learn,

Jemma, a Year 5 teacher, describes how she adapted a well-known legend in order to highlight the key features of the genre. She discusses how oral retellings were used to familiarise children with the structure of the legend, and explains how pupils were able to create adaptations, based on the original plot.

CASE STUDY

Year 5 learning to write legends (I)

I chose the legend of Beowulf as the text the children would learn to retell themselves, as it demonstrated many key features of this genre such as a 'good vs evil' plotline, a truly heroic character and an ending hinting at subsequent stories to come. In addition, it had a clear structure that I could imagine the children finding easy to adapt. I re-wrote the text myself so that I was sure it exhibited the key connectives, vocabulary and language patterns I wanted the children to learn, whilst retaining the essence of the legend and the features of the genre. The children needed to broaden the sentence openers they were currently using, and this unit was an opportunity to study starting sentences with adverbs.

To aid memorisation I produced a text map, mostly using pictures and symbols and as little text as possible, on a large sheet of sugar paper. The children suggested actions throughout the retelling, which helped them to remember key words and phrases. Retellings were whole-class to begin with, with the adults leading them every time. It was necessary to return to it every day over a two-week period in order for the children to learn it fully.

When the children's confidence grew, I moved on to supporting them as they retold the story with actions in small groups. The children made their own version of the story map, which they referred to during each retelling. The class recreated the settings from the legend inside shoeboxes, which was a very engaging activity and helped to deepen their understanding of the text.

The children eventually moved onto paired retellings. By this stage the children were relying less and less on the story maps and referred back to them only occasionally. Language patterns and new vocabulary were becoming embedded. The children helped each other to remember parts they found difficult, and teaching and learning from each other in this way further strengthened their own recall.

Children were finally able to retell the text on their own and they used video recorders to film each other retelling the whole text. They had a specific audience for the films in mind, as we decided to produce them for the Year 4 class to watch. Some children used props to jog their memories, some preferred to use their story maps. It was important that the children understood that they should try to retell the story coherently by trying to include as much of the original language as possible. Some children were ready to add their own embellishments. This was encouraged, as it showed a deepening understanding of the narrative.

I then moved onto adapting the text to show how the plot could be recycled. My adaptation was set in England rather than Denmark, and told of a poor monarch who lived in a castle rather than a hall, and who was being terrorised by a Minodred, a hideous bog monster, instead of Grendel. My heroic protagonist was called Sir Philip rather than Beowulf, and when he was victorious he nailed the monster's leg instead of his arm to the wall.

I took care to retain the text level elements that made the story a legend. For example, I made sure that the 'good' character defeated the 'evil' monster in a heroic battle and the ending hinted that the tale did not end there... I also modelled adapting the stylistic devices and sentence level features such as similes and sentences starting with adverbs to the new context.

The children found it easy to think of alternative ways they could adapt their own stories and all came up with an individual take on the same plot. They drew a story map to help plan their writing and found it relatively easy to write their first draft. After receiving feedback on their work, they edited their writing.

I found that this approach worked particularly well for the less able writers in the class. They were able to focus on the things they struggle with when writing (eg how to hold the pen / write neatly / spell / punctuate sentences).

Units of work such as the one described above embed a 'blueprint' (Corbett, 2007, ix) for a text type in the children's minds on which they will be able to draw again in the future. Moreover, the deep exploration of the story allows for meaningful learning of language patterns as the children are fully engaged in the context in which they find them.

Once the children have learnt a text well enough to retell it orally themselves, the next step is to show them how to adapt it to suit a new purpose. This process is often referred to as 'innovation' (Corbett, 2007, 16). Children find this adaptation easy and they see it as 'playing' with the text. The teacher can model boiling down the text to its core elements, which will be considered a 'blueprint' (Corbett, 2007, ix) for the text type. They then go on to model retaining these features in their new text, whilst crucially changing other elements to suit the new purpose.

Once children have gone through the process of *innovating* on a text themselves in the same way, they should be prepared to write a new text on their own. They should draw on the blueprint in their minds, the newly internalised vocabulary and language patterns and their understanding of how to adapt a model text to a new purpose.

FOCUS ON RESEARCH

Story mapping

The case study above draws on insights from the research undertaken by Lewis (2001). She discusses the strategy of teaching children specific story structures by reading a number of stories with a similar structure, followed by asking children to produce a story map for one of them. This visual representation is then adapted by the children through changing something, such as the setting or viewpoint, which then forms the basis for their own writing. She also advocates the use of picture books when familiarising children with a story structure.

In response to potential criticism that this approach might stifle creativity, Lewis (2001) argues that story mapping teaches children common story structures they can then build on and modify to create their own writing. She found that children became *more explicitly aware of story structure* when different types were studied in isolation (75), and this resulted in children improving the structure of their *own* texts, a strategy advocated by Corbett (2008a).

Similarly, in the case study above, children were taught how to adapt a simple story structure to create their own unique piece of work. Like the old adage that *you must know a rule before you can break it*, learning well-established structures paves the way for our budding writers to go beyond them and create something new.

In the case study below, Jemma explains how the context of the legend was critical in helping to refine children's vocabulary and their knowledge of sentence structure successfully.

CASE STUDY

Year 5 learning to write legends (II)

During the process of learning to retell the legend, we explored the meaning of the text through drama and discussion activities. For example, the children hot-seated characters to deepen understanding of their feelings and reactions.

I picked out particular sentences to study, for example this one, which started with an adverb: *Eventually, King Hrothgar abandoned his banqueting hall*. A colour code was used to help children identify word classes, so nouns were red, adjectives were blue, verbs were green and adverbs purple. The sentence above was displayed on the interactive whiteboard and the children were asked to colour code the words. The children copied out the sentence on mini whiteboards and discussed alternative words that could be used while retaining the same meaning.

Contextualising such sentences had greater impact than studying them in isolation, as they were meaningful, and the children could be reminded to choose words appropriate to the character and setting. In addition, it gave children the opportunity to start writing the new vocabulary they were learning and become familiar with how these new words could be used.

Once the children had internalised sentence structures used in *Beowulf,* they were then able to compose new sentences by keeping the same structure but substituting the vocabulary to suit a new context. This showed that they were beginning to understand the role the words play in the sentences they had been looking at and could identify other words that have the same function (eg substituting *slouched* for *staggered*). As the children became familiar with the plot, we were able to have in-depth conversations about word choices. For example, *which verb would be best to describe how Grendel travels back to the swamp after the fight with Beowulf? 'Staggered'. Why would that not be appropriate for describing him travelling to the hall earlier on? Because he was not injured then. 'Stalked' would be better, because he is moving in a threatening way.* This also sparked a valuable discussion about impact and ways to avoid repetition in stories.

This familiarity with the story allowed for exploration into the role of punctuation too. As the children were fully immersed in the legend, the sentences from the text in which they hunted for punctuation were more meaningful. For example, the children were able to deduce the function of the apostrophe in phrases taken from the text, such as *King Hrothgar's hall* and *Beowulf's grip*. Furthermore, when they learnt the text orally, they retold it with the pauses provided by commas and full stops. So, when they adapted a sentence such as *The soldiers, exhausted and bleeding, gasped in despair*, they were able to 'hear' the pauses and understood that some sort of marker should go there to signal the pause to the reader.

Activity 1

» *Using Jemma's model, described above, try teaching children to retell a story. When they are able to retell it themselves, play a game of substitution with them using a sentence from the text. Can they think of suitable alternatives that retain the essence of the original?*

FOCUS ON RESEARCH

Teaching grammar and punctuation in context

The success of the teaching described in the case study above may be explained in part by the research carried out by Myhill *et al.* (cited in DfE, 2012, 14). Their study found that children who had been taught grammar in context scored more highly in writing assessments than those who had been taught grammar explicitly.

Hall echoes this sentiment in his chapter on *Developing understanding of punctuation with young readers and writers* (2001). With reference to a study by Calkins (1980), he noted that meaningful learning about how and when to use punctuation occurred when children were engaged in meaningful reading and writing activities. They were able to discuss the punctuation they had chosen in terms of the difference it made to a text. By contrast, children who learnt about punctuation by being taught rules and definitions did not appreciate the impact it had on texts. Instead, they included punctuation by following the rules they had been taught.

The above case study indicates that a combination of oral storytelling and story mapping was successful in developing children's writing skills. Could a similar process be successful for much younger children?

In the case study below, David, a Year 2 teacher, explains how it was beneficial for his children to study three books with very similar plotlines, to help embed the structure of a 'cumulative' story (Lewis, 2011, 146).

CASE STUDY

Year 2 looking at different stories by the same author

The *Mrs Armitage* stories are a series of three books written by Quentin Blake. All three books feature Mrs Armitage (and her faithful dog Brakespear) and follow broadly similar plotlines in which Mrs Armitage either adds to, or removes parts from, a mode of transport. This follows Corbett's belief that *narrow reading leads to imitative writing* (2008a, 2).

To familiarise pupils with the character of Mrs Armitage, I read *Mrs Armitage: Queen of the Road* to them. In fours, pupils then discussed what happened in the story and, as a group, had to retell it to an adult to check they had understood its structure. I felt that pupils' anxiety would be reduced through working on a group retelling and that working as a group would improve the understanding of all involved (Jalongo, 1988; Jolliffe, 2008). The pupils were very keen to discuss what they had remembered about the story and the exact order in which they believed the events occurred.

The next book we read was *Mrs Armitage on Wheels*. With very little prompting, pupils were able to spot similarities between the two books, such as: characters, vocabulary and plot. Pupils became more familiar with the concept of *innovating through substitution* (DCSF, 2008, 8) (in this case, substituting one mode of transport for another) through paired discussion.

I created a story map for *Mrs Armitage on Wheels* (Corbett, 2008b). This involved sketching a picture to represent each of the scenes and using arrows to link the different scenes together (Lewis, 2011). The rationale for this was that it enabled pupils to visualise a 'map' of the events that occurred in the story; a method they could then use when planning to write their own text.

I then read *Mrs Armitage and the Big Wave* to the pupils to further familiarise them with the structure of the Mrs Armitage stories. I modelled how to be an 'adjectives detective' and encouraged pupils to spot adjectives as they encountered them throughout the story. For some of the adjectives, I suggested four alternatives and asked the class to vote for their preferred choice. I deliberately suggested some possibilities that would completely change the meaning of the sentence in order to prompt discussions about how careful thought must be given when using 'powerful' word choices, and how they must be appropriate to the context of the story.

I also modelled how to start the story map for this story, and pupils were then, in pairs, asked to complete it. I reduced the size of the groups here because I felt that children could lose focus if they were waiting for a long time for their turn to draw.

After assessing the pupils' work, I found that a particular benefit of the maps was their flexibility. Higher-attaining pupils had recalled a greater a number of events but had not been restricted by a rigid format. Lower-attaining pupils had recalled less, yet could still experience success because there were no minimum criteria to meet.

Subsequently, I asked pupils to work with their partners to tell the story of *Mrs Armitage and the Big Wave.* The rationale for this was that I wanted pupils to experience using a story map as a prompt for their thinking, as this was what they would be doing later when using their *own* story map for writing their *own* text.

Having now experienced three similar plots, I felt it appropriate for the pupils to move onto developing ideas for their own writing. I displayed a photograph of a scooter and explained that this was an *incredible* scooter and that we were going to use adjectives to describe the amazing features that it possessed. As well as being excited by the fact that they could 'invent' their own scooter, the pupils were taking Mrs Armitage's needs into consideration and thinking about how she and Brakespear could use the inventions they created. This was particularly interesting, as I had not mentioned Mrs Armitage during this session.

In the next session, I explained that we were going to write our own story featuring Mrs Armitage: *Mrs Armitage and the Useful Scooter.* With another adult, we modelled how to orally rehearse a story and demonstrated how repeating and revising a given section can help you adjust and improve it. As a class, we then discussed how to start the story and spent time refining this section, with contributions from a number of different pupils, to reinforce how collaboration can create a more powerful story (Carter, 2006). Particularly striking was the children's successful use of pictures at the planning stage; they acted as a point of reference around which pupils could organise their thoughts and then collaborate in order to develop and expand their ideas.

Another advantage of using story maps became clear when pupils began to write their stories. Each picture they drew represented a different scene and thus each individual picture could represent a different paragraph. Corbett (2008b) suggests that a story map structure forms an early introduction to paragraphing.

The stories that were created were of a higher quality than I expected for children of this age and ability. I believe that the interactions children had with their peers when planning their stories helped them to acquire and develop vocabulary (Mandel-Morrow, 1989). Generally, the stories were well-structured, yet children's use of a given structure did not appear to stifle their creative ideas (Lewis, 2001).

FOCUS ON RESEARCH

Collaborative learning

Krant (1991) highlights the importance of teachers sharing their own writing and modelling how to participate in editing conferences. This gives pupils the confidence to make their own independent choices, rather than over-relying on the teacher for support. Crawford *et al.*

(2005, 91) outline a number of techniques that can be used to conduct successful discussions, such as *directed listening-thinking* in which children are encouraged to make and then adjust their predictions based on what they have heard.

Many believe the size of a collaborative group to be of paramount importance (Krant, 1991; Jolliffe, 2008). Jolliffe maintains there should be five or fewer in a group because if the number is any higher the group may divide into smaller sub-groups, leading to a loss of cohesiveness. She also suggests that pupils may benefit from initially working in pairs over a shorter time, in order to help them develop their collaborative skills, before eventually increasing the size of the group and the length of time they are expected to collaborate. Krant (1991) agrees and adds that a circular table can be more conducive to collaborative work.

Crawford *et al.* (2005, 59) explain that children need to experience different roles in a collaborative group in order to become 'better-rounded' in terms of their collaborative skills. Seeing collaborative work from different perspectives should help pupils to gain a greater understanding of each other's viewpoints, ultimately leading to more successful collaborations.

Activity 2

»   *Try using different co-operative learning strategies when asking pupils to collaborate.*

–   *Which do you find to be most successful?*

–   *Is their success affected by the size of the group?*

   You may find Wendy Jolliffe's (2008) co-operative learning ideas of use here.

Broader context

Recently, the literacy curriculum objectives of British primary schools have differed from the objectives of other European countries, especially in the Early Years. The introduction of the *Year 1 Phonics Screening Check* contrasts with Sweden, for example, where, following a review of reading and writing practices, the authors concluded that the optimal conditions necessary for young children to acquire literacy skills involved encouraging children *to participate in communicative processes and actively take part in a dialogue about their own reading and writing* (INCA, 4).

The age when children start their formal schooling is different in Britain compared to Europe. In Britain, pupils start formal schooling at the age of four; across mainland Europe it is more likely to be six or seven. And, as the *Cambridge Primary Review* (2009, 15) notes, *In 14 of the 15 countries that scored higher than England in a major study of reading and literacy in 2006, children did not enter school until they were 6 or 7 (see Chapter 1).*

Thus it could be surmised that the emphasis on dialogue found in other areas of Europe is helpful in improving literacy skills (Andrews, 2001; Reed, 2005).

Talking about texts

Reflecting on the use of pictures to aid writing a story, we might ask ourselves some questions.

* Is it possible that we have underestimated the strength of pictures in assisting children's understanding of a story?

* Could picture books be used to strengthen children's knowledge of story structure and provide an alternative, and perhaps superior, perspective to words?

In fact, *wordless* books appear to be a suitable vehicle for developing knowledge of story structure. Graham (1998) describes how stories that are devoid of words can actually be very powerful tools because they 'force' pupils to use their imagination to articulate the narrative. Also, wordless books can be accessed by pupils with a broad range of reading abilities, making them very appropriate for whole-class teaching (see Chapter 7).

They are useful for other reasons.

* The teacher can model how to tell a story, in terms of the language used in storytelling and how to construct phrases and sentences.

* Children can visualise each scene in the story, making it easier for them to remember.

* Each picture acts as a scene, which can provide an early introduction into paragraphing.

In the following case study, David explains how a wordless book with a clever plot twist stimulated children's imagination and improved their ability to make careful vocabulary choices.

CASE STUDY

Year 2 looking at 'stories with a familiar setting'

The Chicken Thief is a wordless book. The story begins with Fox kidnapping Chicken from his garden. Rabbit and Bear chase Fox day and night in an attempt to save their friend. However, it becomes clear that Fox does not want to eat Chicken; he merely wants a friend to play with. Indeed, in the climax of the story, Chicken makes it clear that he would actually quite like to like to live with Fox! Bear and Rabbit return home empty-handed.

The teaching sequence for the unit followed a similar pattern to that of the Mrs Armitage stories; in fact, it was designed to build upon the knowledge acquired in those sessions. However, there was a different emphasis this time; we studied characterisation, dialogue and time connectives.

The pictures communicated a depth of understanding about the relationships between characters that children of this age would not ordinarily be able to infer from text. Indeed, it was striking that pupils were able to identify subtle changes in the drawings that I had not even noticed. For example, a few pupils saw that the grip of Fox loosened on Chicken as the first day wore on. This led to a discussion about *why*. Some suggested that Fox was tired; others believed it showed that Fox trusted Chicken not to run away. This illustrates the accessibility of wordless books to pupils of all abilities as the depth of the discussion is not affected by their ability to decode words. These subtleties also allow pupils to build up their knowledge of how to 'show not tell' (Jump, 2013, 1) characters' behaviour when writing their own stories.

I found that the retellings (or perhaps 'tellings' is a better term, as wordless books are left open to interpretation) of *The Chicken Thief* were imaginative and incorporated a wide range of vocabulary. In addition, the dialogue between characters was of such high quality that it drove the plot forward. For example, one pupil, in the role of Fox, started to cry and explained to Chicken that he only wanted a friend and that he was crying because he was now feeling guilty. I would assert that the pictures are critical in providing a structure that guides the children down an appropriate path, whilst freeing them to write creatively.

It is possible to make predictions about what could happen in the plot in any type of book, but wordless books may make this process easier. This could be because all pupils can see the picture in front of them and are not having to rely on their memory or their ability to decode. The initial predictions for this story were clearly and understandably based on pupils' prior knowledge of texts; their experiences with traditional tales led them to believe that Fox would eat Chicken. The fact that the book is left open to interpretation may have given pupils greater confidence to make predictions, safe in the knowledge that no answers will be 100 per cent wrong or right.

Encouraging children to describe accurately the illustrations prompted them to use more effective sentence structures and vocabulary choices. For example, the carefully-crafted illustrations initiated much discussion about what time of day or night it could have been. The pupils generated numerous connectives to describe night-time, eg *at midnight, when the moon came out, at nightfall.* In addition to an increased *range* of connectives, I felt that the *quality* of these connectives also improved because they needed to be carefully chosen in order to describe the action in the story effectively.

After immersing themselves in the story, it was time for pupils to orally rehearse and then write their own. We used the structure of *The Chicken Thief,* but also used *substitution* (DCSF, 2008) so that pupils could develop their own 'evil' character and choose their own 'problem'. It was noticeable that many of the words and phrases that were collected whilst discussing *The Chicken Thief* were used in pupils' own stories, indicating that the discussions had certainly broadened their range of vocabulary. Some pupils also included a bitter-sweet ending, similar to the ending of *The Chicken Thief.*

Activity 3

» *Read and then discuss a wordless book with your class. Ask them to collaborate to create their own stories, either oral or written, that involve substitution (DCSF, 2008). Note the impact that the shared story has on the children; are they using what they have learned to develop more powerful stories?*

Graham (1998, 35) found that many children, even fluent storytellers, found it difficult to retell a story, and instead gave a 'running commentary' in the present tense. To help one girl overcome this, the child was asked to start the story with *Once Upon a Time* and to describe the story without showing the pictures to the audience; this led to a much richer retelling. Perhaps paragraph starters or connectives could be used as prompts to support a child's retelling (Lewis, 2011).

FOCUS ON RESEARCH

Wordless books

Communication skills are much enhanced by the use of wordless books (Graham 1998; Marriott 1991). However, as Jalongo (1988, 51) states: *Dialogue about literature need not be children parroting back details recalled from the story. Instead, it can and should be a window on each child's thought process, a means of developing communication skills.* Marriott (1991, 54) emphasises the importance of children listening to stories and responding to them, postulating that *there is no substitute for such a form of reading*.

Graham (1998, 28) explains that the wordless picture book is a generous invitation to the child reader to create the verbal story at will and that, because of this 'openness', the books will retain the attraction for the child that comes from co-creation. This increased ownership (28) of wordless books can be motivating for children (Marriott, 1991). Jalongo (1988) agrees that discussing picture books can be more pleasurable as it is possible to question children in order to deepen their thinking, yet without the possible anxiety caused by their fear of giving the 'wrong' answer. Graham (1998) adds that wordless books can present a greater challenge to children. Is this because they require a greater amount of thought in order to construct meaning? Jalongo argues that the pictures can stimulate both the left side and right side of the brain, giving children more holistic perceptions (61).

Horner and Ryf (2007) believe that the use of illustrations can teach children the importance of subtext, ie characters might not mean what they say they mean, and the reader is therefore a critical part of the story. They suggest that *the real meaning is often hidden in the illustrations as it is here that the depth of meaning can be explored beyond the sometimes brief written text evident in books for younger children* (30). Thus children may not have sufficient opportunities to respond to a text in great depth if their phonic knowledge is at the emergent level.

Conclusion

This chapter has explored ways in which children's writing could be developed by increasing their engagement in reading and interpreting texts. A common theme in all three case studies is the importance of dialogue, both in the telling and retelling of known texts, and its value in the development of new ones. Oral preparation equips children with the skills required to write effectively. Active reading engages children at risk of being turned off reading in an age when increasingly rich stimuli are competing for their attention. Similarly, wordless books offer rich and enjoyable literary experiences for children of all abilities. Their active participation in reading and the construction of meaning empowers them to write and consider themselves authors.

The *National Curriculum in England* (2013:14) presents a similar view: *Pupils should develop a capacity to explain their understanding of books and other reading, and to prepare their ideas before they write*, thereby acknowledging that 'talk' has a vital role to play in the development of key literacy skills.

Critical points

» *Children can be successfully engaged in reading by exploring texts actively.*

» *Increased engagement in reading is likely to result in greater and lasting enjoyment.*

» *Active reading and plenty of 'talk' about texts can be harnessed to improve writing skills at text, sentence and word level.*

Critical reflections

» *How could you use a text to teach children to write? How could the pupils be actively engaged so that they become familiar with the text structure and language patterns? How could pictures and text maps be used to stimulate useful talk which broadens children's understanding of the text?*

Taking it further

Gamble, N. and Yates, S. (2006) *Exploring Children's Literature: Teaching the Language and Reading of Fiction*, London: Paul Chapman.

This explores a number of different story structures, considers language and the impact it has on a reader and also categorises different types of fantasy stories. It might help you develop some additional ideas about how to adapt the ideas presented in the case studies.

Graham, J. (1998) Turning the visual into the Verbal: Children Reading Wordless Books, in Evans, J. (ed) *What's in the Picture: Responding to Illustrations in Picture Books*. London: Paul Chapman Publishing Ltd.

Jolliffe, W. (2008) *Co-operative Learning in the Classroom: Putting it into Practice*. London: SAGE Publications Ltd.

Jolliffe emphasises the importance of talk in the classroom, explores different approaches to co-operative learning and suggests how such an environment can be created within a classroom.

Waugh, D., Neaum, S. and Waugh, R. (2013) *Children's Literature in Primary Schools*. London: Sage.

Chapter 5 on picture books explores different ways of looking at picture books and the importance of visual imagery to children's meaning-making.

References

Andrews, R. (2001) *Teaching and Learning English*. London: Continuum.

Brien, J. (2012) *Teaching Primary English*. London: Sage.

Carter, D. (2000) *Teaching Fiction in the Primary School*. London: David Fulton.

Corbett, P. (2007) *The Bumper Book of Storytelling into Writing: Key Stage 2*. Melksham: Clown Publishing.

Corbett, P. (2008a) *Good Writers: The National Strategies – Primary*.

Corbett, P. (2008b) *Writer-Talk: The National Strategies – Primary*.

Corbett, P. and Strong, J. (2011) *Talk for Writing Across the Curriculum*. Maidenhead: McGraw Hill, Open University Press.

Crawford, A., Saul, W., Mathews, S. and Makinster, J. (2005) *Teaching and Learning Strategies for the Thinking Classroom*. New York: International Debate Education Association.

Cremin, T. (2011) Motivating Children to Write with Purpose and Passion, in Goodwin, P. (ed) *The Literate Classroom*. London: David Fulton.

DCSF (2008) *Talk for Writing*. Nottingham: DCSF Publications.

DfE (2012) *What Is The Research Evidence On Writing?* Education Standards Research Team, Department for Education.

The National Curriculum for England (2013) *The National Curriculum in England: Framework Document For Collaboration*. London: Department for Education: Qualifications and Curriculum Authority. https://media.education.gov.uk/assets/files/pdf/n/national%20curriculum%20consultation%20-%20framework%20document.pdf (accessed 8 April, 2013).

Graham, J. (1998) Turning the Visual into the Verbal: Children Reading Wordless Books, in Evans, J. (ed.) *What's in the Picture: Responding to Illustrations in Picture Books*. London: Paul Chapman Publishing Ltd.

Goodwin, P. (ed) (2011) *The Literate Classroom*. London: David Fulton.

Hofkins, D. and Northen, S. (2009) *Introducing the Cambridge Primary Review*, the Cambridge Primary Review, University of Cambridge Faculty of Education: Cambridge.

www.primaryreview.org.uk/Downloads/Finalreport/CPR-booklet_low-res.pdf (accessed 8 April, 2013).

Horner, C. and Ryf, V. (2007) *Creative Teaching: English in the Early Years and Primary Classroom*. London and New York: Routledge.

Jump, S. (2013) Show Not Tell: What the Heck Is That Anyway? *Foremost Press*. www.foremostpress.com/authors/articles/show_not_tell.html (accessed 6 March, 2013).

Krant, A. (1991) Talk and Peer Conferencing in the Writing Process, in Booth, D. and Thornley-Hall, C. (eds) *Classroom Talk*. Portsmouth, NH: Pembroke.

Jalongo, M.R. (1988) *Young Children and Picture Books, Literature from Infancy to Six*. USA: National Education for the Education of Young Children.

Jolliffe, W. (2008) *Co-operative Learning in the Classroom: Putting it into Practice*. London: SAGE Publications Ltd.

Lewis, M. (2001) From Reading to Writing: Using Picture Books as Models, in Evans, J. (ed) *The Writing Classroom: Aspects of Writing and the Primary Child 3–11*. Trowbridge, Wiltshire: The Cromwell Press.

Lewis, M. (2011) Developing Children's Narrative Writing Using Story Structures, in Goodwin, P. (ed) *The Literate Classroom* (3rd edn). London: David Fulton.

Mandel-Morrow, L. (1989) *Literacy Development in the Early Years: Helping Children Read And Write*. Englewood Cliffs, NJ: Prentice-Hall.

Marriott, S. (1991) *Picture Books in the Primary Classroom*. London: Paul Chapman Publishing Ltd.

Merisuo-Storm, T. (2006) Girls and Boys Like to Read and Write Different Texts. *Scandinavian Journal of Educational Research*, 50:2.

Millard, E. (2001) Aspects of Gender, in Evans, J. (ed) *The Writing Classroom: Aspects of Writing and the Primary Child 3–11*. Trowbridge, Wiltshire: The Cromwell Press.

Reed, M. (2005) Strong Language: The Purpose of Dialogue in the Development of Writing. *Changing English*, 12:1.

Rosen, H. (1988) The Irrepressible Genre, in Maclure, M., Phillips, T. and Wilkinson, A. (eds) *Oracy Matters*. Milton Keynes: Open University Press,.

9 Premier League reading

DANIEL HARRISON

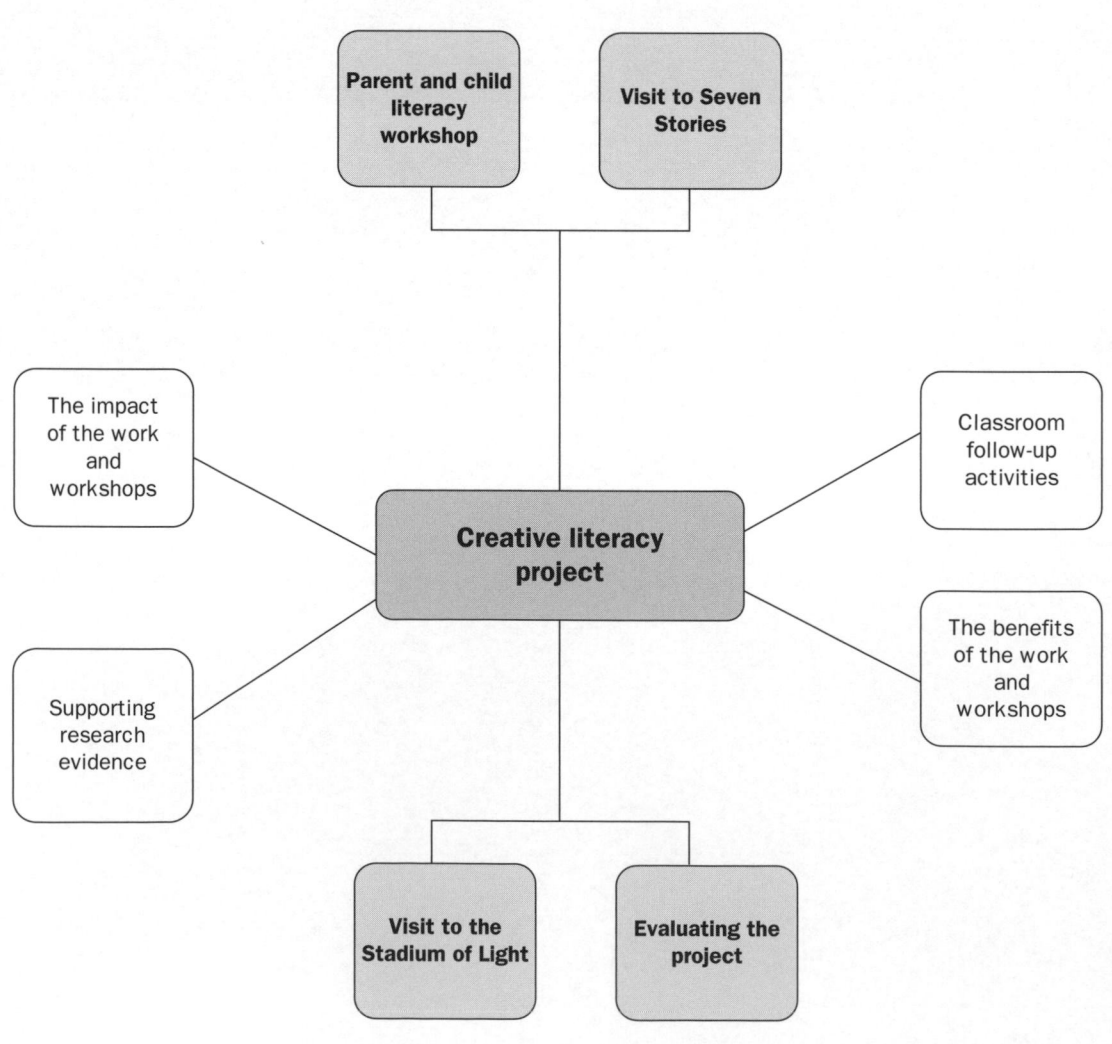

Teachers' standards

3 Demonstrate good subject and curriculum knowledge

- have a secure knowledge of the relevant subject(s) and curriculum areas, foster and maintain pupils' interest in the subject, and address misunderstandings
- demonstrate a critical understanding of developments in the subject and curriculum areas, and promote the value of scholarship

4 Plan and teach well-structured lessons

- contribute to the design and provision of an engaging curriculum within the relevant subject area(s)

Critical questions

» *How can schools develop projects beyond the classroom to develop children's interest and engagement with books and reading?*

» *How can these be followed up in the classroom?*

» *How can parents be encouraged to become involved in, and enthusiastic about reading with their children?*

» *What is the impact of this type of work on children's learning and, importantly, their enthusiasm for learning?*

» *What are children's, teachers' and parents' views on this approach to teaching and learning?*

Introduction

This chapter outlines a school's project to engage their children and parents in reading and writing. The school identified a need to work innovatively to encourage enthusiasm and enjoyment of reading. To achieve this, they planned a series of visits and workshops for the children and their parents. The project aimed to engage children's interest and delight in books, reading and writing, and in doing so raise their attainment. Both during and at the end of the school year, the school evaluated the project through interviews with parents and carers, teachers and pupils. After reading the chapter, you may wish to consider how you could make use of similar initiatives to engage both children and parents/carers with reading.

Background

At the beginning of the 2012 school year, the school embarked upon a 'Creative Literacy' project that aimed to boost the standards of reading and writing within the Year 3 cohort. Data showed that children consistently entered the school in Reception with levels of language and literacy below the national averages. This was despite parents being generally very supportive, and the school falling within the average band in the deprivation index (a way of using a series of measurable aspects of people's lives to identify the most and least deprived areas of England, and to compare whether one area is more deprived than another)

(Department for Communities and Local Government, 2011). Furthermore, the Year 3 cohort had only 5 per cent of children who were in line with national averages in writing when they were in Reception. The children made good progress and by the time that they had exited KS1, 77 per cent were at the national average in reading and 32 per cent in writing. However, staff were determined to narrow the gap further. Additionally, it had also been noted that attainment for boys in this cohort was significantly lower than for girls.

With all of this in mind, staff aimed to create a year-long Creative Literacy project that would involve parents and children working together, and also would involve working with several outside agencies. In light of the analysis of attainment in the cohort, careful regard was given within the project to providing *boy-friendly* activities and texts.

The project's initiatives focused on a number of the factors that have been shown to influence children's literacy development (see Figure 9.1). Initially, the staff met with Seven Stories, the National Centre for Children's Books, based in Newcastle upon Tyne (see Chapter 7). They agreed upon making some visits to the centre and, in line with projects that were being run there, to base much of the learning on Cressida Cresswell's *How to Train Your Dragon* text. A bonus from this was that it would be possible to work with the author when she visited the area. The visits to Seven Stories were planned as family events, aiming to raise awareness of the power of reading using Seven Stories as a resource. In addition, a visit to the

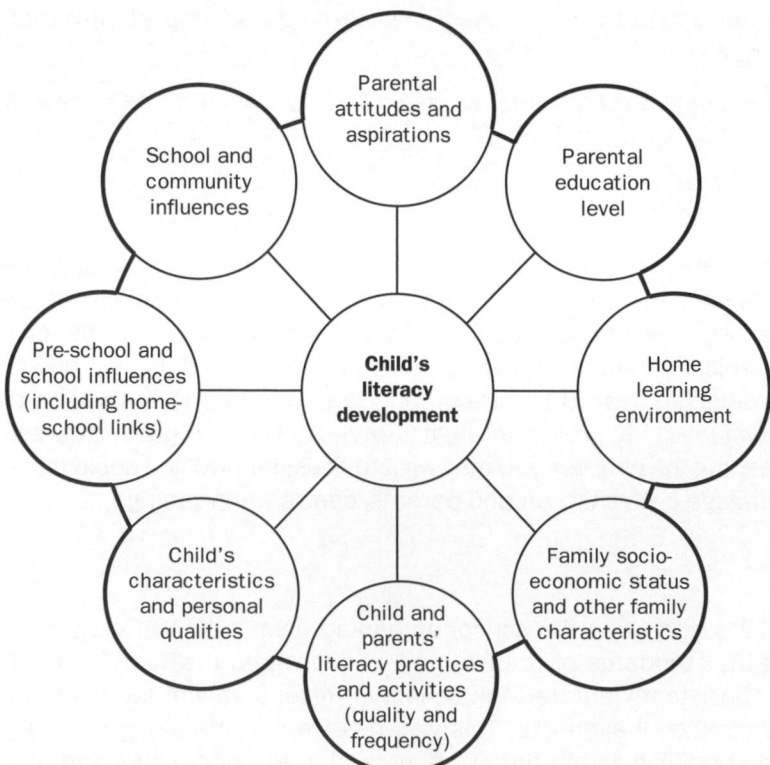

Figure 9.1 Some of the key factors influencing children's literacy development. Diagram from *Bonci et al.*, (2011).

Stadium of Light, Sunderland AFC's football ground, was arranged to work with their learning team – hence the title of the chapter! Finally, the children would also benefit from working with a storyteller and would take part in a celebration event at Spennymoor Town Hall at the end of the year.

FOCUS ON RESEARCH

Why involve parents?

The Creative Literacy project planned to involve parents in all aspects of the project and to elicit their views on the impact of the visits and workshops on their child and family's engagement with books and reading. This approach, of involving parents, has been shown to make a difference to children's learning and literature relating to early literary experience in the home tends to view the practice as wholly positive. *The Impact of Parental Involvement in Children's Education* (DCSF, 2008) states that:

Overall, research has consistently shown that parental involvement in children's education does make a positive difference to pupils' achievement.

Also that

Parental involvement in children's education from an early age has a significant effect on educational achievement, and continues to do so into adolescence and adulthood. (1)

Desforges and Abouchaar (2003) similarly conclude that parental involvement has a significant effect on children's achievement and adjustment even after all other factors, such as social class, maternal education and poverty, have been taken out of the equation. Additionally, they argue that *differences in parental involvement have a much bigger impact on achievement than differences associated with the effects of school in the primary age range* (Desforges and Abouchaar, 2003, 86).

First stages

The following case study documents the first stage of the project, a visit to Seven Stories, The National Centre for Children's Books, and the ways in which this was followed up in school-based activities.

CASE STUDY

Seven Stories family visit

The project began with 28 children in Class 5 (Y2/3) making a visit to Seven Stories. Sixteen of the children were accompanied by an adult, most of whom were parents, with one or two aunts, uncles and grandparents. The bus made two stops on the way – one at *The Angel of the North* (an iconic, contemporary steel sculpture of an angel, 20 metres tall with wings measuring 54 metres across created by Antony Gormley in 1998), and the other at the Newcastle–Gateshead Quayside (a square mile of iconic buildings, such as The Sage, landmark bridges, such as the Millennium Bridge, and a range of galleries and exhibitions). The intention in these visits was to stimulate opportunities for talk, including the use of descriptive vocabulary. Once at Seven Stories, the children engaged in workshop activities, focused in particular upon the Julia Donaldson gallery, and set the scene for the *Cressida Cresswell* work that was to follow. The class teacher commented:

All of the children thoroughly enjoyed the trip to Seven Stories and Newcastle. They worked closely with an adult: the largest group was three children to one adult and many were one to one. All wanted to revisit Seven Stories, and to do more work with their parents' involvement.

Indeed, when interviewed, every child confirmed that they had enjoyed the visit, with one child stating:

I like reading more now and I really want to go back to Seven Stories.

Classroom follow-up

Following the visit, each Wednesday afternoon the children engaged in work linked to the project. Perhaps most significantly, the children enjoyed *How to Train Your Dragon* as a whole-class reading book. The teacher told of how the whole text focus had led to lots of speaking and listening activities and role play. In addition:

> *Writing tasks have included: recounts, character descriptions – both warrior and dragon with lots of description, the use of adjectives, similes and alliteration. There was also artwork around the text, sketches of* The Angel of the North *and labelling of the artwork.*

The impact of the work with Seven Stories

Reading the text and the associated activities certainly engaged the children; responses showed that an impressive 95 per cent thoroughly enjoyed the text and follow up. Several boys indicated that they enjoyed the involvement of dragons and adventure, and three children specifically used the word *exciting* in their responses. This excitement was borne out in responses from parents. For example, one parent commented:

> *Seven Stories was brilliant. It was so visual and that is just what boys need, it makes it easier to understand. He loved it and since going there I feel that it has opened his eyes … with it being visual at Seven Stories, he will now draw a character at home and then write about it.*

All but one of the girls also offered enthusiastic responses, noting the presence of *characters* and *adventures*. Eight children identified the fact that the book contains alliteration as a positive factor. One parent told of how the visit to *The Angel of the North* and sketches had reignited his interest in drawing, and when the school hosted an Art Gallery at Spennymoor Town Hall, he presented the class teacher with an impressive, framed pencil sketch of the Angel.

However, despite this reported enjoyment of the visit, interviews with the children indicated that only 75 per cent of them expressed an enthusiasm for reading. One boy said, *It is boring*, another stated that he did not enjoy reading, *Because I get bored*, and a third boy commented that, *All you do is read, read and read*.

In addition to the children's responses, another telling fact emerged during the reflections on the visit: only 30 per cent of the class reported that an adult read to them at home. Five of the children claimed that they used to have a story read to them *When I was little*. It was also found that there was a direct correlation between those children who disliked reading, and those who received no story reading at home.

On the other hand, the teacher told of how *boys have been more engaged and focused*, and that two children had bought the entire series of *How to Train Your Dragon* books and brought them into school.

In terms of academic statistics, there was evidence at this stage of the project that many of the children were beginning to make progress with their reading. Fifty per cent of the children improved their reading level in the following term and, while this offered some encouragement, more significant progress was hoped for in the next term. The impact on the children's writing was, however, much more tangible. An impressive 95 per cent of the children thought the project and work around the text had helped them to improve their writing. Many said that the book had given them *better ideas for writing,* whilst greater awareness of *alliteration, similes, adjectives* and *powerful words* were mentioned by the children. Furthermore, the class teacher described how:

> one boy directly used vocabulary that he thought up with his Dad, on the visit, in his writing assessment at the end of term [this was 'an iconic landmark'].

Indeed, it was satisfying to note that 84 per cent of the class had improved their writing level in just one term. Given the fact that writing has been a major issue with the cohort throughout their time in school, this progress effectively rendered the initial phase of the project a significant success.

At the end of this initial stage, staff reflected upon the project and noted that, although there were clear signs of success, some changes to the project were needed. It was agreed that more reading response activities would be included in the Wednesday afternoon sessions, and further copies of the book would be purchased so that more children could follow the text. The rationale behind this was to help the children see the link between this work, which they perceived as fun, and reading. Furthermore, staff decided to try and tackle the home storytelling issue. This was to be done by inviting parents into school for story time, providing them with texts to read at home, and sharing findings and experiences as a group. The case study below details how the school planned to improve parental engagement through workshops and storytelling.

CASE STUDY

Improving parental engagement through storytelling and literacy workshops

As the work on *How to Train your Dragon* continued in school with very good effect, a key strategy in stage two of the project was to improve parental engagement through storytelling at a reading club, and at a parent and child literacy workshop. These initiatives were intended to help build partnerships between the school and families, which would aid the children's learning by highlighting to parents the value of reading and writing, and establishing that literacy can be engaging and enjoyable.

Parents were invited into school for a series of six sessions in which the children and parents shared texts from Seven Stories' *Hooks into Books* book recommendations (see Chapter 7), and others. On each occasion, the class teacher read *How to Train Your Dragon* to the children in the presence of the adults, thus modelling this most important art. Attendance at these sessions was very impressive: 77 per cent of the children had an adult who attended at least one of the sessions. Week 6 was the culmination and the teacher and the children dressed in pyjamas for the session, while enjoying hot chocolate with the adults, mimicking a cosy, bedtime read.

Alongside the reading club, a parent literacy workshop was held. Here, parents were shown how aspects of writing are taught in a 'live lesson'. Particular focus and attention was placed upon grammar and punctuation, in light of the introduction of the DfE spelling, punctuation and grammar (SPAG) test (DfE, 2013). These workshops were held across KS2; however, uptake and attendance by the Year 2/3 parents was much more significant than in other classes. Typically, attendance was between 30 per cent and 40 per cent across the Key Stage, but over 70 per cent of the Year 2/3 parents attended. This was an indication that the engagement strategies in stage one of the project had been successful. This was underlined by parental responses. One parent commented:

I enjoyed coming in to the story time when the teacher read the story and we got the chance to read 1:1 to our children. It gave me that special time with him and just him. With having his sister as well that isn't always easy at home.

The impact of the parental engagement work

Ultimately, such engagement would be pointless unless there was some tangible benefit to the children. Pupil responses were very favourable. The enjoyment of reading improved marginally from 75 per cent to 77 per cent, while 100 per cent of the children said that they had enjoyed *How to Train Your Dragon*. Interestingly, when asked about how they had benefited from reading the text, all of the children noted benefits in their writing rather than in reading. Responses included:

*   *I am better at describing now;*
*   *helps with connectives;*
*   *I like the adjectives;*
*   *I can use alliteration.*

Furthermore, 100 per cent of the children indicated that they felt that the activities had helped them to improve as writers. Assessments showed that 86 per cent of the children actually made at least one sub-level of progress in writing within the six weeks of the parental sessions. This meant that the class remained on target to make good progress in writing over the year and, given the low baseline in writing, this was clearly positive news.

There were also definite benefits for the children's reading. Following the parental work-shops, 54 per cent of children indicated that someone read to them at home. This was a huge increase of 24 per cent on the previous figures. An impressive 92 per cent of pupils indicated that they had enjoyed the reading club. One boy commented, *I just loved it*, while another reported that, *I liked spending time reading with my mam.* Importantly, 54 per cent of the children claimed that they now read more at home with a parent as a result of the reading club. The expectation was that the academic results of such improved engagement would be longer term, however, and 71 per cent of those who indicated that they now read more at home with an adult made at least one sub-level of progress within six weeks. Another positive spin-off from the reading club was that 31 per cent of the children said they had started to attend the library more often.

FOCUS ON RESEARCH

The benefits of parental involvement

The positive role that parents play in supporting and encouraging children's engagement with books and stories is well documented. Therefore, encouraging parents to become involved and interested in reading with their children is likely to benefit children's engagement and therefore their learning and development. For example, Colker (2007) observes that, of all the academic subjects, research shows reading is most sensitive to family involvement. She goes on to state that, reading achievement is felt to be more dependent on learning activities in the home than either maths or science.

Gest, Freeman, Domitrivich and Welsh (in Bonci *et al.*, 2011, 3) note the benefits of parental involvement: parental involvement with reading activities at home has significant positive influences on reading achievement, language comprehension and expressive language skills.

Rowe (in Bonci *et al.,* 2011) argues that parental involvement is significant because it affects pupils' levels of interest, their attitudes to reading and can create positive behaviours in the classroom such as attentiveness. This is supported by Clark and Foster (2005) in the National Literacy Trust report on children's reading habits and preferences, in which they report that children who were enthusiastic about reading said they were *encouraged to read a lot by their mother and father* (Clark and Foster, 2005, 4).

The benefits of parental school involvement in literacy are also described by Hill and Taylor (2004). They use the terms *social capital* (parental school involvement increases parents' skills) and *social control* (families and schools work together to provide a consensus of ideas) to describe the impact on children and families. They also note that parental involvement promotes achievement of children, citing Baker and Stevenson's (1996) study, which con-cluded *compared with parents who were not involved, parents who were involved developed more complex strategies for working with schools and their children to promote achievement* (Hill and Taylor, 2004, 62).

Final stage: Premier League reading

The final stage of the project was a visit was made to the 47,000-seat Stadium of Light, the home of Sunderland AFC. The aim of this was two-fold: to maintain the momentum created by earlier aspects of the project, and to actively engage the boys.

CASE STUDY

Visit to the Stadium of Light

This visit was intended to provide further creative stimulus and opportunities for reading and writing. Chiefly, the intention was to get the children to develop their skills of empathy and description. Before the visit, the children were presented with a series of accounts by players describing the atmosphere at the Stadium of Light and at other atmospheric stadia such as Celtic Park.

First, the children were provided with cameras and were given the opportunity to access many different parts of the stadium, from the dressing rooms to the coaches' dugouts, the executive boxes to pitch side, and from the stands to the tunnel from which the teams emerge before matches. At each juncture, the children were given the opportunity to note appropriate adjectives and similes. Following a session of reading poems in a stadium classroom, the children then used their adjectives and similes to write a poem.

Second, the children were lined up in the tunnel, while Prokofiev's evocative *Dance of the Knights* (the music played when Sunderland enter the playing area) was blasted over the stadium tannoy system. The children were asked to imagine that they were about to run out into the arena in front of 47,000 roaring fans. Crucially, they were asked to be aware of what they were thinking, feeling and doing at this point, to get them to think empathetically about the experience. Both the poem and the tunnel work would be followed up back in the classroom, along with further writing activities. There was no doubt that the visit generated enthusiasm, with every one of the children saying that they had enjoyed it.

Classroom follow-up

The follow-up was immediate. The visit was used to stimulate a range of different writing activities, encompassing both fiction and non-fiction texts. In the first instance, the children recapped their learning and produced effective recounts. They were keen to talk about the visit and the teacher used this as a starting point for discussions. In addition, the children used notes that they had taken on the visit to create a Stadium of Light fact file. The children also produced five-line poems using the bank of descriptive vocabulary generated during the visit as the children made their way round the stadium, particularly in the tunnel area. Suitable similes were also identified. The teacher noted that many of the children continued to use the similes long after the visit.

Impact of the visit and activities

Every one of the children felt that this part of the project had helped them with their writing. Six children stated that this part of the project had been their favourite part; two of these pupils were female and four male. When asked how it had helped, *writing poems* was the most common response, and *including similes, using adverbs,* and, *putting commas in* were also mentioned. One boy commented that *I use better sentence openers,* whilst a girl stated that *the teacher knows that my writing is now better because I have been using VCOP* (Vocabulary, Connectives, Openers, Punctuation).

The class teacher noted that the children were now more confident in committing their pencils to the page, and that their vocabulary was increasingly adventurous. Furthermore, the majority of children evidently found it easier to complete follow-up activities, as their writing was based upon a concrete and exciting experience. Academic progress was also extremely pleasing following the visit. Over the period of ten weeks from the visit, 89 per cent of the children made progress in their writing, while 86 per cent made progress in reading over the same period.

Evaluating the project

As the academic year was drawing to a close by this point, the impact of the project was assessed. Certainly, there was evidence of a broad impact. Seventy-five per cent of the children claimed that they now read more at home, while 50 per cent said that they now read more with an adult. Given the profile of the children's experiences at the beginning of the project, this represented a major success. Ten children in the class also reported that they now bought more books. Tellingly, 89 per cent felt that they had improved in both reading and writing. Over two full terms, every single child made progress in these areas. One girl noted that *I am better at writing because I use more connectives such as although,* while another highlighted her use of *adjectives, similes and openers.*

Next steps

Beyond the time frame of the immediate project, several activities were planned to maintain the momentum of the project and children's interest and engagement with books, reading and writing, It was arranged that a storyteller would visit the school to work with the children on the theme of journeys, within a myths and legends theme. Eventually, the aim is to bring all aspects of the project together in an exhibition, in which the children will present their work from across the project to parents.

Conclusion

The project outlined in this chapter demonstrates how using different stimuli can encourage children's engagement and enjoyment of language, books and reading, and in doing so, have an impact on their reading and writing. The visits to iconic landmarks, Seven Stories, *The Angel of the North* and the football stadium all offered the children memorable experiences on which they could draw to support their learning in the classroom. Additionally, the work with the families meant that the children's growing pleasure in books and reading was continued at home.

Critical points

» *Providing exciting and memorable experiences for children has benefits for their engagement and interest in learning.*

» *These experiences can be harnessed to promote reading as an enjoyable and worthwhile activity, at school and at home.*

» *Research evidence points to the importance of involving parents in these activities, to encourage shared enthusiasm for books and learning.*

Critical reflections

» *What are the things that engage and interest the children in your class?*

» *How could these be included in your planning for children's learning?*

» *How could you use these as starting points to provide memorable experiences for the children?*

» *How could you use these experiences to develop their interest in language, and their enthusiasm for books?*

» *How could you involve parents and families in this?*

Note

Most professional football clubs are engaged with 'Football in the Community' projects and welcome visits from schools. Many have designated classrooms and some have homework clubs. It is worth contacting your nearest club if you wish to set up a project similar to the one described in this chapter.

References

Bonci, A., Mottram, E., McCoy, E. and Cole, J. (2011) *A Research Review: The Importance of Families and the Home Environment (Revised 2011)*. London: The National Literacy Trust.

Clark, C. and Foster, A. (2005) *Children's and Young People's Reading Habits and Preferences: The Who, What, Why, Where and When*. Nottingham: The National Literacy Trust.

Colker, L.J. (2007) Family Involvement: A Key Ingredient in Children's Reading Success. Available at: www.education.com/reference/article/Ref_Family_Involvement/ (accessed 31 January, 2013).

Department for Communities and Local Government (2011) *English Indices of Deprivation 2010*. Available at: www.gov.uk/government/uploads/system/uploads/attachment_data/file/6222/1871538.pdf (accessed 20 June, 2013).

DCFS (2008) *The Impact of Parental Involvement in Children's Education*. Nottingham: DCSF Publications.

DfE (2013) 2013 Key Stage 2 Tests: English Grammar, Punctuation and Spelling Test. Available at: www.education.gov.uk/schools/teachingandlearning/assessment/keystage2/b00208296/ks2–2013/english-tests/grammar-punctuation-spelling-test (accessed 17 June, 2013).

Hill, N.E. and Taylor, L.C. (2004) Parental School Involvement and Children's Academic Achievement: Pragmatics and Issues. *Current Directions in Psychological Science*, 13:4, 161–4.

Rose, J. (2006) *Independent Review of the Teaching of Early Reading*. Nottingham: DfES Publications.

10 A perfect storm: literacy in alternative provision

CRAIG SMALL

Teachers' standards

3 Demonstrate good subject and curriculum knowledge

- have a secure knowledge of the relevant subject(s) and curriculum areas, foster and maintain pupils' interest in the subject

- demonstrate an understanding of and take responsibility for promoting high standards of literacy and articulacy

5 Adapt teaching to respond to the strengths and needs of all pupils

- know when and how to differentiate appropriately, using approaches which enable pupils to be taught effectively

- have a secure understanding of how a range of factors can inhibit pupils' ability to learn, and how best to overcome these

- demonstrate an awareness of the physical, social and intellectual development of children, and know how to adapt teaching to support pupils' education at different stages of development

- have a clear understanding of the needs of all pupils, including those with special educational needs; those of high ability; those with English as an additional language; those with disabilities; and be able to use and evaluate distinctive teaching approaches to engage and support them

Critical questions

» *How do we engage disengaged children in reading?*

» *How do we tune into these children's interests and use this in our teaching?*

» *How can we enable them to see the value and pleasure in reading?*

» *How can we make assessments of vulnerable children's learning that emphasises their abilities and progression, rather than using levels and labels?*

» *How can we include reference to their engagement in reading in the assessment process?*

Introduction

On 1 September 2011, the Secretary of State for Education, Michael Gove, made a speech at Durand Academy about the 'educational underclass'. He was referring to pupils outside mainstream education who fail to achieve academically and grow up without skills to become successful adults and members of society: he was referring to the experience of children in *alternative provision* (Taylor, 2012).

For the most part, alternative provision is provided to meet the needs of children with behavioural and emotional difficulties, whose needs are not met by mainstream education, and, although it is difficult to estimate the levels of children in alternative provision who have special educational needs (SEN), we do know that the figure is higher than in mainstream schools.

For example, 79 per cent of those attending Pupil Referral Units (one type of provision for children not in mainstream school) have a special educational need (Taylor, 2012). Often these needs manifest as a behavioural difficulty, but the behaviour frequently masks other issues.

Charlie Taylor, the government's Expert Adviser on Behaviour, conducted a review of alternative provision to provide recommendations for improving the outcomes for these vulnerable children. His review outlined how only 1.4 per cent of children in alternative provision achieve five or more GCSEs at grades A*–C, including English and Maths, compared to 53.4 per cent of their peers.

So what is going wrong? As well as the individual differences, and often complex home and family dynamics that these children bring to the learning situation, there is an interaction between the curriculum offered in schools, and the potential this has for sustained engagement and learning. Many children have had negative experiences of school prior to their placement in alternative provision. This means that engaging and maintaining their interest in learning, in particular the more formal skills of reading and writing, is challenging. This presents a particular issue, because, as Gallagher (2009) observes in his book *Readicide*, struggling readers who do not read voraciously will never catch up.

An additional challenge within alternative provision exists: gender. In the 2011 census, 73 per cent of children in alternative provision were boys (16045 boys, versus 6065 girls), and with this comes a secondary, although significant, issue boys' engagement with reading. Boys' underachievement in reading is a concern for schools across the country. In a National Literacy Trust survey (2012), 76 per cent of UK schools said boys in their school did not do as well in reading as girls, and whilst 82 per cent of schools surveyed had developed their own strategies to tackle this issue, it remains deep-seated, and test results consistently show that this is a long-term and international trend (National Literacy Trust, 2012). The findings of the Boys' Reading Commission (National Literacy Trust, 2012) articulate some of the reasons for the trend in boys' relatively poor engagement with reading. They found that boys' underachievement in reading is associated with the interplay of three factors:

1   the home and family environment, where girls are more likely to be bought books and taken to the library, and where mothers are more likely to support and role-model reading;

2   the school environment, where teachers may have a limited knowledge of contemporary and attractive texts for boys, and where boys may not be given the opportunity to develop their identity as a reader through experiencing reading for enjoyment;

3   male gender identities that do not value learning and reading as a mark of success.

Thus, for many of the children in alternative provision, boys in particular, there is an interplay of factors that contribute to their profiles as disengaged learners. In terms of their literacy, complex learning, social and familial factors often result in these children embodying all the negative trends in reading; and it is this conflation of factors that feels like *a perfect storm*.

Re-thinking engagement and approaches to learning (REAL)

REAL Education is an alternative education provider based in the East Midlands. It was started by a group of teachers who, after many years of experience in providing tailor-made solutions for children with additional needs, decided the best way to use their skills, energy and expertise was to offer education provision themselves.

Since 2008, REAL Education has worked with children excluded from school, and those whose placements have broken down in mainstream or specialist provision, such as special schools and Pupil Referral Units. So, these children arrive in the provision with significant school failure behind them, and often are completely disengaged from every aspect of learning. So, once children are in the provision, the first, and continuing emphasis, is on engagement, as without this, little can be achieved.

In terms of reading and literacy, the profile of the children, who are mainly boys, is often one of incomplete progression through the early stages of literacy, and as a result of this, they have low levels of engagement in reading and uses of literacy in their day-to-day life. In short, literacy is a major risk factor in the life chances for these children. The difficult experiences the children have had before reaching REAL means they often lack both the motivation and the skills to read. The gap between how they engage with reading and literacy, and how they need to engage with reading and literacy to participate in modern society, is often wide. The job to be done is a simple, although challenging one: bridge this gap.

The REAL literacy project

With this in mind, a development project was initiated. The aim was to develop a suitable framework for approaching this complex situation and meeting these children's complex needs.

The aims of the project were:

- to work from an evidence base;

- to develop a framework with the minimal elegance required for it to be delivered in the complex context that is alternative provision;

- to develop tools and approaches that could be used by a team working around a child;

- to embed assessment in the framework, but not become unduly focused on assessment over action.

The assessment aspect of the project was important. Many of the children who are in alternative provision have had difficult previous experiences of being assessed and labelled, and the aim was not to repeat this type of failure. The project therefore began with a commitment to a strengths-based approach, in which the aim was not to label the children, but rather to use assessment to inform what should happen next, to indicate what works and to identify resources that could make a difference.

The project also began with the end in mind. Rather than looking for the deficits that might explain the children's difficulties, literature was reviewed on what works in adult literacy programmes. It quickly became evident that traditional classroom-based teaching was unlikely to reap benefits. It was evident that for children whose experience of school had been broadly negative, a new experience was needed.

The foundation stone: authentic literacy

There is no single solution for turning underachieving and unmotivated children into readers and writers; a sustained approach is required. In this context, the aim for developing children's engagement with learning, and their literacy, uses texts for reading and writing drawn from the children's lives beyond school. The term used for this is *authentic*. The framework is based on the belief that using real life texts for real life purposes provides these children with an education that is meaningful and responsive to their needs. An authentic approach is one that is:

- led by the child's interests;

- builds on competencies of the child and family;

- encourages habits of literacy;

- engages with a range of text formats including new media.

This view contrasts with the reality of many classrooms, where texts often contain little material that is relevant to these children's lives beyond school, and is thus decontextualised. For children in alternative provision, this decontextualisation is often a powerful barrier to learning. For them, the classroom has often become an alien environment; one where they have experienced significant failure. In developing the framework, the assumption was made that reliance on texts from this environment was likely both to reinforce failure, and elicit the very behaviours that led the child to be in alternative provision; indeed, as the saying goes, *if you keep on doing what you've always done, you'll keep on getting what you've always got* (Bateman, ND). So, the framework was to be underpinned by a commitment to relevance, enjoyment and engagement. Given the gender balance in the group (majority boys), it was anticipated that this model would provide a supportive social context to re-engage boys in reading, and counteract the possible negative trigger of decontextualized learning.

FOCUS ON RESEARCH

The impact of using authentic texts in teaching and learning

Several research studies have documented a real relationship between the frequency of engagement in authentic reading and writing, and achievement in reading and writing. In the USA, the TEXT study (Duke *et al.*, 2006) involved 26 second- and third-grade teachers and their children. The teachers made authentic reading and writing an integral part of their science instruction. In the case of the TEXT study, this translated into reading and writing real-life science information texts such as books on snakes, the weather, or force and motion. Real-life science texts also included brochures that one could find at a science museum, procedures for scientific experiments and bookmarks that included scientific facts.

The children were assessed three times a year, for two years, on reading comprehension of these types of science texts, and on their ability to write/compose such science texts.

At the end of the two years of the study, the children who had read and written more real-life texts for real-life purposes scored higher on these assessments that those who had not. Additionally, it was found that for each increase in the frequency of authentic literacy in these classrooms, there was a corresponding increase in literacy achievement.

Purcell-Gates *et al.*, (2002) found similar positive impacts. In their nationwide US study of adult learners, they found that adults in programmes using authentic literacy activities reported:

* reading and writing more often in their daily lives;

* reading and writing more complex texts.

They also found that the longer the students engaged in these programmes, the more this was true.

Activity 1

» *The research studies above found significant benefits for using authentic texts to support children's learning.*

– *Why do you think that the use of authentic texts is beneficial to children's learning?*

– *How does this link to what you know about how children learn?*

– *How could you incorporate authentic texts into your teaching? Consider all curriculum areas.*

Combining an authentic approach with structured reading interventions

Trying something different, something authentic, with the children required some simple tools and resources that staff could use in their day-to-day work. The aim was to encourage the use of structured reading interventions, whilst working within an authentic literacy framework. Additionally, the aim was to audit what worked well, and organise resources and expertise so that staff could use the framework effectively. It was important that in combining these approaches, the structured teaching of reading was embedded within an authentic approach, to ensure that the fundamental aim of engagement and enjoyment of reading remained central to the framework.

In initial discussions, it quickly became evident that the primary issue was not which literacy intervention programme reaped the greatest benefits, but how to engage the children in authentic literacy experiences; that would be the context to address difficulties with reading. Time and again feedback from experienced teachers highlighted the core issues of engagement and motivation; that if the child could become interested in reading, the interventions could deliver on the promise of greater skills in decoding and encoding words. Thus, it was agreed that the framework would have a small number of highly-structured, systematic programmes that would constitute an organised and planned response to support children's phonics skills. The structured programmes would support children's literacy skills, while an authentic literacy approach would provide reasons for engaging with text. The aim was to support the children in developing reasons for reading more texts and so improve their reading and, by getting better at reading, improve their life chances.

A particular programme, *Toe-by-Toe* (Cowling, 2009), was favoured by many experienced teachers. It is a highly systematic intervention that has a page-by-page and step-by-step series of activities in one book, delivered one-to-one, and with instructions provided for each activity. The programme deliberately takes learners right back to the beginning of phonics, and works from there. This approach is based on the observation that many learners with difficulties don't have a good grasp of phonics. The programme has proven to be effective in many schools, in prisons and Young Offender Institutions, and with young people being supervised in the community. This may, initially, seem at odds with an authentic literacy approach, in that it is highly-structured, however, the challenge was to combine such a structured approach, which is necessary to literacy learning, with engagement in real reading for real purposes.

This approach meant that each child's literacy programme required the interplay between highly-structured instruction and a strong focus on their interests, to ensure authenticity in the teaching.

Creating the resources for an authentic literacy approach

In essence, each child's literacy programme required a mini-project, where the teachers focused precisely on the child's interests, getting alongside them and into their world, to ensure authenticity in their teaching. Therefore, efforts were focused on the frameworks, tools and resources that would allow teachers to begin to weave the authentic provision into their teaching. Additionally, assessment resources and tools were developed that enabled staff to assess children's learning and engagement with reading.

The key resources developed included:

* a framework for authentic text types;

* a pedagogy of teachable moments (outlined below);

* competence-based assessment – the literacy ladder;

* a framework for investigating literacy in the child's home to inform planning of authentic literacy experiences.

Authentic text types

The first key tool was one that would prove to be ubiquitous and concrete, as well as highly useful. The authentic text types framework provided a tool that allowed staff to turn away from the standardised curriculum approach, and begin to look at the real, authentic reasons for reading and writing in the children's lives.

An authentic approach to literacy must import, or capitalise upon, children's real-life activities and situations, if it is to engage them in real-life reading and writing. These authentic contexts are then the springboard for authentic literacy; party invitations need a text message or Facebook post, children check e-mail and text messages to keep in touch with friends and make plans, dates and times for cinema showings need to be found out. All authentic literacy activities require authentic contexts within which reading and writing take place. This requires teachers to be acutely aware of the many reasons for reading and writing in children's day-to-day lives, and the myriad forms that these can take. Therefore, as a prompt for teachers to think about and be aware of, a range of different ways in which children use reading and writing functionally and for pleasure were identified and listed (see also Chapter 5).

- Computer interface
- Tablet computer interface
- Phone interface
- Magazines/catalogues/newspapers
- Birthday cards
- Film posters
- Shop signs
- Advertisements
- Forms
- Letters
- Books
- Jokes
- Instructions
- Pamphlets/leaflets
- Street signs
- Cooking instructions/recipes
- Shopping list
- Food labels

Teachable moments

Most of us are familiar with the concept of *teachable moments*, even if we do not label them as such. These are the moments when events converge to create an opportunity for teaching a concept and/or modelling a particular strategy or skill. These are often unplanned moments that occur whilst children are involved in an activity. The teaching and learning that happens during teachable moments can be powerful. This is because learning is easier if teaching is available as it is needed, and in a meaningful context, as in these moments the relevance of the learning is clear and it can be immediately applied.

Capitalising on these real-life activities and situations requires that teachers can identify teachable moments by observing and listening to children's cues. Teachable moments follow the child's lead, focusing on what is interesting and important in that moment. The teacher needs to respond straight away, so that the impact of the teaching is immediate and relates directly to a real context. This creates meaning and purpose in the child's learning.

The key to the success of responding to teachable moments lies in the teacher's ability, first, to recognise when one occurs, and second, to respond appropriately. This involves knowing what the moment calls for and teaching precisely what is needed. To achieve this, teachers must be aware of what a child is currently learning and what the next steps are in their learning. This requires some specific teacher behaviours. They must be present and ready to listen to the cues offered by the child, and follow these cues and teach spontaneously.

Teachable moments can be very productive within authentic literacy instruction. However, authentic literacy revolves around real-life activities and needs, and many of these moments are likely to relate to the lives of the children beyond school. This means that teachers need to be alert to children's cues for developing authentic literacy activities in school, but based on uses for literacy beyond school. For example, a child may be interested in superhero movies and so the teacher should use the need to read posters and cinema times etc. as an authentic 'way in' to supporting the child's reading. Also, and very importantly, teachers must be aware of the specific developmental needs of the children, especially those who have early literacy problems. This rapid and informed response to children's needs requires a careful approach to assessment and this is embedded within the literacy ladder.

Competence-based assessment: the literacy ladder

The literacy ladder (Appendix) is a single-page assessment and guidance tool that presents this complex area of learning in an accessible format. It provides the information needed to make decisions about a child's level of learning and their engagement with literacy, and thus to identify concerns and create goals for individual children. This will enable the team around each child to make a single, shared assessment of a child's abilities and needs, and agree clear, shared goals. It is organised across four straightforward stages of development and focuses on progress as a reader and writer, alongside a child's level of literacy engagement.

Rather than levels, age equivalent or any such proxy, growth in competency is outlined using real-world descriptions: *early, beginning, independent, experienced*. Evidence of progress and development is gathered through observations, narratives or portfolios.

The ladder is a pragmatic and solution-focused tool with the following key features:

* it informs teaching, setting goals and capturing learners' strengths;
* it fits with the philosophy of an authentic approach to literacy. It emphasises activity in which 'real' readers and writers would engage beyond school, and therefore takes an holistic approach to learners' literacy development;
* it demonstrates children's progress over time;
* it identifies children who require intervention or extra support;
* it provides information about performance trends of groups of children to help make decisions about where resources or additional resources are needed.

The four stages of developmental progress are named to reflect a common sense, grounded way of describing competency and progress. For example, with respect to reading this involves the following.

* *Early* stages of literacy: an understanding of concepts about print, such as the overall structure of texts and conventions of the printed word; the ability to attend to the

sounds of language as distinct from its meaning; recognising letters of the alphabet; recognising letter-sound correspondences.

- *Beginning* stage of reading and writing: the child automatically and accurately recognises words frequently found in print and begins to decode unfamiliar words.

- *Independent* and *experienced* stages of reading: this involves extensive use of strategies such as the ability to use the three major cuing systems (syntactic, semantic and phonic) and make sense from print to summarise, sequence, analyse, interpret, predict, infer and enjoy text.

To support the use of the ladder at the early and beginning stages, a variety of prompt tools is provided so that the resources needed to assess and understand children's early and beginning literacy are to hand. These tools include:

- phonological awareness and phonics checklists tools, including: auditory discrimination; skills and knowledge of syllables; rhyme; recognizing graphemes and phonemes; phonics knowledge; blending and segmentation; deleting phonemes;

- high frequency words to assess high frequency word identification (reading and spelling).

The ladder also intentionally places a keen focus on assessing children's engagement with literacy, in terms of the functional, real-world role that reading and writing plays in their lives, as well as the prominence and modelling of literacy in the home, family and community. It sets out engagement across four stages, so a judgment about engagement can be made. The four stages of literacy engagement are evidence-based and constitute development from disengaged through to engaged (Figure 10.1).

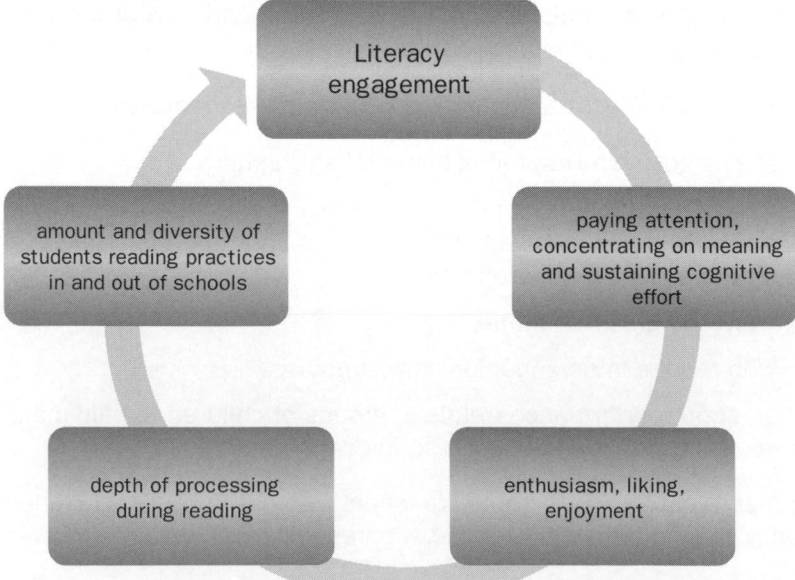

Figure 10.1 The four stages of literacy engagement are evidence-based and constitute development from disengaged through to engaged.

1   First, there is paying attention to text, concentrating on meaning and sustaining cognitive effort (Berliner, 1979; Dolezal *et al.* 2003).

2   A second perspective of engagement emphasises qualities such as enthusiasm, liking and enjoyment that surround the interaction with text (Furrer and Skinner, 2003).

3   A third perspective of engagement refers to cognitive qualities of the reader, emphasising depth of processing during reading. This perspective points toward conceptual learning during reading, which is often facilitated by use of strategies, such as questioning or comprehension monitoring (Meece *et al.*, 1988).

4   A fourth perspective is activity-based, referring to the amount and diversity of students' reading practices in and out of school (Guthrie *et al.*, 2001; Kirsch, *et al.*, 2002).

In line with the approach to assessment of a child's needs, outlined above, the case study demonstrates how staff can assess a child's needs in a way that doesn't replicate the school-based failures that many of these children have experienced. The initial assessment takes place through observation in a context that is meaningful for the child, and therefore offers a purpose for the child to read.

CASE STUDY

Assessing abilities and needs within an authentic approach

Sarah, aged 8, arrived at REAL Education disengaged and disgruntled with her school experience, having been in several schools, and with very little assessment evidence of her literacy abilities. However, Sarah's tutor quickly picked up on her interest in jewellery, including how it is designed and made, and used this area of interest as a way to begin assessing her engagement with learning and her ability and needs in reading. The tutor used catalogues, visits to artisan workshops, websites and jewellery as a starting point for this process. The tutor made careful observations about Sarah's approach to learning and her reading skills as they looked together at the catalogues and websites and visited the workshops. She noticed how Sarah approached reading for meaning, her level of engagement in this process, how she approached decoding words, which letters sounds combinations she knew or could work out, which words she knew by sight, and her ability to comprehend what she was reading. In these ways the tutor was able to begin to build a picture of Sarah's abilities and needs, and place her profile on the literacy ladder. This then provided the basis for discussions with the learning manager and other tutors to develop a bespoke programme for her, based on her interests and using what she currently knew, and could do, as the starting point for her learning.

Using an investigation of literacy in the child's home

There is clear and abundant evidence that the role of literacy in the home can support children's literacy engagement and subsequent achievement (summarised by National Literacy Trust, 2011). Home experiences mediate opportunities for literacy engagement and practice, and therefore have a significant influence on children's attitudes and efforts to engage in literacy activities (see also Chapter 9).

The authentic literacy framework thus needed to include ways of understanding the literacy environment in a child's home. Tools were designed to investigate the 'print richness' in family or care settings. These were specifically targeted to assess environmental features associated with positive literacy outcomes – for example, book reading, general use of reading and writing in daily life – and to investigate attitudes towards literacy in the home.

The aim was not to measure the quality of language and literacy support beyond school, but rather to gauge the quality of the child's engagement with literacy practices that are strongly associated with positive literacy outcomes; this is important. The commitment to an authentic approach required an understanding of engagement with language and literacy in the home, without being judgmental or creating further barriers to learning.

Four parental investigations were developed to be used in an explorative manner with children and parents. These provided the basis for investigating the home context from four overlapping perspectives, using four tools. Each can be adapted to the particular context of the child's home situation.

1 Experiences of literacy

When working authentically, it is useful to know what types of literacy experiences a child has at home. By finding out this information we can connect the kinds of experiences the child is having at home to the literacy experiences provided in school. The following types of questions were designed to elicit what the child sees and understands as literacy practices at home.

* Who do you see reading in your home?

* What kinds of things are they reading? eg texts newspapers novels, cooking instructions.

* What do you (child) like to read?

* Who do you see writing in your home?

* What kinds of things are they writing? eg letters, lists, posting on social media.

2 Types of texts used

The second investigation focuses on the type of texts parents, carers and other family members read and write at home. It is used to tease out the frequency and purposes for literacy that the child is exposed to, and engaged in.

Texts	Frequency	Purpose
Eg newsletters from school	Weekly	To find out what is happening at school
Eg text messages	Daily	Communicating with friends and family

3 Purposes for reading and writing

The third investigation is focused on the purposes for reading and writing and begins to organise literacy into themes. Getting an idea of what children are familiar with, through exposure, allows learning activities to be planned that have meaning because of a connection within the home context. The activity involves mapping out who uses literacy in each theme and what they use it for. Staff were provided with an initial list for use with the children.

- daily tasks

- official purposes

- at work

- information

- entertainment

- internet

- shopping

- relaxation

4 Mapping who, what, where and why

The final activity involves a combination of the activities above. In order to plan activities that reflect the experiences the child has, a conversation is initiated in which the staff member talks with the family, or asks them to complete the following framework. The family is also asked if anyone is willing to have a camera sent home to help document examples of reading and writing activities.

Who	What (reading or writing)	Where	Why
Dad	Reading newspaper	At home	To learn about what is happening in the world
Sister	On Facebook	At home	To keep in touch with her friends

The case study below outlines how a tutor achieved this. He used what he had elicited about the interests and uses of reading at home to draw a child into reading for a purpose, as the first steps of re-engaging him in reading-based learning.

CASE STUDY

Linking home-based literacy experiences to school-based provision

As part of alternative provision, REAL engage children in a range of activities including music, mechanics, sports, outdoors and construction. These experiences are used as vehicles to develop a range of skills, including literacy. Where possible, involvement in these activities is matched to the children's interests and links made with knowledge skills and interest at home, to support parental interest and involvement in their child's learning.

James takes part in the mechanic projects. He is eleven years old and, like his dad, has a strong interest in motor vehicles. The tutor and parents' discussions about literacy in the home found that James' dad had numerous Haynes car maintenance manuals, as well as magazines about motorcycles and cars, which he regularly read for enjoyment. Early assessment of James' engagement and abilities had been mapped onto the literacy ladder and showed that James was an independent reader, a beginning writer and disengaged with all aspects of learning.

His tutors used their assessment of his engagement and needs and tuned into his interest and this use of literacy in the home, to design a programme that involved James in reading for purpose within this context.

Once James had begun to attend the workshops and to enjoy finding out about the cars and motorbikes by working on them, the team began the process of integrating reading into his learning. Initially, the tutors agreed to be alert to all possible teachable moments when James could use and develop his interest and skill in reading. These moments arose regularly and the workshop provided an excellent, authentic context in which to engage James in reading. For example, in the moments that James needed to find things out to inform his work on the cars and motorbikes, the tutors turned to the manuals and modelled use of an index to find the information, and then referred to the labelled diagrams and instructions to inform the work on the vehicles.

In this way, James was drawn into reading that had a clear and specific purpose. This first step provided a springboard for tutors to support James in recognising the importance and value of reading, and in doing so use and develop his literacy skills.

Activity 2

»   *What do you know about children's uses and engagement with reading beyond school?*

»   *How could you find this out in a way that is non-judgmental and elicits information that you can adapt and use in your teaching?*

»   *What do you think are the benefits of making close links with children's reading beyond school?*

»   *How could you use these links with reading and literacy beyond school to plan challenging work for the most able children in your class?*

Conclusion

The use of this framework is in its early stages. The approach being used by REAL is child-centred and attempts to bring an authentic approach to bear on various aspects of learning. There have been some very promising projects that have enabled children to make progress in being in a learning environment alongside other children and tutors. This is an important early step for many of these children: re-engagement with learning.

What has been learned from these early stages is that teachers who are used to working with older children need a firm grounding in how to engage children in reading and weave the teaching of early literacy knowledge and skills into authentic reading experiences. To achieve this, we need to recognise the importance of starting from the child's interests, abilities and needs as a way of providing a relevant and meaningful context for learning. This has proved to be particularly important for children in alternative provision, who have had difficult experiences within the school system, and are therefore often disengaged from most aspects of learning, in particular, from books and reading.

Critical points

» *Engagement in reading is fundamental to all children's learning and progress; therefore re-engaging disengaged readers is essential if they are going to make good progress in learning.*

» *Teaching becomes more relevant and meaningful to disengaged children if we use their interests as a starting point for teaching.*

» *Disengaged children are more likely to engage in reading where the context for reading has a clear relevance to their everyday life.*

» *Assessment of vulnerable children's needs is most useful when it emphasises their abilities and progression, rather than levels and labels, so that next steps in their learning are the focus of assessment rather than a continued emphasis on failure.*

» *An authentic approach to literacy enables these conditions to be met; it is relevant and meaningful to the child, enables assessment of abilities and needs outside of the usual school based experiences and centralises engagement.*

Critical reflections

» *Being authentic means creating experiences for children to learn that resonate with their lives and uses of reading for pleasure. Reflect on the many ways in which you read, for pleasure and other purposes. How could you incorporate this into your planning for children's learning? How can children learn by engaging in real reading, for real purposes, as they would in the real world?*

Appendix

Stage	Reader	Writer	Engagement
1 Early	I am starting to read things I know that a letter makes a sound but I'm not sure of them all yet I understand some reasons why people read I can read some writing,but I might need pictures to help understand it all I'm starting to get how to set out my writing and what all the punctuations mean	The ideas in my writing are not really connected and I use pictures to show what I mean My spelling is just getting going properly, I'm not sure what sounds the letters make I just spell things the way they sound I invent spellings I don't know because I know all my letter-sounds I do know the letters but some words are not spelt as they sound	**Disengaged** I just don't want to read or write I avoid reading and writing if possible We don't have much to read at home I don't have any reasons to write We don't go to the library or places to enjoy reading I do not like writing and I don't think I'm much good at it
2 Beginning	I can read books for beginner readers I read the words but the pictures help a lot I have more than one way of reading a hard word I know some words as soon as I see them I still like someone to help me at times I can tell you about what I've been reading	I am beginning to write about something specific I am starting to get some punctuation and grammar right In spelling I am getting ordinary words right. If I make mistakes on harder spellings I go with the sounds still	**Taking first steps** Occasionally, I pick up a book or something to read but I still don't read regularly at home I still don't read and write if I don't have to but will read for a short while if my tutor says I need to I can do reading or writing for about quarter of an hour, but I get distracted then bored If I do read I can tell you a few things about a story, or some information, but they might not be important ones
3 Independent	I can read detailed stories or information. I don't often need to look at pictures to help me understand I am really good at using clues, besides letter sounds to get what a word means There are a lot of words now which I just know and don't have to work out I think my reading is ok and I'm getting good at it I can read aloud fluently and with expression I can tell you about what I've been reading, in the right order and including some details	I can write quite a lot keeping to the same subject I organise my main ideas with some details in what I write You can tell I plan what order to put things in You can tell I know the main rules of grammar and punctuation I'm getting a real style, you can tell it's me writing In spelling I know if words look wrong. I can break and build words from separate syllables I can spell a lot of words from memory and my guesses of hard words are often right, I don't just spell as it sounds	**Hooked in** I enjoy books and I read other things if it's something I like I really want to work out what everything means I can concentrate really well for 20 to 30 minutes I have favourite topics, but I don't yet read to find out about other things
4 Experienced	I read hard texts and books I use the sounds of letters and the context all the time to work out what something means I can work out hard bits like solving a problem I don't need people with me to help me when I read, I manage on my own If I read aloud I show that I understand it and get listeners interested I can analyse and interpret text	When I write I can say a lot about my subject and make it clear too I use details really well What I write really hangs together well I really get how to set things out and use different features e.g. sub-headings My writer's voice is strong, I can make it sound just like my thinking I can really tell if a word looks wrong and use lots of different rules to get it right I just know many words now without thinking	**Fully engaged** I always have a book on the go, and take my current book with me sometimes I am happy to read for half an hour or more, and I choose to do so myself I read daily, at least thirty minutes per day at home for my own enjoyment, often before going to sleep at night I'm always thinking ahead and testing my ideas with what's on the page I might read something twice, or ask someone to find out what it means I enjoy talking about what I've been reading, and can remember details and main points I have favourite topics e.g. reptiles and football

R.E.A.L
education

References

Bateman W.L. (ND) www.quoteworld.org/quotes/1051 (accessed 23 August, 2013).

Berliner, D.C. (1979) Tempur educare, in Peterson, P.L. and Walber, H. J. (eds), *Research On Teaching*. Berkeley, CA: McCutchan.

Cowling, K. (2009) Toe-by-Toe. Available at www.toe-by-toe.co.uk (accessed 20 June, 2013).

Dolezal, S.E., Welsh, L.M., Pressley, M. and Vincent, M.M. (2003) How Nine Third-Grade Teachers Motivate Student Academic Engagement. *The Elementary School Journal*, 103.

Duke, N., Purcell-Gates, V., Hall L. and Tower, C. (2006) Authentic Literacy Activities for Developing Comprehension and Writing. *The Reading Teacher*, 60:4. Available at

www.academia.edu/165629/Authentic_literacy_activities_for_developing_comprehension_and_ writing (accessed 20 June, 2013).

Furrer, C. and Skinner, E. (2003) Sense Of Relatedness as a Factor in Children's Academic Engagement and Performance. *Journal of Educational Psychology*, 95.

Gallagher, K. (2009). *Readicide: How Schools Are Killing Reading and What You Can Do about It*. Portland, ME: Stenhouse Publishers

Guthrie, J.T., Schafer, W.D. and Huang, C.W. (2001) Benefits of Opportunity to Read and Balanced Instruction on the NAEP. *Journal of Educational Research*, 94.

Haynes car manuals. Available at www.haynes.co.uk/webapp/wcs/stores/servlet/CategoryDis play?catalogId=10001&storeId=10001&categoryId=10215&langId=-1&parent_category_ rn=18501&top_category=10001 (accessed 20 June, 2013).

Kirsch, I., de Jong, J., LaFontaine, D., McQueen, J., Mendelovits, J. and Monseur, C. (2002) *Reading for Change: Performance and Engagement Across Countries*. Paris: OECD.

National Literacy Trust (2011) *A Research Review: The Importance of Families and the Home Environment*. Available at www.literacytrust.org.uk/assets/0000/7901/Research_review-importance_of_families_and_home.pdf (accessed 20 June, 2013).

National Literacy Trust (2012) *Boys' Reading Commission*. Available at www.literacytrust.org.uk/ assets/0001/4056/Boys_Commission_Report.pdf (accessed 20 June, 2013).

Meece, J.L., Blumenfeld, P.C. and Hoyle, R.H. (1988) Students' Goal Orientations and Cognitive Engagement in Classroom Activities. *Journal of Educational Psychology*, 80.

Nichols, M. (2006) *Comprehension Through Conversation: The Power of Purposeful Talk in the Reading Workshop*. New Hampshire: Heinemann Educational Books.

Purcell-Gates, V., Degener, S., Erickson, E. and Soler, M. (2002) Impact of Authentic Literacy Instruction on Adult Literacy Practices. *Reading Research Quarterly*, 37.

Taylor, C. (2012) Improving Alternative Provision. Available at http://media.education.gov.uk/assets/ files/pdf/8/improving%20alternative%20provision.pdf (accessed 20 June, 2013).

11 The modern storyteller: beyond KS2

JAYNE STEAD

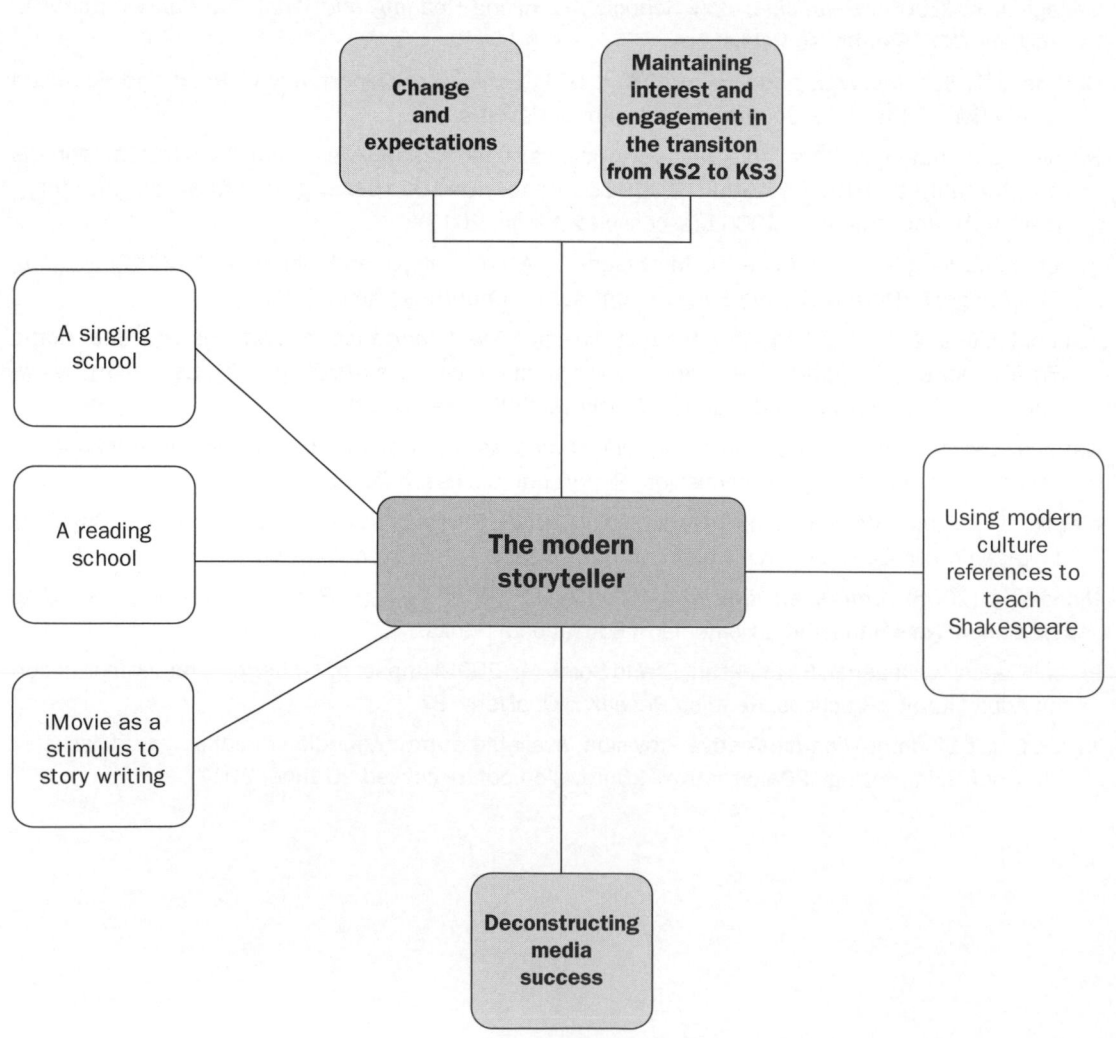

Teachers' standards

3 Demonstrate good subject and curriculum knowledge

- have a secure knowledge of the relevant subject(s) and curriculum areas, foster and maintain pupils' interest in the subject

- demonstrate an understanding of and take responsibility for promoting high standards of literacy and articulacy.

Critical questions

» *How do we tune in to children's interest in different narrative forms and use this to develop their engagement with books and literature?*

» *How do we maintain this interest and engagement in narrative and stories through the transition from primary to secondary school?*

» *How can we understand and deconstruct media successes as a starting point for our work in school?*

Introduction

Ben wants to be a writer. He has a wide vocabulary, an instinctive response to story structure and genre. He is 11. Ben, however, does not read very often. When his teacher suggested he would have to read more if he wanted to be a writer, he looked puzzled because there are lots of ways in which Ben 'reads' and 'writes' stories. He listens to audible stories on CD; he makes videos of stories with his friends on his iPad; he watches a soap opera avidly, and follows the future and past plots online; he still plays with fantasy figures, creating complex plot lines that any writer would be proud of; and he follows complete narrative arcs through on his Xbox and Wii games. This is in addition to reading his favourite books over again and being part of a drama group that reads and performs plays. Ben is a very good example of a modern reader and storyteller.

Ben and his peers love stories. Children always have. Nothing has changed. Murder, mystery, mayhem, romance and betrayal are as significant today as always. Interest in fiction and its structures and genres is still prominent in young people's lives, but their access to them is now unprecedented, and happens through many different platforms (see Chapter 5). This is borne out by the research from the National Literacy Trust (NLT) outlined below, which found that children's on-screen reading has overtaken reading in print (National Literacy Trust, 2013). However, The NLT director, Jonathan Douglas was keen to note that:

> *Our research confirms that technology is playing a central role in young people's literacy development and reading choice. While we welcome the positive impact which technology has on bringing further reading opportunities to young people, it's crucial that reading in print is not cast aside.*

And by way of explanation he adds:

> *We are concerned by our finding that children who only read on-screen are significantly less likely to enjoy reading and less likely to be strong readers. Good reading*

skills and reading for pleasure are closely linked to children's success at school and beyond.

www.literacytrust.org.uk/media/5371

So, how do we, as teachers, connect these worlds in a meaningful way? This chapter considers this issue. How can we engage with children's ever more diverse world of stories and narrative and, in so doing, draw them into the world of the written word? In particular, how can this be achieved in the transition from primary to secondary school?

FOCUS ON RESEARCH

The National Literacy Trust (forthcoming) surveyed 34,910 children and young people from across the UK aged 8 to 16 to find out about their reading habits, and to examine the influence of this on their reading ability and enjoyment.

They found that:

- 39 per cent of children and young people read daily using electronic devices including tablets and e-readers, but only 28 per cent read printed materials daily. The number of children reading ebooks has doubled in the last two years (from 6 per cent to 12 per cent).

- Children say they prefer to read on-screen. Over half (52 per cent) said they would rather read on electronic devices, but only a third (32 per cent) would rather read in print.

- Nearly all children have access to a computer at home and 4 out of 10 now own a tablet or a smartphone, while 3 in 10 do not have a desk of their own.

- Girls are significantly more likely than boys to read in print (68 per cent vs 54 per cent).

- Girls are also more likely to read on a range of on-screen devices including mobile phones (67 per cent girls vs. 60 per cent boys), e-readers (84 per cent girls vs 69 per cen boys), and tablets (70 per cent girls vs 67 per cent boys).

The research also examined the influence of this technology on children's reading abilities and their enjoyment of reading. Significantly, they found that:

- Children who read daily only on-screen are nearly half as likely to be above average readers as those who read daily in print or in print and on-screen (15.5 per cent vs 26 per cent).

- Children who read only on-screen are also less likely to enjoy reading very much (12 per cent vs 51 per cent) and less likely to have a favourite book (59 per cent vs 77 per cent).

Change and expectations

Teachers' expectations of what makes good literature and their knowledge about children's interests and play choices can be very much at odds with what children find engaging and exciting, and with the changing technological world. Children's engagement with narrative and story happens across a wider range than is typically explored in school.

Undoubtedly, the world is changing and history has shown us that fighting the advance of technology is futile. From the smashing of the printing press to the fear of silent movies being replaced by talkies, technology changes the way we are in the world. Rose (2011) observes this, noting how our perception of narrative and the way we absorb those narratives has changed and developed alongside these technological changes.

> *As each of these media achieved production and distribution on an industrial scale, we saw the emergence of 20th-century mass media: newspapers, magazines, movies, music, TV … Then, just as we'd gotten used to consuming sequential narratives in a carefully prescribed, point-by-point fashion, came the internet. The internet is the first medium that can act like all media – it can be text, or audio or video, or all of the above. It's nonlinear … and it is immersive.*

He observes that, the rise of technology has been particularly influential in how our engagement and orientation towards narrative is changing.

> *Under its influence, a new type of narrative is emerging, one that's told through many media at once in a way that's nonlinear, participatory and above all, immersive. We stand now at the intersection of lure and blur. The future beckons, but we're only partway through inventing it. We can see the outlines of a new art form, but its grammar is as tenuous and elusive as the grammar of cinema a century ago. We know this much: People want to be immersed. They want to get involved in a story, to carve out a role for themselves, to make it their own.*
>
> Rose, 2011

So, children are just as enticed and excited by stories, but in different forms, including film, performance and electronic media, and they are living in a world where they have it at their fingertips. Twitter, Facebook, text messaging, websites and emails, as well as the narrative gleaned from television, video games and theatre visits, all play their part in reading for young people. And whilst it would perhaps be unwise to promote total access of visual, electronic and television stimulus, when managed carefully this can provide a valuable resource for teachers.

The *Horrible Histories* series by Terry Deary is an excellent example of how a different approach to stories and narrative can reap rich rewards. This popular brand has become synonymous with hooking children into history. The books dwell on salacious, yet accurate, content, and are presented in cartoon strips, quizzes, imagined conversations and *what ifs*. This provides accurate, bite-sized chunks of entertaining information about the great and, importantly, not so great aspects of history, and the books have sold in their millions, because children can't get enough of them. This process of tuning in to children's interests has created a vehicle with which to engage children in the history curriculum.

In 2009, the BBC commissioned its first series of the television show *Horrible Histories* following the same format; making kings and queens real and accessible, as well as exploring lesser known facts about ordinary citizens. They also moved the whole premise forward by engaging with the social and cultural interests of children who would be watching. They used familiar TV programmes to create sketches with historical characters, for example, *Wife Swap,* popular advertisements and *Ready Steady Cook*. They also used iconic images from social media, such as Facebook conversations, Twitter and texting, and produced original songs in popular music genres, for example, *High School Musical*, boy band and rock ballad. All of these were instantly recognisable to children and provided an engaging and accessible hook into history. The BBC have continued with this approach in the current series by using contemporary programmes and reference points, thus keeping things fresh and current in the eyes of their audience. To date, Deary's work remains very popular, the BBC have been awarded a BAFTA and *Horrible Histories* continues to engage children in learning: surely a win-win situation.

Understanding why we need and appreciate stories

Perhaps a good starting point for understanding what children enjoy about the different narratives and storying in which they engage, is knowing what we gain from our engagement with stories, storytelling and narrative. We need to be aware of what we enjoyed as children, and what currently engages us, as these are good starting points for recommendations, as well as giving us an insight into our enjoyment of narrative. This includes recognising that, as for children, the elements in narrative that engage us can be found in many places.

The list below makes some suggestions about the aspects of texts that may appeal to us across the different ways in which we engage with narrative.

- Meaning
- Patterns
- Immersion
- Relevance
- Character
- Enticing content or concept
- Emotional connection
- Peer currency
- Absorption/Time out
- Subtext
- Recognisable characters
- Education
- Personal journeys

Activity 1

» *In what ways do you engage with stories, storytelling and narrative?*

» *What appeals to you about them? Refer to the suggestions above.*

» *What do you gain from this engagement?*

» *In what ways could this knowledge inform your teaching?*

Alongside an awareness of the ways in which we engage with narrative and our interest in it, it is also worthwhile being familiar with what is currently available and engaging to children, including the technological world that many occupy. Perhaps it is worth turning to children, as they can be an amazing resource if we ask them what they are using, following, discussing and playing. This interest in their worlds is particularly pertinent as they reach the end of the primary phase and move into the secondary phase. It is often at this point that parents begin to allow their children access to a wider range of technology and media and, perhaps, more freedom to explore and engage with it. Additionally, children are exposed to a significantly larger and more diverse peer group. All of which means that, potentially, children's interest and involvement with media and technology is likely to grow. This, coupled with evidence that many children's attainment dips as they move into secondary school, presents both challenges and opportunities for teachers to engage with children in meaningful ways, to maintain interest and engagement in their learning (Galton *et al.*, 1999).

Maintaining interest and engagement in the transition from KS2 to KS3

As children move from primary into secondary school there is, for some, an observable change in their attainment, often referred to as 'the dip'. This has resulted in a range of school-based schemes and initiatives aimed at easing transition and maintaining children's progress. Currently, these schemes and initiatives focus on their social integration and familiarity of location, with the aim of reducing the perceived stress and anxiety associated with moving school. Curriculum continuity has been less of a focus, as there is evidence to suggest that good social adjustment reduces anxiety, and in doing so contributes to academic success. However, looking at transition from an academic standpoint, a number of issues emerge, namely:

- a lack of curriculum continuity in work covered, work already done not acknowledged or used as a starting point;

- a difference in teaching methods not explained or explored;

- a new more competitive environment causing children to give up;

- puberty and relationships becoming dominant;

- children themselves admitting to more distractions from learning.

How then do teachers maintain children's interest in reading and storytelling across this transition? What can be done so that the children feel that the curriculum is designed with them in mind? How can we entice and engage them in reading? Supporting children in their reading through this transition can be achieved by secondary and primary schools working together on curriculum understanding, as well as social concerns. There are, potentially, a number of different levels to this work. There are whole-school considerations around teaching and learning and, for reading, specific considerations within English and other arts subjects. Listed below are some ideas of ways in which academic transition can be achieved at the whole-school level, and in English and the arts.

Transition: whole-school teaching and learning

- Manage children's expectations by preparing them for the 'big' school by introducing them to newer teaching methods and more individualised learning *before* they move – seeing their next phase of learning as 'more adult.'

- Develop a regular and systematic approach where teachers from the secondary school teach their upcoming classes in the primary, after full discussion between teachers about content/teaching style/expected outcomes.

- Have summer schools that explore multiple disciplines; drama: art; music; dance – creative storytelling devices that create, maintain and sustain interest in written/performed/expressed narrative.

Transition: English/arts teachers

Develop projects across the school phases where 'storytelling' is given prominence, and is designed to entice and excite the children, building on what they know and are interested in.

- Create relevant storytelling bridging units; units that can be begun in one form in one school and carried on in another form in another, for example, reading a novel at primary school, with relevant writing for exploration. Then, in the secondary phase, a kinaesthetic exploration through drama, music and art rather than repeating work in English.

- Children receive a reading list of a variety of desirable 'reads' from different media: books; YouTube clips; inspirational people biopics; audible downloads; learning apps for tablets; Xbox/Wii/PlayStation games that have journeys and narratives.

- Primary liaison led by secondary teachers that draws children together to produce a storytelling project to be shown/displayed/read to children across primary feeder schools – helping the social aspect of transition whilst creating academic coherence.

- Reading buddies and mentoring schemes created *before* they get to secondary school. Students in the upper years become involved with mentoring buddies in Year 6 rather than the traditional Year 7/8.

The case studies below continue this theme, illustrating ways in which schools can work together across the phases of education to maintain engagement and momentum in children's learning.

CASE STUDY

A 'Singing School'

A secondary school in the East Midlands has a headteacher who sings. The school has performing arts status, but his previous school did not. That school was also a 'Singing School'. This means that on many occasions the school pupils, teaching staff and non-teaching staff are expected to join in singing. Tutor group singing competitions are held where choice of music is not predefined, and so follows the children's interests. The headteacher leads assembly singing and expects all staff to lead by example, joining in with enthusiasm if not skill. Music has a high take-up in both participation and examination levels. Whole activity days are based on voice and singing for enjoyment. Song-writing competitions are held, with winners' songs being sung and recorded as prizes. Everyone sings whether they can or not, as it is just expected of them. The benefits of singing to personal well-being are explained to the children, and, for the most part, it is a happy and confident school where significant gains in achievement and progress have been made in recent years. There are plans to incorporate the feeder primaries too as 'Singing Schools', and teachers from both phases are meeting to create a structure where this can happen.

Activity 2

» Apply the model above to a 'Reading School' instead. Make a list of all the elements that a school calling itself a 'Reading School' would have.

» Look at the transition ideas. How would you use these ideas to support transition into a 'Reading School'?

» What else could you do?

» Does your 'Reading School' look something like the one outlined below?

CASE STUDY

A 'Reading School'

This is a school where the headteacher reads and is seen to be reading. Bridging units and projects have been carried from one phase into the next. English and arts staff regularly go into primary schools and work with Year 6 children. Continuity of content and teaching styles are genuinely shared and discussed and implemented. All staff are expected to read and have fiction and non-fiction books in their classrooms for reference and cross-school reading projects. Tutor group writing sessions for fun, or competitions, are the norm in guidance and PSHE sessions. Regular talks by staff on their favourite books/films/plays/stories are held, which the children can choose to attend, or they can join in with the silent reading sessions that are held across the school at the same time. Assemblies are focused on personalities who have just published books/autobiographies and reading is discussed as a worthwhile pastime that supports children's self esteem and confidence. Authors are regularly invited into school to work with children. The school enters national reading/writing/presenting competitions with anticipation – for example, BBC Radio 2's 500-word stories and BBC's *School Report*. Older children are given the responsibility of reading to lower school pupils and pupils in the primary school feeders. All avenues of children's interests are exploited, including TV tie-ins and new media, including the loan of Kindles from the school library. Drama in the school is seen as an extension of the literacy language of the school and the reading and writing of play scripts has kudos and rewards attached. The school play is devised and written by the children and staff in a collaborative effort. Imagine...

The changed National Curriculum has a heavy focus on the written word and reading ages. This means that, unfortunately, reading for pleasure can often be reduced to a *desirable* rather than an *essential* in the teaching day – perhaps a book recommendation, a good class reader when time allows, an extract in a literacy session or a book club. So, within this context, and once children have made the transition into secondary school, how do we continue to entice them into reading and to explore a wider range of stories and literature? One of the ways in which this can be achieved is to continue to draw on children's engagement with a range of ways of accessing narrative, and in doing so create a framework where both teacher and child recognise that the two worlds collide. Examples of this, outlined below, show how teachers can deconstruct media successes and use screen-based technologies as starting points for teaching and learning.

Deconstructing media successes: soap operas

Activity 3

» *Read the following elements of narrative structure found in a soap opera such as Eastenders, Coronation Street or Hollyoaks.*

– *Continuing drama*

– *More than one storyline (often with one dominant one)*

– *Short episodes*

– *Two minutes for one scene*

– *Cliffhangers – very little concluded dialogue or action*

– *Look-ins (previous episode clip/reference)*

– *Live – in 'real time' such as Christmas episodes/Olympics, etc.*

– *No music as soundtrack or to create atmosphere or tension*

– *Educational subtext – eg tackling prejudice*

– *Waves of tension*

– *Reflect heightened versions of real life conflicts*

» *Now think about any one of the Harry Potter novels by J.K. Rowling. Apply the above to one of the novels. How many elements of a soap opera can be found in a Harry Potter book? (See also Chapter 6.)*

All stories can be said to have some of the elements listed in the activity above – after all, soap operas have built on traditional storytelling techniques, and, as Christopher Booker (2005) has shown us, there are only seven basic plots in the world's stories. So, perhaps it is no coincidence that some of the more successful stories in recent years have been trilogies or septologies – Suzanne Collins' *The Hunger Games,* Philip Pullman's *His Dark Materials,* Rowling's *Harry Potter,* Stephanie Meyers' *Twilight* series, Malorie Blackman's *Noughts and Crosses,* or book series such as the *Alex Ryder* books by Anthony Horowitz. In these books, the characters occupy the same universe throughout. They are best read sequentially to retain a sense of the building narrative and a fleshing out of a world that becomes familiar.

The reader therefore becomes deeply involved in the world and the characters, just as with television programmes, films and narrative based video games. In short, we love a story that keeps us hooked and rewards us with peril and thrill as well as intimacy and detail, whether it be in the form of TV soap opera or a series of books.

Another good example is the series of books by Simon Mayo, a radio DJ who has turned to writing books for early teenagers whilst bringing up his own teenage children. Itchingham Lofte is a protagonist with a difference. He is obsessed by the elements on the periodic table. He collects the elements and discovers a very important one that people across the world want, and are prepared to kill for. *Itch* goes from being a 'nerd' to a hero and saves the day, but not without a subtext about the environment, strong female and male role models, lots of scenes that are based in teenage lairs – bedrooms, classrooms, places they shouldn't go – and with cliffhangers galore. All the narrative elements that make for a gripping story are used: short chapters, thrilling chases, relationships, mystery, cutting edge technology and politics. And, after reading the first few novels, the reader is more acquainted with the periodic table and the dangers of chemistry gone awry in a modern world where energy is a finite resource. These books draw children in, entertain them, thrill them and make them anxious for the next instalment, all within a context that is relevant to them, and their lives – not unlike many soap operas.

The case study below outlines how one teacher used this approach, deconstructing the narrative elements of soap opera, to engage children's interest and delight in Shakespeare's *Macbeth*. He began from the premise that Shakespeare knew how to engage his audience with the things that concerned them: tales of passion, politics, subterfuge, murder and mayhem, themes that make them universally relevant today.

CASE STUDY

Using modern cultural references to teach Shakespeare

A teacher in the East Midlands decided to use modern cultural references when trying to get Year 7 students engaged in Shakespeare's *Macbeth*. He began by a discussion of who had watched what on the television that week, particularly soap operas or on-going series. Discussions about *Waterloo Road* and *Eastenders* were encouraged, as these seemed to be the most-watched by most children. Eliciting storylines and shock revelations from recent plots soon had the children buzzing and chatting away, making judgements and deciding who was right and wrong, who was currently behaving badly, and whom they were feeling sympathy for. Following the discussion, he laid out large sheets of paper on the floor labelled *intrigue*, *fear*, *jealousy*, *tension*, *fighting (conflict)*, *threat*, *danger* and *love*. He then got the class of children to walk to and stand on/near the one word that they thought best described the element that soap operas need. This provoked great debate as the children made their decision. They were then allowed to add two or three more words to their list, and the children could be observed thinking long and hard about their choices. He then read them a synopsis of *Macbeth* without telling them what it was. The children were encouraged to shout out their word when they recognised it in the plot. It was noisy and a little riotous, but enormous fun, and the children remained engaged throughout. During the plenary section of the lesson, the teacher revealed that the story was the tale of *Macbeth* by William Shakespeare, and that they would be reading the play in the coming week.

Activity 4

»   *Know what you are talking about; research modern children's books aimed at early secondary school children.*

–   *In bookshops, find the relevant age sections and look specifically for the elements of stories that we know attract children and draw them in.*

–   *Search online for the same thing. Use the NLT website, Amazon, book reviews and recommendations from the public.*

–   *Ask children themselves: what books are they reading and what would they recommend you look at?*

–   *Familiarise yourself with the Carnegie Book list every year, looking for new novels and stories that will inspire.*

Screens and their uses

Another way in which teachers can tune in to children's interests and use them to engage them in books and narrative is through the use of mobile technology. Harnessing children's use of screen-based technology can add a different dimension to children's understanding of reading and writing for a purpose, and in doing so, engage them in an enjoyable exploration of narrative (see also Chapter 10). In the case study below, the teacher uses children's interest in developing their own movie clips to encourage children to write and publish their own stories.

CASE STUDY

Making use of technology

On request, Patrick, a Year 7 pupil, brought his iPad in to school to show the movie clips he and his friends had done on the app 'iMovie' – an app that allows children to have great fun acting out different moments of a story to incorporate into a trailer for a fictitious movie or story based on a range of genres. They had chosen the genres 'scary', 'fairy tale' and 'super hero'. The app had cleverly put the clips together in a logical and entertaining way, which added a professional sheen to the play of children in their technological world. The results were highly entertaining and, when played to the class, had them in fits of giggles. Patrick then produced from his bag the first chapter of a book he had written based on the movie genre 'scary'. It was called *The Man in the Cellar* and was clearly inspired by the iMovie app ideas that he and his friends had. He was very proud of his burgeoning novel and wondered what the teacher thought. She read it to the class and the feedback was very positive. The children were interested to know when he was going to write the next instalment.

To follow this up, and capitalise on the children's enthusiasm, the teacher booked out the three iPads currently available in her school and bought the app for the school. During the following lesson, she put the class into groups of three or four and listed the genres available.

- scary/horror
- swashbuckler
- teen
- superhero
- romance
- retro
- narrative/adventure
- fairy tale
- expedition
- coming of age
- Bollywood
- adrenalin/action

She discussed and explained the genres to get a feel for which the children were familiar with. Their explanations were littered with examples from films and stories that they knew within each category. The groups were encouraged to choose a genre that inspired them, then practise and record a 'trailer' for their story. This trailer was the starting point for the children to write an opening chapter to a novel, story or play.

Further drama and practical lessons were then planned to add structure and ideas for content, with the ultimate aim to 'publish' these stories in a class collection, and put it in the school library. Eventually, some of the original trailers were put on the school website and information boards to encourage children from other classes to read the stories in the published collection.

Activity 5

» *Research which apps are available for storytelling using iMovies as a link to gain the interest of pupils:*

  − *Try: iMovie; Intro Designer for iMovie; video clips for iMovie; VidLib (for footage); MovieApp Club; Tunes for iMovie.*

» *Research and make a list of other storytelling apps that may be useful in the classroom, set as homework or just used as suggestions to move children away from the usual fare of* Super Mario Brothers *and* Angry Birds.

– *Try:* Story Shout! *(an app that encourages the child to create a story on the spot, using the symbols given before the symbol fades away);* StoryCorps *(oral history project based on interviewing family members for stories and memories);* Stray Souls: *a dollhouse story (dark and spooky world with great atmosphere ideas);* Nick Chase: *a detective story (clues and puzzles taking you through a mystery story).*

» *Think about the way these apps could be used in the classroom to entice children into storytelling.*

» *Look at movies/game tie-ins as well as more formal apps for writing.*

Conclusion

So, there is an argument that teachers can turn to, and deconstruct, media successes to help children engage with books and narrative. Older children's involvement and interest with screen-based narratives can provide a meaningful starting point with which teachers can draw them into the world of books and literature. To achieve this, we need to know exactly what children are interested in and, when appropriate, start with their experience and tailor what we do, not only to their needs, but also to their interests beyond school. It can be argued that we need to take away the intellectual taboo about video games, television, internet and social media and see them as a tool, a pathway into children's lives and a way to engage them in learning.

Critical points

» *Children are interested in narrative in many different forms.*

» *We can tune in to these interests and use them as starting points for our teaching in order to provide a familiar and relevant context for developing children's engagement with literature.*

» *This requires us, as teachers, to understand children's worlds of narrative and to deconstruct what is interesting and enticing about these worlds, to enable us to develop relevant and engaging starting points for our teaching.*

» *This is particularly important as children get older, and move from primary to secondary school, and have wider access to different forms of technology and media.*

Critical reflections

» *Be aware and alive to the ways in which you engage with stories, storytelling and narrative in your own life. Think carefully about the elements of these narratives that appeal to you; that draw you in and keep you there; that make you want to return to them. Reflect on how you can use these elements of stories in your teaching, to excite children's interest in narrative and begin to draw them into the world of children's print-based literature.*

References

Booker, C. (2005) *The Seven Basic Plots. Why we tell Stories*. London: Continuum.

Blackman, M. (2012) *Noughts and Crosses Boxed set*. London: Corgi Children's.

Collins, S. (2012) *Hunger Games Trilogy*. London: Scholastic.

Deary, T. (2008) *Horrible Histories. Blood Curdling Box Set*. London: Scholastic.

Galton, M., Gray, J. and Ruddock, J. (1999) *The Impact of School Transitions and Transfers on Pupil Progress and Attainment*. London: HMSO. Available at http://webarchive.nationalarchives.gov.uk/20130401151715/https://www.education.gov.uk/publications/eOrderingDownload/RR131.pdf (accessed 20 June, 2013).

Horowitz, A. (2005) *Stormbreaker*. London: Walker Books.

Horowitz, A. (2005) *Point Blank*. London: Walker Books.

Horowitz, A. (2010) *Skeleton Key*. London: Walker Books.

Meyers, S. (2012) *Twilight Saga Book Set*. London: Atom.

Mayo, S. (2012) *Itch*. London: Corgi Children's.

Mayo, S. (2013) *Itch Rocks*. London: Doubleday Children's.

National Literacy Trust (2013) https://www.literacytrust.org

National Literacy Trust (forthcoming) Information available at: www.literacytrust.org.uk/media/5371 (accessed 20 June, 2013).

Pullman, P. (2010) *His Dark Materials Trilogy*. London: Scholastic.

Rowling, J.K. (2010) *Harry Potter Boxed Set*. London: Bloomsbury.

Rose, F. (2011) *The Art of Immersion. Why do we tell stories?* Available at www.wired.com/business/2011/03/why-do-we-tell-stories/ (accessed 20 June, 2013).

Conclusion

We hope that reading this book has prompted you to consider the needs of readers once they have mastered basic skills. Not only do we need to cater for those children who struggle with reading, but we should also be mindful of the importance of developing children's enthusiasm for engaging with a wide range of texts. You have seen that this can be done by sharing texts with children, looking for opportunities to provide reading that is linked to their interests, and ensuring that we take into account what children actually read from day to day.

If this book prompts you to reflect upon your practice as a teacher of reading – and we maintain that every teacher, primary and secondary, is a teacher of reading – then it has been worthwhile.

David Waugh

Sally Neaum

September 2013

Index